Everyday
BAKING
RECIPES

hinkler

hinkler

Published by Hinkler Books Pty Ltd
45–55 Fairchild Street
Heatherton Victoria 3202 Australia
www.hinkler.com.au

© A.C.N. 144 619 894 Pty Ltd 2011

Cover Illustration: Brijbasi Art Press Limited
Prepress: Splitting Image
Typesetting and internal illustrations: MPS Limited

ISBN: 978 1 7418 4126 8

Printed and bound in China

Contents

Introduction

Make Your Own Pastry

Ingredients

Pastry at its simplest is flour mixed with half its weight in some form of fat, then bound with water.

Flour Plain (all-purpose) white flour is the one most commonly used for pastry. For a slightly different texture, a combination of wholemeal (whole wheat) plain (all-purpose) and plain (all-purpose) white flour is used. Store your flour in an airtight container.

Fat Butter is the most commonly used fat for making pastry and gives a wonderful colour to the pastry. Use real butter, not margarine or softened butter blends. Sometimes a mixture of butter and lard is used, sometimes all lard. Lard gives a good flaky texture. Butter and lard are usually chilled and cut into cubes to make it easier to incorporate them into the flour, keeping the pastry cooler and more manageable. Generally, unsalted butter should be used for sweet and salted butter for savory recipes. Olive oil is sometimes used to give pastries a different texture, for example in a traditional spinach pie.

Salt Salt can be added to both sweet and savory pastry to add flavour.

Sugar Caster (berry) sugar is used in sweet shortcrust (pie) pastry as its fine texture ensures that it blends well.

Liquid The usual binding liquid in pastry-making is iced water, but sometimes an egg or an egg yolk will be used to enrich the dough. You will find that most pastry recipes only give an approximate liquid measure because the amount will vary according to the flour, the temperature, the altitude and the humidity. Add a little at a time and work it in until the pastry 'starts to come together' in clumps that can then be pressed together.

Tools of the Trade

Food processor While not essential, a food processor can make pastry-making easy. Pastry should be kept cool and a processor means you don't need to touch the dough as you mix. The processor method is described on page 10. If you prefer, you can use the processor just to combine the butter and flour before continuing to mix by hand.

Marble pastry board Although not strictly necessary, marble boards are favoured by pastry-makers for their cool and hygienic surface. If you don't have one, place a roasting tin full of iced water on your work surface for a while to cool the surface before rolling your pastry.

Rolling pins are an essential tool in pastry-making. They are now available in traditional wood, marble, plastic and stainless steel. Lightly sprinkle your rolling pin with flour to prevent the pastry sticking. You can also use the rolling pin to lift the pastry into the tin and then trim away the excess pastry by rolling over the top.

Baking paper is very useful when rolling out pastry. The dough is rolled out between two sheets of paper, the top sheet is removed and the pastry is inverted into the tin before removing the other sheet. A crumpled sheet of baking paper is also used to line pastry shells when blind baking.

Baking beads Reuseable baking beads are spread in a layer over baking paper and used to weigh down pastry during blind baking. They are available in kitchenware shops and department stores. Dried beans or uncooked rice can also be used and stored in a jar for reuse.

Cutters are available in all shapes and sizes. They are used to cut bases and tops for small pies and to cut out pieces of dough to decorate the pie. Cutters may need to be dusted lightly with flour to prevent them from sticking to the pastry. If you don't have a pastry cutter, a fine-rimmed glass, turned upside-down, is a good substitute.

Pie tins and dishes are available in many styles. While testing the pies for this book we baked with metal, glass and ceramic pie dishes. We found the crispest base crusts were achieved in the metal tins.

Pastry brushes are used for glazing. A glaze gives the pastry crispness and colour. Pastry can also be sealed and joined by brushing the edges with milk or beaten egg. Use only a small amount of liquid or your pastry may become soggy.

Pastry-Makers' Tips

1 Dough must be kept cool. Work in a cool kitchen if possible. If you are baking in summer, chill your work surface by leaving a tin of iced water on it before you start rolling or shaping. Make sure all the ingredients are as cool as possible and that they stay cool during the preparation.

2 Because your hands are warm, try to handle the pastry as little as possible. Cool your hands under cold water. Good pastry-makers work quickly – too much handling will cause the cooked pastry to toughen and shrink.

3 Flours vary in their moisture content. Because of this variation, the liquid (usually iced water) is not added all at once. Test the dough by pinching a little piece together. If it holds together and doesn't crumble, you don't need more liquid. If the pastry is too dry, it will be difficult to put into tins; if too wet it will shrink when cooked.

4 Pastry should be wrapped in plastic and put in the fridge for 20–30 minutes before rolling or shaping. In hot weather, refrigerate the pastry for at least 30 minutes.

5 For ease of rolling, roll out dough between two sheets of baking paper.

6 Pies with a bottom crust benefit from being cooked on a heated metal baking tray (sheet). Put the tray (sheet) in the oven as the oven warms up.

7 Pastry can be stored in the fridge for two days or frozen for up to three months. Ensure that it is well sealed in plastic wrap and clearly labelled and dated. Thaw on a wire rack to let the air circulate.

8 Pastry should always be cooked in a preheated oven, never one that is still warming up. It is a good idea to use an oven thermometer.

9 Pies can be frozen as long as the filling is suitable (don't freeze creamy, egg fillings) and the pastry has not already been frozen. For best results, a frozen pie should be reheated in a slow oven.

10 To test if a pie is cooked, poke a metal skewer into the centre. If the skewer is cold, the pie needs to be baked for longer.

Shortcrust Pastry

This recipe makes 375 g (13¼ oz) of basic shortcrust (pie) pastry, which is enough to line the base of a 23 cm (9 inch) pie dish, or just the top. If you need 750 g (1 lb 10 oz) of pastry, simply double the quantity.

For 375 g (13¼ oz) shortcrust (pie) pastry, you will need 2 cups (250 g/8¾ oz) plain (all-purpose) flour, 125 g (4⅓ oz) chilled butter, chopped into small pieces and 2–3 tablespoons iced water. If you want to line the top and base, you will need 600 g (1 lb 5 oz) and for this you need 400 g (14 oz) plain (all-purpose) flour, 180 g (6⅓ oz) chilled butter, chopped into small pieces, and 3–4 tablespoons iced water.

1 Remove the butter from the fridge 20 minutes before you make the pastry, except in hot weather. Sift the flour and ¼ teaspoon of salt into a large bowl. Sifting the flour will aerate the dough and help make the finished pastry crisp and light.

2 Add the chopped butter and rub the pieces of butter into the flour with your fingertips – your palms will be too warm – until the mixture resembles fine crumbs. As you rub the butter into the flour, lift it up high and let it fall back into the bowl. If applicable, stir in other dry ingredients such as sugar or herbs.

3 Make a well in the centre, add nearly all the water and mix with a flat-bladed knife, using a cutting rather than a stirring action, turning the bowl with your free hand. The mixture will come together in small beads of dough. If necessary, add more water, a teaspoon at a time, until the dough comes together. Test the dough by pinching a little piece between your fingers. If it doesn't hold together, it needs more water. If the pastry is too dry, it will fall apart when rolled. If too wet, it will be sticky and shrink when baked.

4 Gather the dough together and lift out onto a lightly floured work surface or a sheet of baking paper. Press the dough together into a ball. The trick here is not to knead or handle the dough too much, but just to press it together into a ball. Refrigerate, wrapped in plastic or in a plastic bag for 20–30 minutes – this makes it easier to roll and helps prevent shrinkage during cooking. If the weather is hot, refrigerate for at least 30 minutes.

5 Roll out the pastry between two sheets of baking paper or plastic wrap or on a lightly floured surface to prevent sticking. Always roll from the centre outwards, rotating the dough, rather than backwards and forwards.

6 If you used baking paper to roll out the pastry, remove the top sheet and then carefully invert the pastry over the tin. Make sure you centre the pastry, as it can't be moved once in place, and then peel away the paper. If you rolled out on a floured surface, roll the pastry back over the rolling pin so it is hanging, then ease it into the tin.

7 Once the pastry is in the tin, quickly lift up the sides so they don't break over the sharp edges of the tin. Use a small ball of excess dough to press the pastry firmly into the base and side of the tin. Let the excess hang over the side and, if using a tart tin, roll the rolling pin over the top of the tin to cut off the excess pastry. If you are using a glass or ceramic pie dish, use a small sharp knife to trim the excess pastry.

8 However gently you handle dough, it is bound to shrink a little, so let it sit slightly above the side of the tin. If you rolled off the excess pastry with a rolling pin, you may find it has bunched down the sides. Gently press the sides of the pastry with your thumbs to flatten and lift it. Now refrigerate the pastry-lined tin for 15 minutes to relax the pastry and prevent or minimise shrinkage.

Shortcrust Variations

Herb pastry Add 2–3 tablespoons chopped fresh herbs to the flour.

Cheese pastry Add 60 g (2 oz) grated Parmesan to the flour.

Nut pastry Add 2–3 tablespoons ground nuts, such as almonds, walnuts or pecans, to the flour.

Seed pastry Add 2 teaspoons sesame or poppy seeds to the flour.

Mustard pastry Add 1 tablespoon wholegrain mustard to the flour.

Citrus pastry Add 2–3 teaspoons finely grated orange or lemon rind to the flour.

English shortcrust pastry Use half butter and half lard.

Rich shortcrust pastry This is often to give fruit pies, flans and tarts a richer, crisper crust. To transform a basic shortcrust into a rich one, gradually add a beaten egg yolk to the flour with 2–3 tablespoons iced water as above in step 3. Mix with a flat-bladed knife.

Sweet shortcrust pastry This is a variation that can be used for sweet recipes. Follow the directions for rich shortcrust, adding 2 tablespoons caster (berry) or icing (powdered) sugar after the butter has been rubbed into the flour.

Food Processor Shortcrust

A food processor is a useful tool for pastry-making. Shortcrust pastry can be made quickly with a food processor and, because you don't handle the pastry much, it stays cooler than if made by hand. Process the flour and cold chopped butter in short bursts, using the pulse button if your machine has one, until the mixture resembles fine breadcrumbs. While the processor is running, add a teaspoon of water at a time until the dough holds together. Process in short bursts again – don't over-process or the pastry will toughen and shrink on cooking. You will know you have overworked the dough if it forms into a ball in the processor. It should just come together in clumps. Tip it out onto a lightly floured surface, gather into a ball and wrap in plastic wrap, then refrigerate it for 20–30 minutes.

Puff Pastry

Puff pastry is made by layering dough with butter and folding and rolling to create hundreds of layers. When baked, the butter melts and the dough produces steam, forcing the layers apart to make the pastry rise.

For perfect puff pastry that rises evenly, the edges must be cut cleanly with a sharp knife, not torn. Egg glazes give a shine but must be applied carefully – any drips down the side will glue the layers together and prevent them rising evenly.

Always bake puff pastry at a very high temperature – it should rise evenly so, if your oven has areas of uneven heat, turn during baking. When cooked, the top and base should be brown, with only a small amount of under-baked dough inside, and the layers visible.

Puff pastry is not always perfect – it may fall over or not rise to quite the heights you had imagined – but provided you don't burn it, and it is well cooked, it will still be delicious.

The recipe we have given below makes about 500 g (1 lb 2 oz) of puff pastry. You will notice that we've given a range for the butter quantity. If you've never made puff pastry before, you'll find it easier to use the lower amount. You will need 200–250 g (7–8¾ oz) unsalted butter, 2 cups (250 g/8¾ oz) plain (all-purpose) flour, ½ teaspoon salt and ⅔ cup (170 ml/5¾ fl oz) iced water.

1 Melt 30 g (1 oz) butter in a pan. Sift the flour and salt onto a work surface and make a well in the centre. Pour the melted butter and iced water into the well and blend with your fingertips, gradually drawing in the flour until you have a crumb mixture. If it seems a little dry, add a few extra drops of water before bringing it all roughly together with your hands to form a dough.

2 Cut the dough with a pastry scraper, using a downward cutting action, then turn the dough and repeat in the opposite direction. The dough

should now come together in a soft ball. Score a cross in the top to prevent shrinkage, wrap in plastic and refrigerate for 15–20 minutes.

3 Soften the remaining butter by pounding it between two sheets of baking paper with a rolling pin. Then, still between the sheets of baking paper, roll it into a 10 cm (4 inch) square. The butter must be the same consistency as the dough or they will not roll out the same amount and the layers will not be even. If the butter is too soft it will squeeze out of the sides, and if it is too hard it will break through the dough and disturb the layers.

4 Put the pastry on a well-floured surface. Roll it out to form a cross, leaving the centre slightly thicker than the arms. Place the butter in the centre of the cross and fold over each of the arms to make a parcel. Tap and roll out the dough to form a 15 x 45 cm (6 x 18 inch) rectangle. Make this as neat as possible, squaring off the corners – otherwise, every time you fold, the edges will become less neat and the layers will not be even.

5 Fold the dough like a letter, the top third down and the bottom third up, brushing off any excess flour between the layers. Give the dough a quarter turn to your left and press the seam sides down with the rolling pin to seal them. Re-roll and fold as before to complete two turns and mark the dough by gently pressing into the corner with your fingertip for each turn – this will remind you where you're up to. Wrap the dough in plastic wrap and chill again for at least 30 minutes.

6 Re-roll and fold the pastry twice more and then chill, then roll again to complete six turns. If it is a very hot day, you may need to chill for 30 minutes after each turn, rather than doing a double. The pastry should now be an even yellow and is ready to use – if it looks streaky, roll and fold once more. The aim is to ensure that the butter is evenly distributed so that the pastry rises evenly. Chill the pastry for at least 30 minutes before baking to relax it.

Quick Flaky Pastry

Flaky pastry is a member of the puff pastry family. This is a very easy, quick version which will give you a crust with a nice flaky texture with some rise. It is important to use frozen butter and to handle the dough as little as possible. The butter is not worked into the dough at all but left in chunky grated pieces. If the butter starts to soften, it is absorbed into the flour and the flakiness is lost. This is why it is important to keep the pastry chilled. The amount of pastry given here will make enough to cover two pies. Any leftover pastry can be used for decoration, or refrigerated for up to two days, or wrapped in plastic wrap and frozen for up to three months. This recipe makes about 600 g (1 lb 5 oz) pastry.

1 Sift 350 g (12¼ oz) plain (all-purpose) flour and ½ teaspoon salt into a large bowl. Grate 220 g (7¾ oz) frozen unsalted butter into the bowl, using the largest holes on the grater. Mix the butter gently into the flour with a knife, making sure all the pieces are coated in flour. Add 3 tablespoons chilled water and mix with a metal spatula.

2 The pastry should come together in clumps. Test the dough by pinching a little piece between your fingers. If it doesn't hold together, mix in a teaspoon of iced water.

3 When the dough holds together, quickly gather it into a neat ball in the bowl. Cover and refrigerate the dough for 30 minutes, then roll out as required for your recipe.

Ready-Made Pastry

For busy cooks, there is a large range of ready-made frozen or refrigerated pastries available at supermarkets. Standard puff and shortcrust (pie) pastries are available in blocks, and puff, butter puff and shortcrust (pie) pastries also come as ready-rolled sheets. The recipe will simply say '2 sheets puff pastry' or '250 g shortcrust (pie) pastry' and these should be thawed. Thaw frozen block pastry for 2 hours before using. Sheets only take 5–10 minutes to thaw at room temperature.

Lining the Tin

Roll out the dough between two sheets of baking paper, or on a lightly floured surface. Always roll from the centre outwards, rotating the dough, rather than rolling backwards and forwards. Reduce the pressure towards the edges of the dough. If you used baking paper, remove the top sheet and invert the pastry over the tin, then peel away the other sheet. Centre the pastry as it can't be moved once in place. Quickly lift up the sides so they don't break over the edges of the tin. Use a small ball of dough to press the pastry into the side of the tin. Trim away the excess pastry with a small, sharp knife or by rolling the rolling pin over the top. However gently you handle the dough it is bound to shrink slightly, so let it sit a little above the side of the tin. Chill the pastry in the tin for 20 minutes to relax it and minimise shrinkage.

Blind Baking

If a pie or tart is to have a liquid filling, the pastry usually requires blind baking to partially cook it before filling. This prevents the base becoming soggy.

When blind baking, the pastry needs to be weighted down to prevent it rising. Cover the base and side with a crumpled piece of baking paper or greaseproof paper. Pour in a layer of baking beads (also called pie weights), dried beans or uncooked rice and spread out over the paper to cover the pastry base. Bake for the recommended time (usually about 10 minutes), then remove the paper and beads. The beads are reuseable and dried beans or rice can also be kept in a separate jar for reuse for blind baking (but they are not now suitable for eating). Return the pastry to the oven for 10–15 minutes, or as specified in the recipe, until the base is dry with no greasy patches. Let the pastry cool completely.

The filling should also be completely cooled before filling the shell – filling a cold shell with a hot mixture can also cause the pastry to become soggy.

Things
to
Dip

Cheese and Chilli Shapes

- 1¼ cups (155 g/5½ oz) plain (all-purpose) flour
- pinch hot mustard powder (dry hot mustard)
- 90 g (3¼ oz) butter, roughly chopped
- ½ cup (60 g/2 oz) grated vintage Cheddar (American) cheese
- 4 red chillies, seeded and sliced
- 1 egg yolk

Process the flour, mustard and butter until they resemble fine breadcrumbs. Add the cheese and chilli, then the egg yolk and 1 tablespoon water, and process until the mixture comes together. Gather into a ball, cover with plastic wrap and refrigerate for 30 minutes.

Preheat the oven to 190°C (375°F/Gas 5). On a lightly floured surface, roll out the dough to a 5 mm (¼ in) thickness. Cut into 5 cm (2 in) rounds.

Place on lightly greased baking trays (sheets) and bake for 15–20 minutes, or until golden. Cool.

Makes 12

Crispy Vegetable Treats

- **250 g (8¾ oz) orange sweet potato (yam)**
- **250 g (8¾ oz) beetroot, peeled**
- **250 g (8¾ oz) potato**
- **oil, for deep-frying**

Preheat the oven to moderate 180°C (350°F/Gas 4). Run a sharp vegetable peeler along the length of the sweet potato (yam) to create ribbons. Cut the beetroot into paper-thin slices with a sharp vegetable peeler or knife. Cut the potato into thin slices, using a mandolin slicer or knife with a crinkle-cut blade. If you don't have a mandolin or crinkle-cut knife at home, simply use a sharp knife to cut fine slices.

Fill a deep heavy-based saucepan one third full of oil and heat until a cube of bread dropped into the oil browns in 10 seconds. Cook the vegetables in batches for about 30 seconds, or until golden and crispy. You may need to turn them with tongs or a long-handled metal spoon. Drain on paper towels and season with salt.

Place all the vegetable chips on a baking tray (sheet) and keep warm in the oven while cooking the remaining vegetables. Serve with drinks.

Serves 6–8

15

Grissini

- 7 g (¼ oz) sachet dried yeast
- 1 teaspoon sugar
- 4 cups (500 g/1 lb) plain (all-purpose) flour
- ¼ cup (60 ml/2 fl oz) olive oil
- ¼ cup (15 g/½ oz) chopped basil
- 4 cloves garlic, crushed
- 50 g (1¾ oz) Parmesan, grated
- 2 teaspoons sea salt flakes
- 2 tablespoons grated Parmesan, extra

Put the yeast, sugar and 1¼ cups (315 ml/11 fl oz) warm water in a small bowl and leave in a warm place for about 5–10 minutes, or until frothy. Sift the flour and 1 teaspoon salt into a bowl and stir in the yeast and oil. Add more water if the dough is dry.

Gather the dough into a ball and turn out onto a lightly floured surface. Knead for 10 minutes, or until soft and elastic. Divide into two portions and flatten into rectangles. Put the basil and garlic on one portion and the Parmesan on the other. Fold the dough to enclose the fillings, then knead for a few minutes to incorporate evenly.

Place the doughs into two lightly oiled bowls and cover with plastic wrap. Leave in a warm place for about 1 hour, or until doubled in volume. Preheat the oven to very hot 230°C (450°F/Gas 8) and lightly grease two large baking trays (sheets).

Punch down the doughs and knead each again for 1 minute. Divide each piece of dough into 12 portions, and roll each portion into a stick 30 cm (12 inches) long. Place on the baking trays (sheets) and brush with water. Sprinkle the basil and garlic dough with the sea salt, and the cheese dough with the extra Parmesan. Bake for 15 minutes, or until crisp and golden brown. These can be kept in an airtight container for up to a week.

Makes 24

Herb Grissini

- 7 g (¼ oz) sachet dried yeast
- 1 teaspoon sugar
- 4 cups (500 g/1 lb) plain (all-purpose) flour
- ¼ cup (60 ml/2 fl oz) olive oil
- ½ cup (15 g/½ oz) chopped fresh flat-leaf parsley
- ¼ cup (15 g/½ oz) chopped fresh basil
- 2 teaspoons sea salt flakes

Combine the yeast, sugar and 1¼ cups (315 ml/11 fl oz) warm water in a small bowl and leave in a warm place for 5–10 minutes, or until it is foamy. If the mixture does not foam, the yeast is dead and you will need to start again with another sachet of yeast. Sift the flour and 1 teaspoon salt into a bowl. Stir in the yeast mixture and oil to form a dough, adding more water if necessary.

Gather into a ball and turn out onto a lightly floured surface. Knead for 10 minutes, or until soft and elastic. Add the parsley and basil, and knead for 1–2 minutes to incorporate evenly.

Place the dough in a lightly oiled bowl and cover with plastic wrap. Leave in a warm place for 1 hour, or until doubled in volume. Preheat the oven to very hot 230°C (450°F/Gas 8) and lightly grease two large baking trays (sheets).

Punch down the dough and knead for 1 minute. Divide into 24 portions, and roll each portion into a 30 cm (12 inch) long stick. Place the dough sticks on the trays (sheets)and lightly brush with water. Sprinkle with the sea salt flakes. Bake for 15 minutes, or until crisp and golden. Ideal with white bean dip or hummus.

Makes 24

Cheese Treats

- 1 cup (125 g/4⅓ oz) plain (all-purpose) flour
- 2 tablespoons self-raising flour
- 1 teaspoon curry powder
- 125 g (4⅓ oz) butter
- ½ cup (50 g/1¾ oz) grated Parmesan
- ⅔ cup (85 g/3 oz) grated Cheddar (American) cheese
- 20 g (⅔ oz) crumbled blue-vein cheese
- 1 tablespoon lemon juice
- ¼ cup (25 g/¾ oz) finely grated Parmesan, extra

Place the flours, curry powder and butter in a food processor. Process until the mixture resembles fine breadcrumbs.

Stir in the cheeses and the lemon juice. Bring the mixture together into a ball.

Roll into a 30 cm (12 inch) log. Wrap in plastic wrap and chill for 1 hour. Slice into 5 mm (¼ inch) slices. Reshape if necessary. Preheat the oven to moderately hot 200°C (400°F/Gas 6).

Makes about 60

Orange Sweet Potato Wedges

- 1.3 kg (2 lb 10 oz) orange sweet potato (yam), peeled and sliced into 6 cm × 2 cm (2½ inch × ¾ inch) wedges
- 2 tablespoons olive oil
- 1 tablespoon fennel seeds
- 1 tablespoon coriander seeds
- ½ teaspoon cayenne (red) pepper
- 1 teaspoon sea salt flakes

Preheat the oven to moderately hot 200°C (400°F/Gas 6). Place the sweet potato (yam) in a large baking dish and toss with the oil.

In a mortar and pestle, pound together the fennel and coriander seeds until they are roughly crushed. Add to the orange sweet potato (yam) along with the cayenne (red) pepper and sea salt flakes.

Toss well and bake for about 30 minutes, or until browned and crisp. Serve warm. Ideal with red capsicum (pepper) skordalia or white bean dip. Also great on their own.

Serves 6–8

Herbed Lavash

- ½ cup (125 ml/4¼ fl oz) olive oil
- 3 cloves garlic, crushed
- 6 slices lavash bread
- 2 teaspoons sea salt flakes
- 2 teaspoons dried mixed Italian herbs

Preheat the oven to moderate 180°C (350°F/Gas 4). Heat the oil and garlic in a small saucepan over low heat until the oil is warm and the garlic is fragrant but not browned.

Lightly brush the lavash bread on both sides with the garlic oil. Cut each piece of bread into eight triangular wedges and position them side-by-side on baking trays (sheets).

Sprinkle the upper side of the bread with the sea salt and herbs. Bake the lavash for 10 minutes, or until crisp. Ideal with hummus or dhal.

Makes about 48 pieces

Thai Rice Crackers with Dip

- 370 g (13 oz) long-grain or jasmine rice
- 2 cups (500 ml/17 fl oz) oil

Chilli Jam (Jelly)
- 3 tablespoons dried shrimp
- 2 cups (500 ml/17 fl oz) oil
- 2 cups (220 g/7¾ oz) sliced red Asian shallots

- 35 garlic cloves, thinly sliced
- 4–5 long red chillies, seeded and finely chopped
- ½ cup (90 g/3¼ oz) grated light palm sugar
- 3 tablespoons tamarind syrup
- 2 tablespoons fish sauce

Wash the rice several times in cold water until the water runs clear. Put the rice and 3 cups (750 ml/26 fl oz) water in a saucepan over high heat. When the water boils, reduce the heat to low, cover with a tight-fitting lid and cook for 15 minutes, or until the rice is cooked. Allow the rice to cool.

Preheat the oven to very slow 140°C (275°F/Gas 1) and lightly grease a flat baking tray (sheet) with oil. Spread the cooked rice over the bottom of the tray in a thin layer. Use wet hands to prevent the rice from sticking and spread the rice to a thickness of about two or three grains. Use a knife to score a grid in the rice forming 4 cm (1½ in) squares.

Put the tray of rice in the oven and bake for 1 hour, or until the rice is completely dry. When cool enough to handle, break the rice along the scored lines and store in an airtight container.

To cook the rice squares, heat the vegetable oil in a wok or deep-fat fryer over high heat to 180°C (350°F), or until a cube of bread dropped in the oil browns in 15 seconds. When hot, add several of the rice squares at a time and cook for 1–2 minutes, or until golden. Remove and drain on paper towels. Serve immediately with the chilli jam (jelly) and Tamarind and pork dip.

To make the chilli jam (jelly), soak the dried shrimp in hot water for 5 minutes, drain well, then dry and roughly chop. Heat the oil in a saucepan over medium–high heat, add the shallots and garlic and cook for 10 minutes, stirring constantly, until the shallots and garlic turn golden. Add the shrimp and chillies and cook for 5 minutes, stirring constantly. Remove from the heat. Drain and reserve the oil.

Put the fried mixture in a food processor and blend, gradually adding ¼ cup (60 ml/2 fl oz) of the reserved cooking oil to form a paste. Put the mixture in a saucepan over medium heat and when it begins to simmer add the palm sugar, tamarind syrup and fish sauce. Cook for 5 minutes, stirring frequently, until it thickens. Cool before serving.

Serves 8–10 as a starter

Crispy Tex-Mex Cheese Bites

- 1¾ cups (215 g/7½ oz) plain (all-purpose) flour
- 1 teaspoon chilli powder
- 1 teaspoon garlic salt
- ½ teaspoon ground paprika
- 200 g (7 oz) butter, chopped
- 1 egg, lightly beaten
- 200 g (7 oz) Cheddar (American) cheese, grated

Preheat the oven to hot 210°C (415°F/Gas 6–7). Lightly brush two baking trays (sheets) with melted butter.

Sift the flour, chilli powder, garlic salt and paprika into a large bowl. Rub the butter into the flour with your fingertips until the mixture resembles fine breadcrumbs. Add the egg and cheese and stir until the mixture comes together. Turn onto a lightly floured surface and gather together into a ball. Cover the dough with plastic wrap and refrigerate for 20 minutes.

Roll the dough on a lightly floured surface to 3 mm (⅛ inch) thickness. Cut into shapes with a 6 cm (2½ inch) star-shaped biscuit (cookie) cutter. Place on the trays, allowing room for spreading. Bake for 12 minutes, or until crisp and golden brown. Leave on the trays for 2 minutes before transferring to a wire rack to cool.

Makes 80

Parmesan Puff Straws

- **4 sheets ready-rolled puff pastry**
- **50 g (1¾ oz) butter, melted**
- **1⅔ cups (165 g/5¾ oz) finely grated Parmesan**
- **1 egg, lightly beaten**

Preheat the oven to moderately hot 200°C (400°F/Gas 6). Lightly brush the puff pastry with the butter, then sprinkle each sheet with ¼ cup (25 g/¾ oz) of the cheese and season with salt and pepper.

Fold each sheet in half, bringing the top edge down towards you. Brush the tops of each sheet with the egg. Sprinkle each with 2 tablespoons of extra grated Parmesan and season with salt.

Using a very sharp knife, cut the dough vertically into 1 cm (½ inch) wide strips. Transfer each of the strips to a baking tray (sheet) lined with baking paper, spacing them evenly apart. Leave room for them to puff up without touching each other.

Grab each end of the pastry and stretch and twist in the opposite direction. Bake for 8–10 minutes or until lightly browned. Ideal with warm cheese dip or warm crab and lemon dip. Also good on their own.

Makes 80

Mediterranean Twists

- 2 tablespoons olive oil
- 2 onions, thinly sliced
- ⅓ cup (80 ml/2¾ fl oz) dry white wine
- 3 teaspoons sugar
- 1 cup (30 g/1 oz) chopped fresh flat-leaf parsley
- 8 anchovies, drained and finely chopped
- 1 cup (130 g/4½ oz) coarsely grated Gruyère
- 6 sheets filo (phyllo) pastry
- 60 g (2 oz) unsalted butter, melted

Preheat the oven to hot 220°C (425°F/Gas 7) and warm a baking tray (sheet). Heat the oil in a medium frying pan and cook the onion over low heat for 5 minutes. Add the white wine and sugar, and cook for 10–15 minutes, or until the onion is soft and golden. Remove from the heat and cool.

Combine the parsley, anchovies, grated Gruyère and cooled onion mixture in a bowl.

Keeping the filo (phyllo) covered while you work, take one sheet, brush lightly with the butter, cover with another sheet and repeat until you have three buttered sheets. Spread the parsley mixture over the pastry and top with the remaining three sheets, buttering each layer as before. Press down firmly, then cut the pastry in half widthways, then cut each half into strips 1.5–2 cm (⅝–¾ inch) wide. Brush with butter, then gently twist each strip. Season with black pepper, place on a baking tray (sheet) and bake for 10 minutes, or until crisp and golden.

Think Ahead: Make the Mediterranean twists up to 2 days ahead and store them in an airtight container lined with thick paper towels to absorb any excess butter. To refresh them, warm them in a moderate 180°C (350°F/Gas 4) oven for 10 minutes before serving.

Variation: There are many variations to these twists, but a great one to try is Parmesan and thyme twists. Simply substitute the Gruyère with ¾ cup (75 g/2½ oz) of coarsely grated Parmesan and replace the parsley with 2 teaspoons of thyme.

Makes 24

Herbed Cheese Delights

Biscuit (Cracker) Pastry
- 1 cup (125 g/4⅓ oz) plain (all-purpose) flour
- ½ teaspoon baking powder
- 60 g (2 oz) butter
- 1 egg, lightly beaten
- 60 g (2 oz) Cheddar (American) cheese, grated
- 1 teaspoon chopped fresh chives
- 1 teaspoon chopped fresh parsley

Cheese Filling
- 80 g (2¾ oz) cream cheese, softened
- 20 g (⅔ oz) butter
- 1 tablespoon chopped fresh chives
- 1 tablespoon chopped fresh parsley
- ¼ teaspoon lemon pepper
- 90 g (3¼ oz) Cheddar (American) cheese, grated

Preheat the oven to moderately hot 190°C (375°F/Gas 5). Line two baking trays (sheets) with baking paper.

To make the biscuit (cracker) pastry, sift the flour and baking powder into a large bowl and add the chopped butter. Rub in with your fingertips, until the mixture resembles fine breadcrumbs.

Make a well in the centre and add the egg, cheese, herbs and 1 tablespoon iced water. Mix with a flat-bladed knife, using a cutting action until the mixture comes together in beads. Gently gather together and lift out onto a lightly floured surface. Press together into a ball.

Roll the pastry between sheets of baking paper to 3 mm (⅛ inch) thickness. Remove the top sheet of paper and cut the pastry into rounds, using a 5 cm (2 inch) cutter. Place the rounds onto the trays. Re-roll the remaining pastry and repeat cutting. Bake for about 8 minutes, or until lightly browned. Transfer to a wire rack to cool.

To make the filling, beat the cream cheese and butter in a small bowl with electric beaters until light and creamy. Add the herbs, pepper and cheese and beat until smooth. Spread half a teaspoon of filling on half of the biscuits (crackers) and sandwich together with the remaining biscuits (crackers).

Note: You can use freshly chopped lemon thyme instead of parsley.

In Advance: The biscuits (crackers) can be made 2 days ahead and stored in an airtight container, or frozen. The filling can be made a day ahead and stored, covered, in the refrigerator.

Makes 20

Bite-Sized
Treats

Ham, Leek and Port Fig Treats

- 2 cups (250 g/8¾ oz) plain (all-purpose) flour
- 3 teaspoons baking powder
- 110 g (3¾ oz) chilled butter
- 100 g (3½ oz) Stilton cheese
- 2 tablespoons chopped fresh chives
- ¾ cup (185 ml/6½ fl oz) milk

Filling
- 1 cup (250 ml/8½ fl oz) port
- 6 large dried figs, stems removed
- 1 teaspoon sugar
- 1 large leek
- 1 teaspoon Dijon mustard
- 2 teaspoons red wine vinegar
- 1 tablespoon olive oil
- 150 g (5¼ oz) shaved ham

Sift the flour, baking powder and ¾ teaspoon salt into a large bowl. Coarsely grate the butter and cheese into the flour and rub in with your fingertips until the pieces are the size of coarse breadcrumbs. Stir in the chives. Pour in the milk and combine with a fork until large clumps form. Turn onto a floured surface and press into a ball.

On a floured surface, roll the dough into a 15 × 25 cm (6 × 10 inch) rectangle. With the long edge of the dough facing you, fold in both ends so they meet in the centre, then fold the dough in half widthways. Roll again into a 15 × 25 cm (6 × 10 inch) rectangle, about 1 cm (½ inch) thick. Cut rounds close together with a 3 cm (1¼ inch) cutter. Push the scraps together and roll and cut as before. Place 2.5 cm (1 inch) apart on a baking tray (sheet) and refrigerate for 20 minutes. Preheat the oven to hot 220°C (425°F/Gas 7) and bake for 10–12 minutes, or until lightly browned.

In a small pan, heat the port, figs and sugar. Bring to the boil, reduce the heat and simmer for 15 minutes. Remove the figs and, when cooled, roughly chop. Simmer the liquid for about 3 minutes, until reduced and syrupy. Put the figs back in and stir to combine. Set aside.

Discard any tough leaves from the leek, then rinse the leek. Trim off the dark green tops. Slit the leek lengthways, almost to the bottom, roll a quarter turn and slit again. Wash well, drain and steam for about 10 minutes, or until very soft. Roughly chop, then combine with the mustard, vinegar and oil. Season with salt and pepper.

Cut the scones (biscuits) in half. Put a folded piece of ham on each bottom half, top with a teaspoon each of leek and fig mixture, then replace the tops.

Makes about 40

Lamb Korma Pies

- 3 cups (375 g/13¼ oz) plain (all-purpose) flour, sifted
- 2 tablespoons caraway seeds
- 180 g (6⅓ oz) butter, chopped
- 1 tablespoon olive oil
- 1 small onion, finely chopped
- 1 clove garlic, crushed
- 2 tablespoons bottled mild curry paste
- 250 g (8¾ oz) lamb fillets, trimmed, finely diced
- 1 small potato, finely diced
- ¼ cup (40 g/1½ oz) frozen baby peas
- ¼ cup (60 g/2 oz) natural yoghurt
- 1 egg, lightly beaten
- 2 tablespoons chopped fresh coriander (cilantro)

Combine the flour and caraway seeds in a large bowl. Rub in the butter using just your fingertips, until the mixture resembles fine breadcrumbs. Make a well, add 4 tablespoons water and mix with a flat-bladed knife, using a cutting action, until the mixture comes together in beads. Lift onto a floured surface and gather into a ball. Flatten slightly into a disc, wrap in plastic wrap and chill for 20 minutes.

Heat the oil in a heavy-based pan, add the onion and garlic and stir over medium heat for 3–4 minutes, or until the onion is soft. Add the curry paste and stir for 1 minute. Increase the heat to high and add the lamb, potato and peas, stirring for 5 minutes, or until the lamb is well browned all over. Add the yoghurt, bring to the boil, then reduce the heat and simmer, covered, for 30 minutes, or until the lamb is tender. Uncover and simmer for 10 minutes, or until the sauce thickens. Remove from the heat and allow to cool.

Preheat the oven to 180°C (350°F/Gas 4). Lightly grease two 12-hole mini muffin tins. Roll two-thirds of the dough between baking paper to 2 mm (¹⁄₁₆ inch) thick. Cut 24 rounds with a 7 cm (2¾ inch) cutter and ease into the tins. Spoon the lamb into the cases. Roll out the remaining pastry into a rectangle. Cut 24 strips 1 × 20 cm (½ × 8 inches) and twist onto the top of each pie. Brush with the egg and bake for 25–30 minutes, or until golden brown. Cool slightly before removing from the tins. Serve warm, sprinkled with fresh coriander (cilantro).

Makes 24

Lahm Bi Ajeen (Lamb Pastry Fingers)

- 1 tablespoon olive oil
- 350 g (12¼ oz) lean lamb mince (ground lamb)
- 1 small onion, finely chopped
- 2 cloves garlic crushed
- 1 tablespoon ground cumin
- 1 teaspoon ground ginger (ginger root)
- 1 teaspoon paprika
- 1 teaspoon ground cinnamon
- pinch of saffron threads, soaked in a little warm water
- 1 teaspoon harissa (Tunisian hot chilli (pepper) sauce)
- 2 tablespoons chopped fresh coriander (cilantro)
- 2 tablespoons chopped fresh flat-leaf parsley
- 3 tablespoons pine nuts, toasted
- 1 egg
- 6 sheets filo (phyllo) pastry
- 60 g (2 oz) butter, melted
- 1 tablespoon sesame seeds

Yoghurt Sauce
- 1 cup (250 g/8¾ oz) natural yoghurt
- 2 tablespoons chopped fresh mint
- 1 clove garlic, crushed

Preheat the oven to moderate 180°C (350°F/Gas 4). Lightly grease a large baking tray (sheet).

Heat the oil in a large frying pan, add the lamb and cook for 5 minutes, breaking up any lumps with the back of a wooden spoon. Add the onion and garlic and cook for 1 minute. Add the spices, harissa (Tunisian hot chilli (pepper) sauce), chopped coriander (cilantro) and parsley and cook for 1 minute, stirring to combine. Transfer to a sieve and drain to remove the fat.

Place the mixture in a bowl and allow to cool slightly. Mix in the pine nuts and egg.

Place a sheet of filo (phyllo) on the bench with the shortest side facing you. Cover the remaining sheets with a damp tea towel to prevent them from drying out. Cut the sheet of filo (phyllo) into four equal strips lengthways. Brush one of the strips with melted butter and place another on top. Do the same with the other two pieces. Place 1 tablespoon of the lamb mixture on each at the short end of the filo (phyllo) and roll each up, tucking in the ends to hold the mixture in and form each into a cigar shape. Repeat this process until you have used up all the filo (phyllo) and meat mixture.

Place the lamb fingers on the baking tray (sheet). Brush with any remaining melted butter and sprinkle with sesame seeds. Bake for 15 minutes, or until lightly golden.

For the yoghurt sauce, stir all the ingredients together in a small bowl. Serve the filo (phyllo) fingers warm with the sauce on the side.

Makes 12

Pesto Palmiers

- 1 cup (50 g/1¾ oz) fresh basil leaves
- 1 clove garlic, crushed
- ¼ cup (25 g/¾ oz) grated Parmesan
- 1 tablespoon pine nuts, toasted
- 2 tablespoons olive oil
- 4 sheets ready-rolled puff pastry, thawed

Preheat the oven to hot 220°C (425°F/Gas 7). Roughly chop the basil leaves in a food processor with the garlic, Parmesan and pine nuts. With the motor running, gradually add the oil in a thin stream and process until smooth.

Spread each pastry sheet with a quarter of the basil mixture. Roll up one side until you reach the middle then repeat with the other side. Place on a baking tray (sheet). Repeat with the remaining pastry and basil mixture. Freeze for 30 minutes.

Slice each roll into 1.5 cm (⅝ inch) slices. Curl each slice into a semi-circle and place on a lightly greased baking tray (sheet). Allow room for the palmiers to expand during cooking. Bake in batches for 15–20 minutes, or until golden brown.

Note: Palmiers are delicious bite-sized specially shaped pastry snacks which traditionally were sweet. They were made by sprinkling sugar between the pastry folds and then cutting into slices before baking until crisp and golden. Sometimes they were dusted with icing sugar and served as a petit four with coffee. Other savoury variations include spreading with a prepared tapenade paste made with olives, capers, anchovies, oil and garlic, or with tahini, a sesame seed paste. Another simple version is to sprinkle just the grated Parmesan between the pastry layers.

Makes 60

Seafood Parcels

- 250 g (8¾ oz) skinless white fish fillets (eg. cod, snapper, coley, ocean perch)
- 100 g (3½ oz) scallops
- 400 g (14 oz) cooked medium prawns (shrimps)
- 30 g (1 oz) butter
- 1 tablespoon lemon juice
- 1 tablespoon plain (all-purpose) flour
- 1 cup (250 ml/8½ fl oz) milk
- 60 g (2 oz) Cheddar (American) cheese, grated
- 1 tablespoon chopped fresh chives
- 1 tablespoon chopped fresh dill (dill weed)
- 10 sheets filo (phyllo) pastry
- 60 g (2 oz) butter, melted
- 2 teaspoons poppy seeds or sesame seeds

Preheat the oven to moderate 180°C (350°F/Gas 4). Line a baking tray (sheet) with baking paper.

Cut the fish into 1 cm (½ inch) wide strips. Wash the scallops and slice or pull off any vein, membrane or hard white muscle, leaving any roe attached. Peel the prawns (shrimps) and pull out the dark vein from each prawn back, starting at the head.

Melt the butter in a heavy-based pan. Add the fish, scallops and lemon juice. Cook over medium heat for 1 minute, or until tender. Remove from the pan with a slotted spoon, place in a bowl and keep warm.

Stir the flour into the butter and cook for 1 minute, or until pale and foaming. Remove from the heat and gradually stir in the milk. Return to the heat and stir constantly until the mixture boils and thickens. Reduce the heat and simmer for 2 minutes. Stir in the Cheddar (American) cheese, chives, dill (dill weed), fish, scallops and prawns (shrimps). Remove from the heat and season, to taste, with salt and pepper. Cover the surface with plastic wrap.

Layer 2 sheets of pastry together with melted butter, then cut into 4 equal strips. Cover unused pastry with a damp tea towel. Place 2 tablespoons of seafood mixture on one short end of each pastry strip. Fold in the edges and roll up. Repeat with the remaining pastry, seafood and some of the remaining butter. Place the parcels seam-side-down on the baking tray (sheet). Brush with the remaining melted butter, sprinkle with poppy seeds and bake for 20 minutes.

Note: You can make the sauce a day ahead and refrigerate until required.

Makes 20

Seafood Toasts

- 350 g (12¼ oz) raw medium prawns (shrimps)
- 1 clove garlic
- 75 g (2½ oz) canned water chestnuts, drained
- 1 tablespoon chopped fresh coriander (cilantro)
- 2 cm × 2 cm (¾ inch × ¾ inch) piece fresh ginger (ginger root), roughly chopped
- 2 eggs, separated
- ¼ teaspoon white pepper

- 12 slices white bread, crusts removed
- 1 cup (155 g/5½ oz) sesame seeds
- oil, for deep-frying

Dipping Sauce
- ½ cup (125 ml/4¼ fl oz) tomato sauce (ketchup)
- 2 cloves garlic, crushed
- 2 small fresh red chillies, seeded and finely chopped
- 2 tablespoons hoisin sauce
- 2 teaspoons Worcestershire sauce

To make the dipping sauce, combine all the ingredients in a small bowl.

Peel the prawns (shrimps) and gently pull out the dark vein from each prawn (shrimp) back, starting at the head end. Put the prawns (shrimps) in a food processor with the garlic, water chestnuts, coriander (cilantro), ginger (ginger root), egg whites, pepper and ¼ teaspoon salt, and process for 20–30 seconds, or until smooth.

Brush the top of each slice of bread with lightly beaten egg yolk, then spread evenly with the prawn (shrimp) mixture. Sprinkle generously with sesame seeds. Cut each slice of bread into three even strips.

Fill a large heavy-based saucepan or deep-fryer one-third full of oil and heat to 180°C (350°F), or until a cube of bread dropped into the oil browns in 15 seconds. Deep-fry the toasts in small batches for 10–15 seconds, or until golden and crisp. Start with the prawn (shrimp) mixture facing down, then turn halfway through. Remove the toasts from the oil with tongs or a slotted spoon and drain on crumpled paper towels. Serve with the dipping sauce.

Makes 36

Tamale Beef and Bean Pies

- 1 tablespoon oil
- 1 small onion, finely chopped
- 250 g (8¾ oz) beef mince (ground beef)
- 1 clove garlic, crushed
- ¼ teaspoon chilli powder
- 200 g (7 oz) canned crushed tomatoes
- 1½ cups (375 ml/13 fl oz) beef stock (broth)
- 300 g (10½ oz) can red kidney beans, drained
- 2½ cups (360 g/12¾ oz) masa harina
- 1 teaspoon baking powder
- 125 g (4⅓ oz) butter, cut into cubes and chilled
- 125 g (4⅓ oz) Cheddar (American) cheese, grated
- sour cream, for serving

Heat the oil in a frying pan. Add the onion and cook over low heat for 3–4 minutes, or until soft. Increase the heat, add the mince (ground beef) and cook until browned all over. Add the garlic, chilli, tomato and ½ cup (125 ml/4¼ fl oz) stock (broth). Bring to the boil, then reduce the heat and simmer for 35 minutes, or until the liquid has evaporated to a thick sauce. Stir in the beans and cool.

Lightly grease 30 holes in deep mini muffin tins. Sift the masa harina, baking powder and ½ teaspoon salt into a bowl. Rub the butter into the flour with your fingertips until it resembles fine breadcrumbs. Make a well in the centre and, with a flat-bladed knife, mix in the remaining stock, then use your hands to bring the mixture together into a ball. Divide into thirds and roll two thirds between 2 sheets of baking paper and cut out rounds with a 7 cm (2¾ inch) cutter. Line the muffin tins. Trim the edges and reserve any leftover pastry.

Preheat the oven to moderately hot 200°C (400°F/Gas 6). Spoon the filling into the pastry cases and sprinkle with the Cheddar (American) cheese. Roll out the remaining pastry and reserved pastry as above. Cut into 4 cm (1½ inch) rounds to cover the tops of the pies. Brush the edges with water and place over the filling. Trim the edges and press the pastry together to seal. Bake for 20–25 minutes, or until the pastry is crisp and lightly browned. Serve with sour cream.

Makes 30

Mini Meat Pies

- 6 sheets ready-rolled shortcrust pastry (pie pastry)
- 2 small tomatoes, sliced
- ½ teaspoon dried oregano leaves

Filling
- 1 tablespoon oil
- 1 onion, chopped
- 2 cloves garlic, crushed

- 500 g (1 lb) beef mince (ground beef)
- 2 tablespoons plain (all-purpose) flour
- 1½ cups (375 ml/13 fl oz) beef stock (broth)
- ⅓ cup (80 ml/2¾ fl oz) tomato sauce (ketchup)
- 2 teaspoons Worcestershire sauce
- ½ teaspoon dried mixed herbs

Preheat the oven to moderately hot 200°C (400°F/Gas 6). Cut the pastry into 48 circles (if making traditional pies, only 24 if making uncovered pies) using a 7 cm (2¾ inch) round cutter. Press 24 circles into two lightly greased 12-hole patty tins.

To make the filling, heat the oil in a heavy-based pan, add the onion and garlic and cook over medium heat for 2 minutes, or until the onion is soft. Add the mince (ground beef) and stir over high heat for 3 minutes, or until well browned and all the liquid has evaporated. Use a fork to break up any lumps of mince (ground beef).

Add the flour, stir until combined, then cook over medium heat for 1 minute. Add the stock (broth), sauces and herbs and stir over the heat until boiling. Reduce the heat to low and simmer for 5 minutes, or until the mixture has reduced and thickened; stir occasionally. Allow to cool.

Divide the filling among the pastry circles. Top each with two half slices of tomato and sprinkle with oregano. Bake for 25 minutes, or until the pastry is golden brown and crisp. For traditional pies, place the remaining pastry rounds over the tomato and oregano topping and seal the edges with beaten egg before baking. Serve hot.

Makes 24

Smoked Salmon Bread Baskets

- 250 g (8¾ oz) smoked salmon
- 1 loaf white sliced bread
- ¼ cup (60 ml/2 fl oz) olive oil
- ⅓ cup (90 g/3¼ oz) whole-egg mayonnaise
- 2 teaspoons extra virgin olive oil
- 1 teaspoon white wine vinegar
- 1 teaspoon finely chopped fresh dill (dill weed)
- 3 teaspoons horseradish cream
- 3 tablespoons salmon roe

Preheat the oven to 180°C (350°F/Gas 4). Cut the salmon into strips. Flatten the bread to 1 mm (1⁄32 inch) with a rolling pin. Cut out 24 rounds with a 7 cm (2¾ inch) cutter. Brush both sides of the rounds with olive oil and push into the holes of two 12-hole flat-based patty (bun) tins. Bake for 10 minutes, or until crisp. Cool.

Stir the mayonnaise in a bowl with the extra virgin olive oil, vinegar, dill (dill weed) and horseradish until combined.

Arrange folds of salmon in each cooled bread case and top each with 1 teaspoon of mayonnaise mixture. Spoon ½ teaspoon of salmon roe on top of each before serving.

Note: The bread cases can be made a day in advance and, when completely cold, stored in an airtight container. If they soften, you can crisp them on a baking tray (sheet) in a moderate oven for 5 minutes. Cool before filling.

Makes 24

Pumpkin and Hazelnut Pesto Bites

- **750 g (1½ lb) butternut pumpkin (squash)**
- **3 tablespoons oil**
- **35 g (1¼ oz) roasted hazelnuts**
- **35 g (1¼ oz) rocket (arugula)**
- **3 tablespoons grated Parmesan**

Preheat the oven to moderately hot 200°C (400°F/Gas 6). Peel the pumpkin (squash) and cut into 2 cm (¾ inch) slices, then cut into rough triangular shapes about 3 cm (1¼ inches) along the base. Toss with half the oil and some salt and cracked black pepper, until coated. Spread on a baking tray (sheet) and bake for 35 minutes, or until cooked.

For the hazelnut pesto, process the hazelnuts, rocket (arugula), 1 tablespoon of the Parmesan and the remaining oil, until they form a paste. Season with salt and cracked black pepper.

Spoon a small amount of the hazelnut pesto onto each piece of pumpkin (squash) and sprinkle with the remaining Parmesan and black pepper if desired. Serve warm or cold.

In Advance: Pesto can be made several days ahead. Pour a film of oil over the surface to prevent discoloration. Tip the oil off before using the pesto.

Makes 48

Turkey Pastry Parcels

- 20 g (⅔ oz) butter
- 200 g (7 oz) button mushrooms, sliced
- 4 rashers bacon, diced
- 350 g (12¼ oz) cooked turkey, chopped
- 150 g (5¼ oz) ricotta
- 2 spring (green) onions, sliced
- 3 tablespoons shredded fresh basil
- 24 sheets filo (phyllo) pastry
- butter, melted, extra, for brushing
- sesame seeds, for sprinkling

Melt the butter in a large saucepan and add the mushrooms and bacon. Cook over high heat for 5 minutes, or until the mushrooms are soft and there is no liquid left. Combine the turkey, ricotta, spring (green) onion and basil in a bowl, add the mushroom mixture, then season, to taste.

Preheat the oven to moderate 180°C (350°F/Gas 4). Cover the pastry with a damp tea towel to prevent drying out. Working with 3 sheets at a time, brush each layer with melted butter. Cut into 3 strips. Place 1 tablespoon of filling at the end of each strip and fold the pastry over to form a triangle. Fold until you reach the end of the pastry. Repeat with the remaining pastry and filling. Place on a greased baking tray (sheet), brush with butter and sprinkle with sesame seeds. Bake for 30–35 minutes, or until golden.

Makes 24

Pumpkin and Pesto Chicken in Pastry

- 4 chicken breast fillets
- 1 tablespoon oil
- 250 g (8¾ oz) pumpkin
- 1 bunch English (common) spinach
- 12 sheets filo (phyllo) pastry

- 100 g (3½ oz) butter, melted
- ¼ cup (25 g/¾ oz) dry breadcrumbs
- 100 g (3½ oz) ricotta
- ⅓ cup (90 g/3¼ oz) pesto (see Note)
- 1 tablespoon pine nuts, chopped

Preheat the oven to moderately hot 200°C (400°F/Gas 6). Season the chicken fillets with salt and pepper. Heat half the oil in a frying pan and fry the chicken until browned on both sides, then remove from the pan.

Cut the peeled pumpkin into 5 mm (¼ inch) slices. Heat the remaining oil in the same pan and fry the pumpkin until lightly browned on both sides. Allow to cool.

Put the spinach leaves into a bowl of boiling water and stir until just wilted. Drain well and pat dry with paper towels. Layer 3 sheets of filo (phyllo) pastry, brushing each with some of the melted butter, sprinkling between layers with some of the breadcrumbs.

Wrap each chicken breast in a quarter of the spinach and place on one short side of the filo (phyllo), leaving a 2 cm (¾ inch) gap. Top the chicken with a quarter of the pumpkin slices, then spread a quarter of the ricotta down the centre of the pumpkin. Top with a tablespoon of the pesto.

Fold the sides of the pastry over the filling, then roll the parcel up until it sits on the unsecured end. Repeat with the remaining ingredients. Place the parcels on a lightly greased baking tray (sheet), brush with any remaining butter and sprinkle with the pine nuts. Bake for 15 minutes, then cover loosely with foil and bake for a further 20 minutes, or until the pastry is golden brown.

Note: Bottled pesto is not suitable for this recipe – you can either make your own or use fresh pesto from a delicatessen.

Serves 4

Bacon and Whole Egg Pies

- 1 teaspoon oil
- 4 spring (green) onions, chopped
- 6 lean bacon rashers, chopped
- ½ cup (125 ml/4¼ fl oz) milk
- ¼ cup (60 ml/2 fl oz) cream
- 2 tablespoons chopped fresh parsley
- pinch of ground nutmeg
- 7 eggs
- 10 sheets filo (phyllo) pastry
- melted butter, for brushing

Heat the oil in a pan and cook the spring (green) onion and bacon for 2–3 minutes, then set aside to cool. Mix together the milk, cream, parsley, ground nutmeg and 1 egg and season with salt and pepper.

Brush 1 sheet of filo (phyllo) pastry with the melted butter, then brush another sheet and lay it on top. Repeat until you have a stack of 5 sheets. Cut into 6 squares. Repeat with the remaining 5 sheets of pastry. Place 2 squares together at an angle to form a rough 8-pointed star and fit into a 1 cup (250 ml/8½ fl oz) muffin tin. Repeat with the remaining squares.

Preheat the oven to 200°C (400°F/Gas 6). Divide the spring (green) onion and bacon mixture evenly between the filo (phyllo) pastry cups. Then pour over the egg and cream mixture and carefully break an egg on the top of the pie. Bake for 10 minutes, then reduce the oven to moderate 180°C (350°F/Gas 4) and bake for a further 10–15 minutes, or until the pastry is lightly crisp and golden and the egg is just set. Serve the pies immediately.

Makes 6

Cocktail Tartlets

- 1½ cups (185 g/6½ oz) plain (all-purpose) flour
- 100 g (3½ oz) chilled butter, chopped
- 30 g (1 oz) Parmesan, grated
- 1 egg, lightly beaten

Fillings
- pesto, sun-dried tomato and black (ripe) olives
- olive tapenade, hard-boiled quail eggs and fresh flat-leaf parsley
- cream cheese, shredded sliced smoked salmon, thinly sliced Lebanese cucumber, and chopped fresh chives

Sift the flour and ¼ teaspoon salt into a large bowl, add the butter and rub into the flour with your fingertips until the mixture resembles fine breadcrumbs. Stir in the Parmesan, then make a well in the centre. Add the egg and a little water and mix with a flat-bladed knife, using a cutting action, until the mixture comes together in beads. Gently gather together and lift out onto a lightly floured surface. Press together into a ball. Wrap in plastic wrap and refrigerate for 30 minutes.

Preheat the oven to hot 210°C (415°F/Gas 6–7). Lightly grease two 12-hole round-based patty (bun) tins. Roll the pastry out very thinly and using an 8 cm (3 inch) cutter, cut 30 rounds from the pastry. Press the pastry into the tins and prick lightly all over. Bake for 8–9 minutes, or until golden. Allow to cool in the tins. Remove and repeat with the remaining pastry.

Fill the cooled shells with the different fillings.

In Advance: The tartlet shells can be made up to a few days ahead and stored in an airtight container. If necessary, re-crisp briefly in a moderate 180°C (350°F/Gas 4) oven before use.

Makes about 30

Mini Oyster Pies

- 2 cups (500 ml/17 fl oz) fish stock (broth)
- 1 tablespoon olive oil
- 2 leeks, chopped
- 30 g (1 oz) butter
- 1 tablespoon plain (all-purpose) flour
- 1 teaspoon lemon juice
- 1 teaspoon chopped fresh chives
- 8 sheets puff pastry
- 30 fresh oysters
- 1 egg, lightly beaten, to glaze

Pour the stock into a saucepan and simmer over medium heat for 15 minutes, or until reduced by half – you will need 1 cup (250 ml/8½ fl oz).

Heat the oil in a saucepan over medium heat. Add the leek and cook, stirring well, for 5 minutes, or until soft and lightly coloured. Transfer to a small bowl to cool slightly.

Melt the butter in a small saucepan over low heat. Add the flour and cook, stirring well, for 2 minutes, or until the flour is golden. Remove from the heat and gradually add the fish stock (broth), stirring well. Return to the heat and bring to the boil, stirring constantly for 2 minutes, or until thickened. Add the lemon juice, chives and leek and season well. Set aside to cool for 20 minutes. Preheat the oven to 200°C (400°F/Gas 6) and grease two baking trays (sheets).

Using a 6 cm (2½ inch) round cutter, cut out 30 circles of pastry and put one oyster and a heaped teaspoon of the filling on top of each, leaving a narrow border. Lightly brush the edges with beaten egg.

Cut thirty 8 cm (3 inch) circles from the remaining pastry. Cover the filling with these rounds and press the edges with a fork to seal. Brush the tops with the remaining beaten egg, put on the trays (sheets) and bake for 15–20 minutes, or until golden and well puffed.

Makes 30

Mushrooms en Croûte

- 8 slices white bread, crust removed
- 80 g (2¾ oz) butter, melted
- 1 tablespoon olive oil
- 1 clove garlic, crushed
- ½ small onion, finely chopped
- 375 g (13¼ oz) small button mushrooms, finely sliced
- 1 tablespoon dry sherry
- ⅓ cup (80 g/2¾ oz) sour cream
- 2 teaspoons cornflour (cornstarch)
- 1 tablespoon finely chopped fresh parsley
- 1 teaspoon finely chopped fresh thyme
- 30 g (1 oz) Parmesan, grated

Preheat the oven to moderate 180°C (350°F/Gas 4). Brush both sides of the bread with the butter. Cut each slice in half vertically, then each half into three horizontally. Bake on a baking tray (sheet) for 5–10 minutes, or until golden and crisp.

Heat the oil in a large frying pan, add the garlic and onion and cook, stirring, over low heat until the onion is soft. Add the mushrooms and cook over medium heat for 5 minutes, or until tender. Season with salt and pepper.

Pour the sherry into the pan. Blend the sour cream and cornflour (cornstarch), add to the mushrooms and stir until the mixture boils and thickens. Remove from the heat and stir in the herbs. Allow to cool.

Spread the mushroom mixture onto each croûte and sprinkle with the Parmesan. Place on a baking tray (sheet) and bake for 5 minutes, or until heated through. Serve decorated with small sprigs of fresh herbs, if desired.

In Advance: Bake the bread up to 4 days in advance and store in an airtight container. Make the topping and assemble just prior to serving.

Makes 48

Oregano and Prosciutto Pinwheels

- 1 red capsicum (pepper)
- 1 green capsicum (pepper)
- 1 yellow capsicum (pepper)
- 125 g (4⅓ oz) cream cheese, softened
- 25 g (¾ oz) Parmesan, grated
- 2 spring (green) onions, finely chopped
- ¼ cup (7 g/¼ oz) chopped fresh oregano
- 1 tablespoon bottled capers, drained and chopped
- 1 tablespoon pine nuts, chopped
- 12 thin slices prosciutto

Cut the capsicums (peppers) into quarters and remove the seeds and membrane. Cook, skin-side-up, under a hot grill (broiler) until the skin blackens and blisters. Place in a plastic bag until cool, then peel.

Mix together the cream cheese, Parmesan, spring (green) onion, oregano, capers and pine nuts.

Place the capsicum (pepper) pieces on the prosciutto slices and trim the prosciutto to the same size. Remove the capsicum (pepper) and spread some cheese mixture on the prosciutto. Top with the capsicum (pepper) and spread with a little more cheese mixture. Roll up tightly from the short end. Cover and refrigerate for 1 hour, or until firm. Slice into 1 cm (½ inch) rounds and serve on toothpicks.

Makes about 40

Thai Chicken Sausage Rolls

- 200 g (7 oz) chicken breast fillet, roughly chopped
- 150 g (5¼ oz) mild pancetta, chopped
- 1 clove garlic, crushed
- 3 spring (green) onions, chopped
- 2 tablespoons chopped fresh coriander (cilantro)
- 2 bird's eye chillies, seeded and finely chopped
- 1 teaspoon fish sauce
- 1 egg
- 1 teaspoon grated fresh ginger (ginger root)
- 375 g (13¼ oz) block frozen puff pastry
- 1 egg yolk
- 2 tablespoons sesame seeds
- sweet chilli sauce (jalapeno jelly), to serve
- fresh coriander (cilantro), to serve

Preheat the oven to moderate 180°C (350°F/Gas 4). Put the chicken, pancetta, garlic, spring (green) onion, coriander (cilantro), chilli, fish sauce, whole egg and ginger (ginger root) in a food processor and process until just combined.

Roll out the pastry to a rectangle 30 cm × 40 cm (12 inches × 16 inches). Halve lengthways. Take half the filling and, with floured hands, roll it into a long sausage and place along the long edge of one piece of pastry. Brush the edges with water and fold the pastry over, pressing down to seal. Place the sealed edge underneath. Repeat with the remaining pastry and filling.

Using a sharp knife, cut the sausage rolls into 3 cm (1¼ inch) lengths on the diagonal; discard the end pieces. Brush the tops with egg yolk, then sprinkle with sesame seeds. Bake for 10–15 minutes, or until golden. Serve with sweet chilli sauce (jalapeno jelly) and garnished with fresh coriander (cilantro).

Think Ahead: You can make the sausage rolls a day ahead. Reheat in a moderate 180°C (350°F/Gas 4) oven for 10–12 minutes, or until they are warmed through.

Variation: For spicy lamb sausage rolls, follow the method outlined for the basic sausage roll, but change the filling. Mix 375 g (13¼ oz) lamb mince, ½ cup (40 g/1½ oz) fresh breadcrumbs, ½ small grated onion, 2 teaspoons soy sauce, 1 teaspoon grated fresh ginger (ginger root), 1 teaspoon soft brown sugar, ½ teaspoon ground coriander (cilantro), ¼ teaspoon each of ground cumin and sambal oelek. Lightly sprinkle the uncooked sausage rolls with poppy seeds after glazing and bake for 10–15 minutes.

Makes 24

Borek of Asparagus

- 16 fresh asparagus spears
- ½ teaspoon salt
- ½ teaspoon black pepper
- 2 tablespoons finely grated lemon rind

- 2 sheets ready-rolled puff pastry
- 1 egg yolk
- 1 tablespoon sesame seeds

Preheat the oven to moderately hot 200°C (400°F/Gas 6).

Add the asparagus to a large pan of lightly salted boiling water and simmer for about 3 minutes, then drain and refresh under cold running water. Trim to 10 cm (4 inch) lengths.

Combine the salt, black pepper and lemon rind in a shallow dish and roll each asparagus spear in this mixture.

Cut the puff pastry sheets into 12 × 6 cm (4¾ × 2½ inch) rectangles and place one asparagus spear on each piece of pastry. In a bowl, combine the egg yolk with 2 teaspoons water and brush some on the sides and ends of the pastry. Roll the pastry up like a parcel, enclosing the sides so that the asparagus is completely sealed in. Press the joins of the pastry with a fork.

Place the parcels on lightly greased baking trays (sheets). Brush with the remaining egg and sprinkle with sesame seeds. Bake for 15–20 minutes, or until golden.

Makes 16

Little Chicken and Vegetable Pot Pies

- 1¼ cups (150 g/5¼ oz) plain (all-purpose) flour
- 90 g (3¼ oz) butter, chilled and cubed
- 1 tablespoon finely chopped fresh thyme
- 1 tablespoon finely chopped fresh flat-leaf parsley
- 3–4 tablespoons iced water

Filling
- 750 g (1½ lb) chicken breast fillets
- 1 lemon, quartered
- 5 spring (green) onions
- 2 bay leaves
- 1½ cups (375 ml/13 fl oz) chicken stock (broth)

- ¼ cup (60 ml/2 fl oz) dry white wine
- 60 g (2 oz) butter
- 1 large onion, thinly sliced
- 1 tablespoon finely chopped fresh tarragon
- 100 g (3½ oz) button mushrooms, thinly sliced
- ¾ cup (90 g/3¼ oz) plain (all-purpose) flour
- 2 large carrots, cut into small cubes
- 1 celery stick, cut into small cubes
- ½ cup (90 g/3¼ oz) peas
- 1 egg, lightly beaten, to glaze

To make the pastry, sift the flour and ¼ teaspoon salt into a large bowl. Add the butter and rub it into the flour with your fingertips until the mixture resembles fine breadcrumbs. Stir in the chopped herbs. Make a well in the centre of the mixture, add almost all the water and mix with a flat-bladed knife, using a cutting action, until the mixture comes together in beads, adding a little more water if necessary.

Gently gather the dough together and lift it out onto a lightly floured work surface. Press together into a ball. Flatten slightly into a disc, wrap in plastic wrap and refrigerate for at least 20 minutes to let the dough relax.

Preheat the oven to 180°C (350°F/Gas 4). Place the chicken, lemon, 4 of the spring (green) onions, the bay leaves, chicken stock (broth), wine, 1½ cups (375 ml/13 fl oz) water and ½ teaspoon salt in a large saucepan. Bring to the boil over high heat. Reduce the heat and simmer for 20 minutes, or until the chicken is cooked through. Remove the chicken from the liquid with a slotted spoon and set aside. Return the liquid to the heat and boil for 10 minutes, or until it has reduced to 2 cups (500 ml/17 fl oz), then strain into a bowl and set aside. Roughly cut the chicken into small pieces.

Melt the butter in a large saucepan over medium heat. When it is sizzling, add the onion and cook for 2–3 minutes, or until soft. Add the tarragon and mushrooms and cook, stirring occasionally, for 3–4 minutes, or until the mushrooms are soft. Add the flour and cook, stirring constantly, for 3 minutes. Pour in the reserved poaching liquid, bring to the boil and cook, stirring often, for 2 minutes, or until slightly thickened. Remove from the heat, then stir in the carrot, celery, peas and chicken. Divide the filling evenly among six 1½ cup (375 ml/13 fl oz) ramekins.

Divide the dough into six even portions. Roll out each portion into a flat disc, 12 cm (4¾ inches) in diameter (or use a cutter). Moisten the ramekin rims and cover with pastry rounds, pressing down firmly to seal the edges. Re-roll any pastry trimmings to make decorations. Prick the pie tops with a fork, then brush with the egg. Bake for about 30 minutes, or until the pies are golden.

Makes 6

Cornish Pasties

- 2½ cups (310 g/11 oz) plain (all-purpose) flour
- 125 g (4⅓ oz) butter, chilled and chopped
- 160 g (5⅔ oz) round steak, finely chopped
- 1 small potato, finely chopped
- 1 small onion, finely chopped
- 1 small carrot, finely chopped
- 1–2 teaspoons Worcestershire sauce
- 2 tablespoons beef stock (broth)
- 1 egg, lightly beaten

Grease a baking tray (sheet). Place the flour, butter and a pinch of salt in a food processor and process for 15 seconds, or until crumbly. Add 4–5 tablespoons of water and process in short bursts until the mixture comes together (add more water if needed). Turn out onto a floured surface and gather together into a ball. Cover with plastic wrap and refrigerate for 30 minutes. Preheat the oven to hot 210°C (415°F/Gas 6–7).

Place the steak, potato, onion, carrot, Worcestershire sauce and stock (broth) in a large bowl and combine well. Season with salt and pepper.

Divide the dough into six portions. Roll out each portion to 3 mm (⅛ inch) thick and use a 16 cm (6⅓ inch) diameter plate as a guide to cut out 6 circles. Divide the filling evenly and put in the centre of each pastry circle.

Brush the edges of the pastry with beaten egg and form into a semicircle. Pinch the edges to form a frill and arrange on the tray (sheet). Brush with the remaining beaten egg and bake for 15 minutes. Lower the heat to moderate 180°C (350°F/Gas 4). Cook for 25–30 minutes, or until golden.

Makes 6

Chinese Barbecued Pork Pies

- 2 tablespoons cornflour (cornstarch)
- ¼ cup (60 ml/2 fl oz) oyster sauce
- ¼ cup (60 ml/2 fl oz) rice wine
- 2 tablespoons kecap manis (Indonesian soy sauce)
- 2 tablespoons lime juice
- 1 tablespoon grated fresh ginger (ginger root)
- ½ teaspoon ground white pepper
- 400 g (14 oz) Chinese barbecued pork, cut into 1 cm (½ inch) dice
- 150 g (5¼ oz) snow peas (mange tout), sliced
- 2 cups (100 g/3½ oz) thinly sliced Chinese cabbage
- 375 g (13¼ oz) shortcrust (pie) pastry
- 375 g (13¼ oz) puff pastry
- milk, for brushing
- 1 teaspoon sesame seeds

Preheat the oven to moderate 180°C (350°F/Gas 4). Grease four 11 cm (4⅓ inch) top, 9 cm (3⅓ inch) base and 3 cm (1¼ inch) deep metal pie dishes. Mix the cornflour (cornstarch) with 2 tablespoons water. Heat a large frying pan over low heat and add the oyster sauce, rice wine, kecap manis (Indonesian soy sauce), lime juice, ginger (ginger root), white pepper and the cornflour (cornstarch) mixture. Simmer for 2 minutes, or until very thick. Add the pork, snow peas (mange tout) and cabbage. Cook, stirring, for 5 minutes. Cool, then refrigerate for 1 hour, or until cold.

Meanwhile, roll out the shortcrust (pie) pastry between two sheets of baking paper until it is 3 mm (⅛ inch) thick. Cut out four 16 cm (6½ inch) rounds. Line the pie dishes with the pastry, then refrigerate.

When the filling is cold, fill the pastry shells. Roll out the puff pastry between the baking paper to 3 mm (⅛ inch) thick and cut out four rounds large enough to cover the tops of the pie dishes. Cover the pies with the puff pastry rounds and trim any excess. Use a fork to seal the edges and prick a few holes in the top. Brush the lids with milk, sprinkle with sesame seeds, and bake for 35 minutes, or until golden.

Makes 4

Potato and Salmon Parcels

- **750 g (1½ lb) floury potatoes, peeled**
- **40 g (1¼ oz) butter**
- **¼ cup (60 ml/2 fl oz) cream**
- **1 cup (125 g/4⅓ oz) grated Cheddar (American) cheese**
- **210 g (7½ oz) can red salmon, skin and bones removed, flaked**
- **1 tablespoon chopped fresh dill (dill weed)**
- **4 spring (green) onions, finely chopped**
- **3 sheets puff pastry**
- **1 egg, lightly beaten, to glaze**

Cut the potatoes into small pieces and cook in a pan of boiling water until tender. Mash with the butter and the cream until there are no lumps. Lightly grease two oven trays (sheets).

Add the cheese, salmon, dill (dill weed) and spring (green) onion to the potato and mix well. Preheat the oven to 200°C (400°F/Gas 6). Cut each pastry sheet into four squares. Divide the mixture among the squares (approximately ¼ cup in each). Lightly brush the edges with beaten egg. Bring all four corners to the centre to form a point and press together to make a parcel.

Put the parcels on the greased trays (sheets) and glaze with egg. Bake for 15–20 minutes, or until the pastry is golden brown.

Note: Before removing the pastries from the oven, lift them gently off the tray (sheet) and check that the bottom of the parcels are cooked through. Take care not to overcook the parcels or they may burst open.

Hint: If you like your puff pastry to taste extra buttery, brush it with melted butter before baking.

Makes 12

Breads

Parmesan and Prosciutto Loaf

- 7 g (¼ oz) dried yeast
- 1 teaspoon caster (berry) sugar
- ½ cup (125 ml/4¼ fl oz) warm milk
- 2 cups (250 g/8¾ oz) plain (all-purpose) flour
- 1 teaspoon salt
- 1 egg, lightly beaten

- 30 g (1 oz) butter, melted and cooled slightly
- 1 tablespoon milk, extra
- 60 g (2 oz) sliced prosciutto, finely chopped
- ½ cup (50 g/1¾ oz) grated Parmesan

Mix the yeast, sugar and milk in a bowl. Cover and set aside in a warm place for 10 minutes, or until frothy.

Mix the flour and salt in a bowl. Make a well in the centre and add the egg, butter and frothy yeast. Mix to a soft dough and gather into a ball; turn out onto a floured surface and knead for 8 minutes, or until elastic.

Put in an oiled bowl, cover loosely with greased plastic wrap and leave in a warm place for 1¼ hours, or until doubled in size.

Punch down the dough, turn out onto a floured surface and knead for 30 seconds, or until smooth. Roll out to a rectangle, 30 × 20 cm (12 × 8 inches), and brush with some extra milk. Sprinkle with the prosciutto and Parmesan, leaving a border. Roll lengthways into a log shape.

Lay on a greased baking tray (sheet) and brush with the remaining milk. Slash the loaf at intervals. Leave to rise in a warm place for 30 minutes. Bake at 220°C (425°F/Gas 7) for 25 minutes.

Serves 6

Rosemary Bread Trios

- 7 g (¼ oz) sachet dried yeast
- 1 teaspoon caster (berry) sugar
- 4 cups (500 g/1 lb) plain (all-purpose) flour
- 1 tablespoon caster (berry) sugar, extra
- 1 teaspoon salt
- 1 cup (250 ml/8½ fl oz) warm milk
- ¼ cup (60 ml/2 fl oz) vegetable oil
- 10 small sprigs of rosemary
- 1 egg yolk
- sea salt flakes, to sprinkle

Combine the yeast, caster (berry) sugar and ½ cup (125 ml/4¼ fl oz) of warm water in a small bowl. Cover and set aside in a warm place for 10 minutes, or until frothy.

Sift the flour into a large bowl and stir in the extra caster (berry) sugar and salt. Make a well in the centre and pour in the warm milk, oil and frothy yeast. Mix to a soft dough, gather into a ball then turn out onto a lightly floured surface and knead for 10 minutes, or until smooth and elastic. Add a little extra flour if the dough becomes too sticky. Place in a large, oiled bowl, cover loosely with greased plastic wrap and leave in a warm place for 1 hour, or until doubled in size.

Punch down the dough, then turn out onto a lightly floured surface and knead for 1 minute. Lightly grease 2 large baking trays (sheets). Divide the dough into 10 pieces. Form each piece into three balls – keeping the remaining pieces covered – and place close together on the prepared baking tray (sheet); add a sprig of rosemary to the centre of each trio. Repeat with the remaining pieces of dough, and lay each set separately on the baking tray (sheet).

Cover the trios with a damp tea towel and set aside for 20 minutes, or until well risen. Preheat the oven to moderate 180°C (350°F/Gas 4). Brush the trios lightly with the combined egg yolk and 1 teaspoon of water and sprinkle with the sea salt flakes. Bake for 15 minutes, or until golden brown. Allow to cool on a wire rack and replace the rosemary sprigs with fresh ones, if you want.

Makes 10

Fougasse

- **7 g (¼ oz) sachet dried yeast**
- **1 teaspoon sugar**
- **4 cups (500 g/1 lb) white bread flour**
- **2 teaspoons salt**
- **¼ cup (60 ml/2 fl oz) olive oil**

Place the yeast, sugar and ½ cup (125 ml/4¼ fl oz) warm water in a small bowl and stir until dissolved. Leave in a warm, draught-free place for 10 minutes, or until bubbles appear on the surface. The mixture should be frothy and slightly increased in volume. If your yeast doesn't foam it is dead, so you will have to discard it and start again.

Sift the flour and salt into a bowl and make a well in the centre. Add the yeast mixture, olive oil and ¾ cup (185 ml/6½ fl oz) warm water. Mix to a soft dough and gather into a ball with floured hands. Turn out onto a floured surface and knead for 10 minutes, or until smooth.

Place in a large, lightly oiled bowl, cover loosely with plastic wrap or a damp tea towel and leave in a warm place for 1 hour, or until doubled in size.

Punch down the dough and knead for 1 minute. Divide the mixture into four equal portions. Press each portion into a large, oval shape 1 cm (½ inch) thick and make several cuts on either side of all of them. Lay on large, floured baking trays (sheets), cover with plastic wrap and leave to rise for 20 minutes.

Preheat the oven to hot 210°C (415°F/Gas 6–7). Bake the fougasse for 35 minutes, or until crisp. To assist the crust to crispen, after 15 minutes cooking, spray the oven with water.

Makes 4

Roasted Vegetable Buns

- 2 red capsicums (peppers), cut into large flat pieces
- 7 g (¼ oz) dried yeast
- 2 teaspoons sugar
- 4 cups (500 g/1 lb) plain (all-purpose) flour
- 1 teaspoon salt
- 1 tablespoon olive oil
- 1 egg, lightly beaten

Place the capsicum (pepper) skin-side-up under a hot grill (broiler), until the skins blacken. Cool in a plastic bag, then peel away the skin and dice the flesh.

Combine the dried yeast, sugar and ½ cup (125 ml/4¼ fl oz) of warm water in a bowl and leave in a warm place for 10 minutes, or until frothy.

Sift the flour and salt into a bowl, make a well in the centre and pour in the oil, the frothy yeast and 1¼ cups (315 ml/11 fl oz) of warm water. Mix to a soft dough, gather into a ball and knead on a floured surface until smooth. Add a little extra flour if needed. Place in a lightly oiled bowl, cover loosely with greased plastic wrap and leave in a warm place for 1 hour, or until doubled.

Punch down the dough, turn out onto a floured surface and knead for 10 minutes, adding the capsicum (pepper) half-way through. Divide the dough into eight and form into rounds. Lay apart on a greased baking tray (sheet). Cover with a damp tea towel and leave for 30 minutes, or until well risen. Preheat the oven to 180°C (350°F/Gas 4). Brush the buns with beaten egg. Bake for 40–45 minutes, or until the bases sound hollow when tapped.

Makes 8

Beer Bread with Sun-Dried Tomato and Herbs

- 1 tablespoon finely chopped fresh oregano, or 1½ teaspoons dried
- 3 tablespoons finely chopped fresh parsley
- 2 tablespoons finely chopped fresh basil
- 3 tablespoons chopped sun-dried tomato
- 1 teaspoon cracked black pepper
- 3 tablespoons grated Parmesan
- 2 cloves garlic, crushed
- 3 cups (375 g/13¼ oz) self-raising flour
- 1 teaspoon salt
- 2 teaspoons sugar
- 1½ cups (375 ml/13 fl oz) beer (not bitter), at room temperature
- 2 teaspoons olive oil

Preheat the oven to 210°C (415°C/Gas 6–7). Brush a 25 × 15 cm (10 × 6 inch) loaf tin with melted butter. Mix the oregano, parsley, basil, sun-dried tomato, pepper, cheese and garlic.

Sift the flour, salt and sugar into a large mixing bowl. Make a well in the centre and add the herb mixture and beer. Stir with a wooden spoon for 1 minute. (It should be very moist – add a little more beer if necessary.)

Spoon into the tin and smooth the surface. Bake for 10 minutes, then reduce to 180°C (350°F/Gas 4) and bake for 30 more minutes. Brush the top with oil and cook for 5 more minutes or until well browned and cooked through. Turn out onto a wire rack to cool.

Serves 8

Cheese and Herb Pull-Apart Loaf

- 7 g (¼ oz) dried yeast
- 1 teaspoon sugar
- 4 cups (500 g/1 lb) plain (all-purpose) flour
- 1½ teaspoons salt
- 2 tablespoons chopped fresh parsley
- 2 tablespoons chopped chives
- 1 tablespoon chopped fresh thyme
- 60 g (2 oz) Cheddar (American) cheese, grated
- milk, to glaze

Combine the yeast, sugar and ½ cup (125 ml/4¼ fl oz) of warm water in a small bowl. Cover and set aside in a warm place for 10 minutes, or until frothy.

Sift the flour and salt into a bowl. Make a well in the centre and pour in 1 cup (250 ml/8½ fl oz) warm water and the frothy yeast. Mix to a soft dough. Knead on a lightly floured surface for 10 minutes, or until smooth. Put the dough in an oiled bowl, cover loosely with greased plastic wrap and leave for 1 hour, or until doubled in size.

Punch down and knead for 1 minute. Divide the dough in half and shape each half into 10 flat discs, 6 cm (2½ inches) in diameter. Mix the fresh herbs with the Cheddar (American) cheese and put 2 teaspoons on a disc. Press another disc on top. Repeat with the remaining discs and herb mixture.

Grease a 21 × 10.5 × 6.5 cm (8½ × 4¼ × 2½ inch) loaf tin. Stand the filled discs upright in the prepared tin, squashing them together. Cover the tin with a damp tea towel and set aside in a warm place for 30 minutes, or until well risen. Preheat the oven to hot 210°C (415°F/Gas 6–7).

Glaze with a little milk and bake for 30 minutes, or until brown and crusty.

Serves 8

Moroccan Flatbread

- 2½ cups (375 g/13¼ oz) wholemeal (whole wheat) flour
- 1 teaspoon caster (berry) sugar
- 7 g (¼ oz) sachet dried yeast
- ½ teaspoon sweet paprika
- ⅓ cup (50 g/1¾ oz) polenta (cornmeal)
- 1 tablespoon oil
- 1 egg, lightly beaten
- 2 tablespoons sesame seeds

Preheat the oven to moderate 180°C (350°F/Gas 4). Lightly grease a baking tray (sheet). Put ½ cup (75 g/2½ oz) of the flour, the sugar, yeast, 1 teaspoon salt and 1¼ cups (315 ml/11 fl oz) tepid water in a bowl and stir until dissolved. Cover and leave in a warm place for 10 minutes, or until bubbles appear. The mixture should be frothy and slightly increased in volume. If your yeast doesn't foam, it is dead and you will have to start again.

Sift the paprika, polenta (cornmeal) and remaining flour into a bowl. Add the oil, then stir in the yeast mixture. Mix to a firm dough and knead until smooth. Cover and leave in a warm, draught-free place for 20 minutes.

Divide into 16 portions, roll each into a ball, then flatten into 8 cm (3 inch) rounds. Place on the baking tray (sheet), brush with egg and sprinkle with sesame seeds. Cover and set aside for 10 minutes, or until puffed up. Bake for 12 minutes, or until golden.

Makes 16

Pitta Bread

- **7 g (¼ oz) sachet dried yeast**
- **1 teaspoon caster (berry) sugar**
- **3½ cups (435 g/15⅓ oz) plain (all-purpose) flour**
- **2 tablespoons olive oil**

Place the yeast, sugar and 1½ cups (375 ml/13 fl oz) lukewarm water in a bowl and stir until dissolved. Leave in a warm place for 10 minutes, or until bubbles appear on the surface. The mixture should be frothy and slightly increased in volume. If your yeast doesn't foam it is dead and you will have to start again.

Process the flour, yeast mixture and oil in a food processor for 30 seconds, or until the mixture forms a ball. Or, if you prefer, place the ingredients in a bowl and mix with a wooden spoon, or with your hand, until the mixture forms a smooth dough.

Turn the dough onto a well-floured surface and knead until smooth and elastic. Place in a well-oiled bowl, cover with plastic wrap, then a tea towel and leave in a warm place for 20 minutes, or until almost doubled in size.

Punch down the dough and divide into twelve equal portions. Roll each portion into a 5 mm (¼ inch) thick round. Place on greased baking trays (sheets) and brush well with water. Stand and allow to rise for another 20 minutes.

Preheat the oven to very hot 260°C (500°F/Gas 10). If the dough has dried, brush again with water. Bake for 4–5 minutes. The pitta bread should be soft and pale, slightly swollen, and hollow inside. Eat warm with kebabs or falafel, or cool on wire racks and serve with salad.

Makes 12

Lemon Pepper Bread

- 2 cups (250 g/8¾ oz) self-raising flour
- 1 teaspoon salt
- 2 teaspoons lemon pepper, or
  1 teaspoon grated lemon rind and
  2 teaspoons black pepper
- 45 g (1⅔ oz) butter, chopped
- 1 tablespoon chopped fresh chives
- ¾ cup (90 g/3¼ oz) grated Cheddar
  (American) cheese
- 2 teaspoons white vinegar
- ¾ cup (185 ml/6½ fl oz) milk

Preheat the oven to hot 210°C (415°F/Gas 6–7). Brush two oven trays (sheets) with melted butter or oil. Sift the flour and salt into a large bowl and add the lemon pepper, or lemon rind and pepper. Using your fingertips, rub in the butter until the mixture resembles coarse breadcrumbs. Stir in the chives and cheese.

Stir vinegar into milk (it should look slightly curdled). Add to flour mixture and mix to a soft dough, adding more milk if dough is too stiff.

Turn the dough onto a lightly floured surface and knead until smooth. Divide dough into two. Place on prepared trays (sheets) and press out into a circle approximately 2.5 cm (1 inch) thick. Score each with a knife into 8 wedges, cutting lightly into the top of the bread. Dust lightly with flour. Bake for 20–25 minutes, or until a deep golden colour and sounds hollow when tapped on the base. Serve warm with butter.

Serves 8

Olive Bread

- 3 cups (375 g/13¼ oz) plain (all-purpose) flour
- 7 g (¼ oz) sachet dry yeast
- 2 teaspoons sugar
- 2 tablespoons olive oil
- 110 g (3¾ oz) Kalamata olives, pitted, halved
- 2 teaspoons plain (all-purpose) flour, extra, to coat
- 1 small sprig of fresh oregano, leaves removed and torn into small pieces, optional
- olive oil, to glaze

Place a third of the flour in a large bowl and stir in 1 teaspoon salt. Place the yeast, sugar and 1 cup (250 ml/8½ fl oz) warm water in a small bowl and stir well. Set aside in a warm, draught-free place for 10 minutes, or until bubbles appear on the surface. The mixture should be frothy and slightly increased in volume. If your yeast doesn't foam, it is dead and you will have to start again.

Add the yeast mixture to the flour and salt mixture in the bowl and stir to make a thin, lumpy paste. Cover with a tea towel and set aside in a warm, draught-free place for 45 minutes, or until doubled in size.

Stir in the remaining flour and the oil and ½ cup (125 ml/4¼ fl oz) warm water. Mix with a wooden spoon until a rough dough forms. Transfer to a lightly floured work surface and knead for 10–12 minutes, incorporating as little extra flour as possible to keep the dough soft and moist, but not sticky. Form into a ball. Oil a clean large bowl and roll the dough around in it to lightly coat in the oil. Cut a cross on top, cover the bowl with a tea towel and set aside in a warm place for 1 hour, or until doubled in size.

Lightly grease a baking tray (sheet) and dust with flour. Punch down the dough on a lightly floured surface. Roll out to 30 × 25 × 1 cm (12 × 10 × ½ inch). Squeeze any excess liquid from the olives and toss to coat in the extra flour. Scatter over the dough and top with the oregano. Roll up tightly lengthways, pressing firmly to expel any air pockets as you roll. Press the ends together to form an oval loaf 25 cm (10 inches) long. Transfer to the prepared tray (sheet), join-side-down. Make 3 shallow diagonal slashes across the top. Slide the tray (sheet) into a large plastic bag and leave in a warm place for 45 minutes, or until doubled in bulk.

Preheat the oven to hot 220°C (425°F/Gas 7). Brush the top of the loaf with olive oil and bake for 30 minutes. Reduce the heat to moderate 180°C (350°F/Gas 4) and bake for another 5 minutes. Cool on a wire rack. Serve warm or cold.

Makes 1 loaf

Walnut Bread

- 2½ teaspoons dried yeast
- ¼ cup (90 g/3¼ oz) liquid malt
- 2 tablespoons olive oil
- 3 cups (300 g/10½ oz) walnut halves, lightly toasted
- 4¼ cups (530 g/1 lb 1 oz) white bread flour
- 1½ teaspoons salt
- 1 egg, lightly beaten

Grease a baking tray (sheet). Place the yeast, liquid malt and 1⅓ cups (350 ml/11¾ fl oz) warm water in a small bowl and stir well. Leave in a warm, draught-free place for 10 minutes, or until bubbles appear on the surface. The mixture should be frothy and slightly increased in volume. If your yeast doesn't foam it is dead, so you will have to discard it and start again. Stir in the oil.

Process 2 cups (200 g/7 oz) of the walnuts in a food processor to a coarse meal. Combine 4 cups (500 g/1 lb) of the flour and the salt in a large bowl and stir in the walnut meal. Make a well and add the yeast mixture. Mix with a large metal spoon until just combined. Turn out onto a lightly floured surface and knead for 10 minutes, or until smooth, incorporating enough of the remaining flour to keep the dough from sticking – it should be soft and moist, but it won't become very springy. Shape the dough into a ball. Place in a lightly oiled bowl, cover with plastic wrap or a damp tea towel and leave in a warm place for up to 1½ hours, or until doubled.

Punch down the dough and turn out onto a lightly floured surface. With very little kneading, shape the dough into a 25 × 20 cm (10 × 8 inch) rectangle. Spread with the remaining walnuts and roll up firmly from the short end. Place the loaf on the baking tray (sheet), cover with plastic wrap or a damp tea towel and leave to rise for 1 hour, or until well risen and doubled in size.

Preheat the oven to moderately hot 190°C (375°F/Gas 5). Glaze the loaf with the egg and bake for 45–50 minutes, or until golden and hollow sounding when tapped. Transfer to a wire rack to cool.

Note: Use good-quality pale and plump walnuts as cheaper varieties can be bitter.

Makes 1 loaf

Pepper and Almond Bread

- **2 teaspoons black peppercorns**
- **2 egg whites**
- **⅓ cup (90 g/3¼ oz) caster (berry) sugar**
- **¾ cup (90 g/3¼ oz) plain (all-purpose) flour**

- **¼ teaspoon ground ginger (ginger root)**
- **¼ teaspoon ground cinnamon**
- **1 cup (155 g/5½ oz) almonds**

Preheat the oven to moderate 180°C (350°F/Gas 4). Grease an 8 × 26 cm (3 × 10½ inch) bar tin. Line the base and sides with baking paper. Lightly crush the peppercorns with the back of a spoon or in a mortar and pestle.

Beat the egg whites and sugar with electric beaters for 4 minutes, or until the mixture turns white and thickens. Sift the flour, ginger (ginger root) and cinnamon and fold in with the almonds and the crushed peppercorns.

Spread the mixture into the tin. Bake for 35 minutes, or until lightly browned. Cool in the tin for at least 3 hours, before turning out onto a board. (You can wrap the bread in foil and slice the next day at this stage.) Using a serrated knife, cut the bread into 3 mm (⅛ inch) slices. Place the slices in a single layer on baking trays (sheets). Bake in a slow 150°C (300°F/Gas 2) oven for about 25–35 minutes, or until the slices are dry and crisp. Allow to cool completely before serving. Serve with soups as an alternative to plain bread.

Note: To make a traditional sweet almond bread, simply omit the peppercorns.

Makes about 70 pieces

Focaccia

- ½ teaspoon caster (berry) sugar
- 7 g (¼ oz) sachet dry yeast
- 1 kg (2 lb 3 oz) bread flour
- ¼ cup (60 ml/2 fl oz) olive oil

Put the sugar, yeast and 2 tablespoons warm water in a small bowl, mix well and leave in a warm, draught-free place for 10 minutes, or until bubbles appear on the surface. The mixture should be frothy and slightly increased in volume. If your yeast doesn't foam it is dead and you will have to start again.

Place the flour and 2 teaspoons salt in a large bowl and mix well. Add 2 tablespoons of the olive oil, the yeast mixture and 3 cups (750 ml/26 fl oz) warm water. Mix with a wooden spoon until the mixture comes together in a loose dough, then turn out onto a lightly floured surface. Start kneading to form a soft, moist, but non-sticky dough, adding a little extra flour or warm water as needed. Knead for 8 minutes, or until smooth, or until the impression made by a finger springs straight back out.

Lightly oil a large bowl. Place the dough in the bowl and roll around to coat. Cut a cross on top with a sharp knife. Cover the bowl with a clean tea towel and leave in a dry, warm place for 1 hour 30 minutes, or until doubled in size.

Punch down the dough on a lightly floured surface and divide in half. One or both portions can be frozen at this point. Roll one portion out to 28 × 20 cm (11 × 8 inches). Use the heels of your hands to work from the middle outwards and shape to measure 38 × 28 cm (15 × 11 inches).

Lightly oil a baking tray (sheet) and dust with flour. Place the dough in the centre and slide the tray (sheet) inside a large plastic bag. Leave in a dry, warm place for 2 hours, or until doubled in size.

Preheat the oven to hot 220°C (425°F/Gas 7). Brush the surface of the dough with some of the remaining olive oil and bake for 20 minutes, or until golden. Transfer to a wire rack to cool. Allow plenty of air to circulate under the loaf to keep the crust crisp. Repeat with the remaining dough. Best eaten within 6 hours of baking.

Makes 2 loaves

Pizza-Topped Focaccia

- 7 g (¼ oz) sachet dry yeast
- 1 teaspoon sugar
- 2 tablespoons olive oil
- 2½ cups (310 g/11 oz) plain (all-purpose) flour, sifted

Pizza Topping
- 1 tablespoon tomato paste (tomato puree)

- 1 large red capsicum (pepper), thinly sliced
- 125 g (4⅓ oz) marinated artichoke hearts, quartered
- ¼ cup (30 g/1 oz) black (ripe) olives, pitted
- 200 g (7 oz) bocconcini, thickly sliced

Combine the yeast, ¾ cup (185 ml/6½ fl oz) of warm water and the sugar in a bowl and set aside in a warm place for 5–10 minutes, or until frothy. Put the oil, flour and 1 teaspoon salt in a large bowl, add the frothy yeast and mix to a soft dough.

Turn the dough out onto a lightly floured surface and knead for 10 minutes, or until smooth and elastic. Roll into a ball and place in a large oiled bowl. Cover with oiled plastic wrap and set aside in a warm place for 1 hour, or until the dough has doubled in size.

Preheat the oven to moderate 180°C (350°F/Gas 4). Punch down the dough with your fist to expel any air, and knead for 1 minute. Roll into a flat disc large enough to fit into a greased 23 cm (9 inch) springform tin. Press into the tin, cover with a tea towel and leave to rise for about 20 minutes.

Spread the tomato paste (tomato puree) over the dough and arrange the other topping ingredients, except for the bocconcini, on top. Bake for 20 minutes, remove from the oven and spread the slices of bocconcini over the top, then bake for a further 20 minutes, or until the dough is well risen and firm to the touch in the centre. Cool on a wire rack before cutting and serving.

Serves 4

Malt Bread

- **1 cup (250 ml/8½ fl oz) lukewarm water**
- **7 g (¼ oz) sachet dried yeast**
- **1 teaspoon sugar**
- **2 cups (300 g/10½ oz) plain wholemeal (whole wheat) flour**
- **1 cup (125 g/4⅓ oz) plain (all-purpose) flour**

- **2 teaspoons ground cinnamon**
- **½ cup (60 g/2 oz) raisins (dark raisins)**
- **30 g (1 oz) butter, melted**
- **1 tablespoon treacle (molasses)**
- **1 tablespoon liquid malt extract, plus ½ teaspoon**
- **1 tablespoon hot milk**

Brush a 21 × 14 × 7 cm (8½ × 5½ × 2¾ inch) loaf tin with oil; line the base with baking paper. Combine the water, yeast and sugar in a small bowl. Cover with plastic wrap and set aside in a warm place for 10 minutes or until foamy. Sift the flours and cinnamon into a large bowl; add raisins (dark raisins) and stir. Make a well in the centre. Add melted butter, treacle (molasses), tablespoon of malt extract and the yeast mixture.

Using a knife, mix to a soft dough.Turn onto lightly floured surface; knead 10 minutes or until smooth. Shape into a ball and place in a lightly oiled bowl. Set aside, covered with plastic wrap, in a warm place for 1 hour or until well risen. Punch down. Knead 3 minutes or until smooth.

Roll into a 20 cm (8 inch) square and then roll up. Place in tin, with the seam underneath, and set aside, covered with plastic wrap, in a warm place for 40 minutes or until well risen.

Preheat oven to moderate 180°C (350°F/Gas 4). Brush with combined milk and remaining malt. Bake for 40 minutes or until a skewer comes out clean. Set aside for 3 minutes in tin before transferring to a wire rack to cool.

Makes 1 loaf

Pies, Pastries and Pizzas

Chicken Pie

- 1 kg (2 lb 3 oz) boneless skinless chicken breasts
- 2 cups (500 ml/17 fl oz) chicken stock (broth)
- 60 g (2 oz) butter
- 2 spring (green) onions, trimmed and finely chopped
- ½ cup (60 g/2 oz) plain (all-purpose) flour
- ½ cup (125 ml/4¼ fl oz) milk
- 8 sheets filo (phyllo) pastry (40 × 30 cm/16 × 12 inches)
- 60 g (2 oz) butter, extra, melted
- 200 g (7 oz) feta, crumbled
- 1 tablespoon chopped fresh dill (dill weed)
- 1 tablespoon chopped fresh chives
- ¼ teaspoon ground nutmeg
- 1 egg, lightly beaten

Cut the chicken into bite-sized pieces. Pour the stock (broth) into a saucepan and bring to the boil over high heat. Reduce the heat to low, add the chicken and poach gently for 10–15 minutes, or until the chicken is cooked through. Drain, reserving the stock (broth). Add water to the stock (broth) to bring the quantity up to 2 cups (500 ml/17 fl oz). Preheat the oven to moderate 180°C (350°F/Gas 4).

Melt the butter in a saucepan over low heat, add the spring (green) onion and cook, stirring, for 5 minutes. Add the flour and stir for 30 seconds. Remove the pan from the heat and gradually add the chicken stock (broth) and milk, stirring after each addition. Return to the heat and gently bring to the boil, stirring. Simmer for a few minutes, or until the sauce thickens. Remove from the heat.

Line a baking dish measuring 25 × 18 × 4 cm (10 × 7 × 1½ inches) with 4 sheets of filo (phyllo) pastry, brushing one side of each sheet with melted butter as you go. Place the buttered side down. The pastry will overlap the edges of the dish. Cover the unused pastry with a damp tea towel to prevent it drying out.

Stir the chicken, feta, dill (dill weed), chives, nutmeg and egg into the sauce. Season, to taste, with salt and freshly ground black pepper. Pile the mixture on top of the pastry in the dish. Fold the overlapping pastry over the filling and cover the top of the pie with the remaining 4 sheets of filo (phyllo), brushing each sheet with melted butter as you go. Scrunch the edges of the pastry so they fit in the dish. Brush the top with butter. Bake for 45–50 minutes, or until the pastry is golden brown and crisp.

Serves 6

Creamy Chicken, Sage and Tarragon Pie

- 1.5 kg (3 lb 5 oz) chicken thigh fillets
- 2 tablespoons olive oil
- 2 slices bacon, finely chopped
- 1 onion, roughly chopped
- 4 fresh sage leaves, chopped
- 1 tablespoon chopped fresh tarragon
- 45 g (1⅔ oz) butter, melted
- 2 tablespoons plain (all-purpose) flour
- ½ cup (125 ml/4¼ fl oz) milk
- 220 g (7¾ oz) can creamed corn (corn, cream style)
- 2 sheets ready-rolled puff pastry
- 1 egg, lightly beaten

Preheat the oven to hot 210°C (415°F/Gas 6–7). Brush a 23 cm (9 inch) pie dish with butter. Cut the chicken into bite-sized pieces. Heat the oil in a large frying pan. Add the chicken, bacon and onion, and cook over medium heat for 5 minutes, or until browned. Add the sage, tarragon, 1 cup (250 ml/8½ fl oz) water, salt and pepper. Bring to the boil, then reduce the heat and simmer, covered, for 25 minutes, or until the chicken is tender. Drain, reserving the juices.

Melt the butter in a heavy-based pan. Add the flour and stir over low heat for 1 minute. Remove from the heat and gradually add the milk and reserved juice, stirring until smooth. Return to the heat and stir over medium heat until thickenened. Stir in the chicken mixture and corn. Spoon into the dish.

Brush a sheet of pastry with egg and top with a second sheet. Brush the rim of the pie dish with egg and place the pastry over the filling. Trim any excess.

Decorate the pie with pastry. Brush with egg and make a few slits in the top. Bake for 15 minutes, then reduce the heat to 180°C (350°F/Gas 4) and bake for 10–15 minutes, or until crisp and golden. Leave for 5 minutes.

Serves 4–6

Chicken and Ham Pie

Pastry
- 3 cups (375 g/13¼ oz) plain (all-purpose) flour
- 180 g (6⅓ oz) butter, chopped
- ⅓ cup (80 ml/2¾ fl oz) iced water

Filling
- 1 kg (2 lb 3 oz) chicken mince (ground chicken)
- ½ teaspoon dried thyme
- ½ teaspoon dried sage
- 2 eggs, lightly beaten
- 3 spring (green) onions, finely chopped
- 2 teaspoons finely grated lemon rind
- 1 teaspoon French mustard
- ⅓ cup (80 ml/2¾ fl oz) cream
- 100 g (3½ oz) sliced leg ham, finely chopped
- 1 egg, lightly beaten, extra

Preheat the oven to moderate 180°C (350°F/Gas 4). Process the flour and butter in a food processor for 20 seconds, or until the mixture is fine and crumbly. Add almost all the water and process for 20 seconds, or until mixture comes together. Add more water if needed. Turn onto a lightly floured surface and press together until smooth. Roll out two-thirds of the pastry and line a 20 cm (8 inch) springform tin, bringing the pastry up 2 cm (¾ inch) higher than the sides. Cover with plastic wrap. Set the pastry trimmings aside.

To make the filling, place the chicken, thyme, sage, eggs, spring (green) onion, lemon rind, mustard and cream in a large bowl and stir with a wooden spoon until well combined. Place half the chicken mixture into the pastry-lined tin and smooth the surface. Top with the chopped ham, then the remaining chicken mixture.

Brush around the inside edge of the pastry with the egg. Roll out the remaining pastry and lay over the top of the mixture. Press the edges of the pastry together. Trim the pastry edges with a sharp knife.

Turn the pastry edges down. Use your index finger to make indentations around the inside edge. Decorate the top of the pie with pastry trimmings. Brush the top of the pie with beaten egg and bake for 1 hour, or until golden brown. Serve the pie warm or at room temperature.

Serves 6

Moroccan Chicken Pie

- 1 tablespoon olive oil
- 1 red onion, chopped
- 2–3 cloves garlic, crushed
- 2 teaspoons grated fresh ginger (ginger root)
- 1 teaspoon ground turmeric
- 1 teaspoon ground cumin
- 1 teaspoon ground coriander
- 500 g (1 lb 2 oz) cooked chicken, shredded
- 60 g (2 oz) slivered almonds, toasted
- 1 cup (50 g/1¾ oz) chopped fresh coriander (cilantro)
- ⅓ cup (20 g/⅔ oz) chopped fresh parsley
- 1 teaspoon grated lemon rind
- 2 tablespoons stock (broth) or water
- 1 egg, lightly beaten
- 9 sheets filo (phyllo) pastry
- 50 g (1¾ oz) butter, melted
- 1 teaspoon caster (berry) sugar
- ¼ teaspoon ground cinnamon

Heat the oil in a large heavy-based frying pan and cook the onion, garlic and ginger (ginger root), stirring, for 5 minutes, or until the onion is soft. Stir in the turmeric, cumin and ground coriander and cook, stirring, for 1–2 minutes. Remove from the heat and stir in the chicken, almonds, coriander (cilantro), parsley and lemon rind. Leave to cool for 5 minutes, then stir in the stock (broth) or water and the beaten egg.

Preheat the oven to moderate 180°C (350°F/Gas 4). Grease a baking tray (sheet). Cut 6 sheets of filo (phyllo) into approximately 30 cm (12 inch) squares, retaining the extra strips. Cut each of the remaining sheets into 3 equal strips. Cover with a damp cloth. Brush 1 square with the melted butter and place on the baking tray (sheet). Lay another square at an angle on top and brush with melted butter. Repeat with the other squares to form a rough 8-pointed star. Spoon the chicken mixture into the centre, leaving a 5 cm (2 inch) border.

Turn the pastry edge in over the filling, leaving the centre open. Brush the pastry strips with melted butter and lightly scrunch and lay them over the top of the pie. Sprinkle with the combined caster (berry) sugar and cinnamon. Bake for 25 minutes, or until the pastry is cooked and golden brown.

Serves 4–6

Raised Pork Pie

- 1.2 kg (2 lb 10 oz) minced pork (ground pork)
- ⅔ cup (90 g/3¼ oz) pistachio nuts, chopped
- 2 green apples, peeled and finely chopped
- 6 fresh sage leaves, finely chopped
- 4 cups (500 g/1 lb 2 oz) plain (all-purpose) flour
- 150 g (5¼ oz) butter
- 2 eggs, lightly beaten
- 1 egg yolk
- 1 cup (250 ml/8½ fl oz) vegetable stock (broth)
- ⅔ cup (170 ml/5¾ fl oz) unsweetened apple juice
- 2 teaspoons powdered gelatine

Preheat the oven to moderately hot 200°C (400°F/Gas 6). Put the pork, pistachio nuts, apple and sage leaves in a bowl, mix well and season. Fry a small piece of the mixture, taste and adjust the seasoning, to taste. Cover the mixture and refrigerate.

Wrap a piece of plastic wrap around a 6 cm (2½ inch) high, 20 cm (8 inch) diameter straight-sided tin, then turn the tin over and grease the plastic on the outside base and side of the tin.

Put the flour and 1 teaspoon salt in a bowl and make a well in the centre. Put the butter in a saucepan with ¾ cup (185 ml/6½ fl oz) water. Bring to the boil and add to the flour, with the beaten eggs. Mix with a wooden spoon until combined, then turn out onto a lightly floured work surface and bring the mixture together, adding another 1–2 tablespoons boiling water if necessary to form a smooth dough. Wrap in plastic wrap and refrigerate for 10 minutes.

Wrap a third of the pastry in plastic wrap – do not refrigerate. Roll the remaining pastry into a circle large enough to just cover the outside of the tin. Lift onto a rolling pin and place over the tin, pressing to the shape of the tin and working quickly before the pastry sets. Refrigerate for about 2 hours, until the pastry hardens, then carefully pull out the tin and remove the plastic wrap. Put the pastry on a lightly greased baking tray (sheet). Attach a paper collar made of 2 layers of greased baking paper around the outside of the pastry so it fits snugly and supports the pastry. Secure it with a paper clip at the top and bottom. Fill the pastry with the pork mixture, then roll out the remaining pastry to form a lid. Brush the rim of the base with a little water and press the lid on to attach. Pinch to seal. Cut a small hole in the top of the pie to fit a funnel.

Bake for 40 minutes and check the pastry top. If it is still pale, bake for another 10 minutes, then remove the paper. Brush with egg yolk mixed with 1 tablespoon water and bake for another 15 minutes, or until the sides are brown. Cool completely.

Bring the vegetable stock (broth) and half the apple juice to the boil in a saucepan, then remove from the heat. Sprinkle the gelatine over the surface of the remaining apple juice in a jug, leave to go spongy, then pour into the stock (broth) and mix well until the gelatine dissolves. Place a small funnel (large icing nozzles work well) in the hole of the pie, pour in a little of the gelatine mixture, leave to settle and then pour in a little more until the pie is full. It is important to fill the pie completely to ensure there are no gaps when the gelatine mixture sets. You may not need to use all the liquid. Refrigerate for several hours, or overnight, until the gelatine has set completely. Serve cold.

Serves 6

Welsh Lamb Pie

- 750 g (1 lb 10 oz) boned lamb shoulder, cubed
- ¾ cup (90 g/3¼ oz) plain (all-purpose) flour, seasoned
- 2 tablespoons olive oil
- 200 g (7 oz) bacon, finely chopped
- 2 cloves garlic, chopped
- 4 large leeks, sliced
- 1 large carrot, chopped
- 2 large potatoes, diced
- 1¼ cups (315 ml/11 fl oz) beef stock (broth)
- 1 bay leaf
- 2 teaspoons chopped fresh parsley
- 375 g (13¼ oz) quick flaky pastry
- 1 egg, lightly beaten, to glaze

Toss the meat in the flour. Heat the oil in a large frying pan over medium heat and brown the lamb in batches for 4–5 minutes, then remove from the pan. Cook the bacon in the pan for 3 minutes. Add the garlic and leek and cook for 5 minutes, or until soft.

Put the lamb in a large saucepan, add the leek and bacon, carrot, potato, stock (broth) and bay leaf and bring to the boil, then reduce the heat, cover and simmer for 30 minutes. Uncover and simmer for 1 hour, or until the meat is cooked and the liquid has thickened. Season to taste. Remove the bay leaf, stir in the parsley and set aside to cool.

Preheat the oven to 200°C (400°F/Gas 6). Place the filling in an 18 cm (7 inch) pie dish. Roll out the pastry between two sheets of baking paper until large enough to cover the pie. Trim the edges and pinch to seal.

Decorate the pie with pastry trimmings. Cut two slits in the top for steam to escape. Brush with egg and bake for 45 minutes, or until the pastry is crisp and golden.

Serves 6

Lamb Shank Pie

- 8 lamb shanks
- ½ cup (60 g/2 oz) plain (all-purpose) flour
- 2 tablespoons olive oil
- 4 red onions, quartered
- 8 cloves garlic, peeled
- 1 cup (250 ml/8½ fl oz) red wine
- 1 litre (1.1 US qt/1.75 UK pt) beef stock (broth)
- 2 tablespoons finely chopped fresh rosemary
- 6 whole black peppercorns
- ¼ cup (30 g/1 oz) cornflour (cornstarch)
- 375 g (13¼ oz) puff pastry
- 1 egg, lightly beaten

Preheat the oven to 220°C (425°F/Gas 7). Lightly dust the shanks with flour, shaking off the excess. Heat the oil in a large frying pan and cook the shanks for 2 minutes each side, or until well browned. Transfer to a deep roasting tin and add the onion, garlic, wine, stock, rosemary and peppercorns. Cover and bake for 1 hour.

Stir the mixture, uncover and return to the oven for 1 hour 10 minutes, stirring occasionally, until the meat falls off the bones.

Remove the lamb bones with tongs. Mix the cornflour (cornstarch) with 2 tablespoons water, then stir into the tin. Return to the oven for 10 minutes, or until thickened. Transfer to a large bowl, cool, then refrigerate for at least 2 hours, or overnight.

Preheat the oven to moderate 180°C (350°F/Gas 4). Grease a 23 cm (9 inch) pie plate with a rim. Spoon in the filling. Roll the pastry out between two sheets of baking paper until a little wider than the plate. Cut a 2 cm (¾ inch) strip around the edge of the pastry, brush with water and place damp-side-down on the rim. Cover with the pastry circle, pressing down on the edges. Use the back of a knife to make small slashes around the edge. Trim, then re-roll the scraps to decorate. Brush with egg and bake for 45 minutes, or until the pastry is golden and has risen.

Serves 6

Shepherd's Pie

- **750 g (1 lb 10 oz) lean cooked roast lamb**
- **25 g (¾ oz) butter**
- **2 onions, finely chopped**
- **¼ cup (30 g/1 oz) plain (all-purpose) flour**
- **½ teaspoon mustard powder (dry mustard)**
- **1½ cups (375 ml/13 fl oz) chicken stock (broth)**
- **2 tablespoons Worcestershire sauce**

Potato Topping
- **4 large potatoes**
- **½ cup (125 ml/4¼ fl oz) hot milk**
- **30 g (1 oz) butter**

Brush a 2 litre (2.1 US qt/1.75 UK qt) casserole with melted butter or oil. Preheat the oven to hot 210°C (415°F/Gas 6–7). Trim the meat of excess fat, then mince (grind) or finely chop. Melt the butter in a large pan, add the onion and stir over medium heat for 5–10 minutes, until golden.

Add the flour and mustard to the pan and cook for 1 minute, or until pale and foaming. Remove from the heat and gradually stir in the stock (broth). Return to the heat and stir constantly until the sauce boils and thickens. Reduce the heat and simmer for 2 minutes.

Add the meat and Worcestershire sauce to the pan and stir. Season, to taste. Remove from the heat and spoon into the casserole dish.

For the potato topping, steam or boil the potatoes for 10–15 minutes, or until just tender (pierce with the point of a small sharp knife – if the potato comes away easily, it's ready). Drain and mash well. Add the milk, butter, and salt and pepper, to taste, to the mashed potato and mix until smooth and creamy. Spread evenly over the meat and rough up the surface with the back of a spoon. Bake for 40–45 minutes, or until the meat is heated through and the topping is golden.

Serves 6

Veal Pie with Jerusalem Artichoke and Potato Topping

- 1 tablespoon olive oil
- 500 g (1 lb 2 oz) lean veal mince (ground veal)
- 2 onions, finely chopped
- 3 cloves garlic, crushed
- 150 g (5¼ oz) bacon, diced
- ½ teaspoon dried rosemary
- 2 tablespoons plain (all-purpose) flour
- pinch of cayenne (red) pepper

- ½ cup (125 ml/4¼ fl oz) dry white wine
- 150 ml (5 fl oz) cream
- 1 egg, lightly beaten
- 2 hard-boiled eggs, roughly chopped

Topping
- 500 g (1 lb 2 oz) Jerusalem artichokes
- 400 g (14 oz) potatoes
- 100 g (3½ oz) butter

To make the filling, heat the oil in a large frying pan and cook the mince (ground veal), onion, garlic, bacon and rosemary, stirring often, for 10 minutes, or until the veal changes colour. Stir in the flour and cayenne (red) pepper and cook for 1 minute. Pour in the wine and ½ cup (125 ml/4¼ fl oz) water. Season well. Simmer for 5 minutes, or until the sauce is very thick, then stir in the cream, beaten egg and chopped egg.

Preheat the oven to 210°C (415°F/Gas 6–7). Lightly grease a 21 cm (8¼ inch) springform tin. Peel and chop the artichokes and potatoes and boil together for 12–15 minutes until tender. Drain, add the butter, then mash until smooth.

Spoon the filling into the tin then spread with the topping. Bake for 15 minutes, then reduce the heat to 180°C (350°F/Gas 4) and bake for 30 minutes, or until golden on top.

Serves 4–6

Burgundy Beef Pie

- 2 tablespoons olive oil
- 40 g (1½ oz) butter
- 185 g (6½ oz) bacon, diced
- 1.25 kg (2 lb 12 oz) chuck steak, trimmed and cut into 2.5 cm (1 inch) cubes
- 2 onions, diced
- 3 cloves garlic, crushed
- 2 carrots, cut into 1.5 cm (⅝ inch) cubes
- ¼ cup (30 g/1 oz) plain (all-purpose) flour
- 1¼ cups (315 ml/11 fl oz) red (Burgundy) wine
- 1½ cups (375 ml/13 fl oz) beef stock (broth)
- 2 tablespoons tomato paste (tomato puree)
- 1 teaspoon chopped fresh thyme
- 1 bay leaf
- 275 g (9⅔ oz) small Swiss brown mushrooms, halved
- pinch of ground nutmeg
- 3 tablespoons chopped fresh flat-leaf parsley
- 375 g (13¼ oz) puff pastry
- 1 egg, lightly beaten

Heat 1 tablespoon of oil and 20 g (⅔ oz) of butter in a large, heavy-based, flameproof casserole dish or saucepan over medium heat. Add the bacon and cook for 2–3 minutes. Transfer to a plate. Increase the heat to high, add the beef to the pan in batches and cook, turning, for 7–8 minutes, or until browned. Add to the bacon.

Heat the remaining oil in the pan over medium heat, add the onion and garlic and cook for 4–5 minutes. Add the carrot and cook, stirring once or twice, for 5 minutes. Stir in the flour, add the beef, bacon, wine, stock (broth) and tomato paste (tomato puree) and stir for 5 minutes, or until the sauce has thickened slightly and is smooth. Add the thyme and bay leaf and season. Reduce the heat, cover and cook for 1¼ hours, or until the meat is tender, adding ¼ cup (60 ml/2 fl oz) hot water, if necessary, to make a thick gravy.

Meanwhile, melt the remaining butter in a frying pan over low heat. Add the mushrooms and fry until golden. Stir in the nutmeg and parsley.

Preheat the oven to moderately hot 200°C (400°F/Gas 6) and grease a 2 litre (2.1 US qt/1.75 UK qt) oval ovenproof dish that has 5–6 cm (2–2½ inch) sides. Roll out the pastry between two sheets of baking paper until about 5 mm (¼ inch) thick and slightly larger than the dish. Roll out the scraps to a 35 cm × 10 cm (14 inch × 4 inch) strap, 5 mm (¼ inch) thick. Cut into 1.5 cm (⅝ inch) strips.

Remove the bay leaf from the meat, then stir in the mushrooms. Spoon into the dish. Cover with the pastry lid, press the edges firmly down onto the lip of the dish, then trim any excess. Brush the edges with egg. Make three 2.5 cm (1 inch) slits in the centre. Take a strip of pastry and twist a tight scroll. Repeat with the other strips. Run them around the rim, pressing joins together. Brush with egg and bake for 1 hour, or until golden.

Serves 6

Cottage Pie

- 2 tablespoons olive oil
- 2 onions, chopped
- 2 carrots, diced
- 1 celery stick, diced
- 1 kg (2 lb 3 oz) beef mince (ground beef)
- 2 tablespoons plain (all-purpose) flour
- 1½ cups (375 ml/13 fl oz) beef stock (broth)
- 1 tablespoon soy sauce
- 1 tablespoon Worcestershire sauce
- 2 tablespoons tomato sauce (ketchup)
- 1 tablespoon tomato paste (tomato puree)
- 2 bay leaves
- 2 teaspoons chopped fresh flat-leaf parsley

Topping
- 800 g (1 lb 12 oz) potatoes, diced
- 400 g (14 oz) parsnips, diced
- 30 g (1 oz) butter
- ½ cup (125 ml/4¼ fl oz) milk

Heat the oil in a large frying pan over medium heat and cook the onion, carrot and celery, stirring occasionally, for 5 minutes, or until softened and lightly coloured. Add the mince (ground beef) and cook for 7 minutes, then stir in the flour and cook for 2 minutes. Add the stock, soy sauce, Worcestershire sauce, tomato sauce (ketchup), tomato paste (tomato puree) and bay leaves and simmer over low heat for 30 minutes, stirring occasionally. Leave to cool. Remove the bay leaves and stir in the parsley.

To make the topping, boil the potato and parsnip in salted water for 15–20 minutes, or until cooked through. Drain, return to the pan and mash with the butter and enough of the milk to make a firm mash.

Preheat the oven to 180°C (350°F/Gas 4) and lightly grease a 2.5 litre (2.6 US qt/2.2 UK qt) ovenproof dish. Spoon the filling into the dish and spread the topping over it. Fluff with a fork. Bake for 25 minutes, or until golden.

Serves 6–8

Beef Wellington

- 1.2 kg (2 lb 10 oz) beef fillet or rib-eye in 1 piece
- 1 tablespoon oil
- 125 g (4⅓ oz) pâté
- 60 g (2 oz) button mushrooms, sliced
- 375 g (13¼ oz) block puff pastry, thawed
- 1 egg, lightly beaten
- 1 sheet ready-rolled puff pastry, thawed

Preheat the oven to hot 210°C (415°F/Gas 6–7). Trim the meat of any excess fat and sinew. Fold the thinner part of the tail end under and tie the meat securely with kitchen string at regular intervals to form an even shape.

Rub the meat with freshly ground black pepper. Heat the oil over high heat in a large frying pan. Add the meat and brown well all over. Remove from the heat and allow to cool. Remove the string.

Spread the pâté over the top and sides of the beef. Cover with the mushrooms, pressing them onto the pâté. Roll the block pastry out on a lightly floured surface to a rectangle large enough to completely enclose the beef.

Place the beef on the pastry, brush the edges with egg, and fold over to enclose the meat completely, brushing the edges of the pastry with the beaten egg to seal, and folding in the ends. Invert onto a greased baking tray (sheet) so the seam is underneath. Cut leaf shapes from the sheet of puff pastry and use to decorate the Wellington. Use the egg to stick the shapes on. Cut a few slits in the top to allow the steam to escape. Brush the top and sides of the pastry with egg, and cook for 45 minutes for rare, 1 hour for medium or 1½ hours for well done. Leave in a warm place for 10 minutes before cutting into slices for serving.

Serves 6–8

Snapper Pies

- 2 tablespoons olive oil
- 4 onions, thinly sliced
- 1½ cups (375 ml/13 fl oz) fish stock (broth)
- 3½ cups (875 ml/30 fl oz) cream
- 1 kg (2 lb 3 oz) skinless snapper fillets, cut into large pieces
- 2 sheets ready-rolled puff pastry, thawed
- 1 egg, lightly beaten

Preheat the oven to hot 220°C (425°F/Gas 7). Heat the oil in a large deep-sided frying pan, add the onion and stir over medium heat for 20 minutes, or until the onion is golden brown and slightly caramelised.

Add the fish stock (broth), bring to the boil and cook for 10 minutes, or until the liquid is nearly evaporated. Stir in the cream and bring to the boil. Reduce the heat and simmer for about 20 minutes, until the liquid is reduced by half, or until it coats the back of a spoon.

Divide half the sauce among four 2-cup (500 ml/17 fl oz) capacity, deep ramekins. Put some fish in each ramekin, then top each with some of the remaining sauce.

Cut the pastry sheets into rounds slightly larger than the tops of the ramekins. Brush the edges of the pastry with a little of the egg. Press onto the ramekins. Brush lightly with the remaining beaten egg. Bake for 30 minutes, or until crisp, golden and puffed.

Note: You can substitute bream, sea perch or garfish for the snapper fillets.

Serves 4

Freeform Seafood Pies

- 2 cups (250 g/8¾ oz) plain (all-purpose) flour
- 125 g (4⅓ oz) chilled butter, cubed
- 1 kg (2 lb 3 oz) raw medium prawns (shrimps)
- 1 tablespoon oil
- 5 cm (2 inch) piece fresh ginger (ginger root), grated
- 3 cloves garlic, crushed

- ⅓ cup (80 ml/2¾ fl oz) sweet chilli sauce (jalapeno jelly)
- ⅓ cup (80 ml/2¾ fl oz) lime juice
- ⅓ cup (80 ml/2¾ fl oz) thick (double/heavy) cream
- 25 g (¾ oz) chopped fresh coriander (cilantro)
- 1 egg yolk, lightly beaten, to glaze
- strips of lime rind, to garnish

Sift the flour into a large bowl, add the butter and rub into the flour with your fingertips until the mixture resembles fine breadcrumbs. Make a well, add 3 tablespoons water and mix with a flat-bladed knife, using a cutting action, until the mixture comes together in beads. Gather the dough together and lift out onto a lightly floured surface. Press into a ball and flatten into a disc. (Alternatively, make in a food processor.) Wrap in plastic wrap and chill for 15 minutes.

Preheat the oven to moderately hot 200°C (400°F/Gas 6). Peel the prawns (shrimps) and gently pull out the dark vein from each prawn (shrimp) back, starting at the head end.

Heat the oil in a large frying pan and fry the ginger (ginger root), garlic and prawns (shrimps) for 2–3 minutes. Remove the prawns (shrimps) and set aside. Add the chilli sauce (jalapeno jelly), lime juice and cream to the pan and simmer over medium heat, until the sauce has reduced by about one third. Return the prawns (shrimps) to the pan and add the coriander (cilantro); cool.

Grease 2 baking trays (sheets). Divide the pastry into 4 and roll out each portion, between sheets of baking paper, into a 20 cm (8 inch) circle. Divide the filling into 4 and place a portion in the centre of each pastry, leaving a wide border. Fold the edges loosely over the filling. Brush the pastry with egg yolk. Bake for 25 minutes, or until golden. Serve garnished with lime rind.

Serves 4

Coulibiac

- 60 g (2 oz) butter
- 1 onion, finely chopped
- 200 g (7 oz) button mushrooms, sliced
- 2 tablespoons lemon juice
- 225 g (8 oz) salmon fillet, skin and bones removed, cut into 1.5 cm (⅝ inch) chunks
- 2 hard-boiled eggs, chopped
- 2 tablespoons chopped dill (dill weed)
- 2 tablespoons chopped parsley
- 1 cup (185 g/6½ oz) cooked, cold long-grain rice
- ¼ cup (60 ml/2 fl oz) thick (double/heavy) cream
- 370 g (13 oz) block puff pastry
- 1 egg, lightly beaten

Melt half the butter in a frying pan, add the onion and cook over medium heat until soft. Add the mushrooms and cook for 5 minutes. Stir in the lemon juice and transfer to a bowl.

Melt the remaining butter in a pan, then add the salmon and cook for 2 minutes. Transfer to a bowl, cool slightly and add the egg, dill (dill weed) and parsley. Season, combine gently and set aside. In a small bowl, combine the rice and cream, and season with salt and pepper.

Roll out half the pastry to an 18 × 30 cm (7 × 12 inch) rectangle and put it on the baking tray (sheet). Spread half the rice mixture onto the pastry, leaving a 3 cm (1¼ inch) border all around. Top with the salmon mixture, then the mushrooms and, finally, the remaining rice.

Roll out the remaining pastry to 20 × 32 cm (8 × 12½ inch) and put it over the filling. Press the pastry edges together, then crimp to seal. Decorate with pastry cut-outs, if you like, then refrigerate for 30 minutes. Preheat the oven to hot 210°C (415°F/Gas 6–7).

Brush the pastry top with the beaten egg and bake for 15 minutes. Reduce the heat to moderate 180°C (350°F/Gas 4) and bake for another 15–20 minutes.

Serves 6

Salmon Pie

- 60 g (2 oz) butter
- 1 onion, finely chopped
- 200 g (7 oz) button mushrooms, sliced
- 2 tablespoons lemon juice
- 200 g (7 oz) cooked poached salmon fillet, broken into small pieces, or 220 g (7¾ oz) can red salmon
- 2 hard-boiled eggs, chopped
- 2 tablespoons chopped fresh dill (dill weed)

- 3 tablespoons chopped fresh parsley
- 1 cup (185 g/6½ oz) cooked long-grain brown rice (see Note)
- ¼ cup (60 ml/2 fl oz) cream
- 375 g (13¼ oz) packet frozen puff pastry
- 1 egg, lightly beaten
- sour cream, optional, for serving

Melt half the butter in a frying pan and cook the onion for 5 minutes until soft but not brown. Add the mushrooms and cook for 5 minutes. Stir in the juice, then remove from the pan.

Melt the remaining butter in the pan, add the salmon and stir for 2 minutes. Remove from the heat, cool slightly and add the egg, dill (dill weed), parsley, and salt and pepper, to taste. Mix gently and set aside. Mix the rice and cream in a small bowl.

Roll out half the pastry to 15 × 25 cm (6 × 10 inches). Trim the pastry neatly, saving the trimmings, and put on a greased baking tray (sheet).

Layer the filling onto the pastry, leaving a 3 cm (1¼ inch) border. Put half the rice into the centre of the pastry, then the salmon and egg mixture, followed by the mushrooms, then the remaining rice. Brush the border with egg.

Roll out the other pastry half to 20 × 30 cm (8 × 12 inches) and place over the filling. Seal the edges. Make two slits in the top. Decorate with the trimmings and chill for 30 minutes.

Preheat the oven to hot 200°C (400°F/Gas 6). Brush the pie with egg and bake for 15 minutes. Reduce the oven to 180°C (350°F/Gas 4) and bake the pie for 25–30 minutes, or until crisp and golden. Serve with sour cream.

Note: You will need to cook about ½ cup (100 g/3½ oz) brown rice for this recipe.

Serves 4–6

Fish Pie

- 2 large potatoes (500 g/1 lb 2 oz), chopped
- ¼ cup (60 ml/2 fl oz) milk or cream
- 1 egg, lightly beaten
- 60 g (2 oz) butter
- 60 g (2 oz) Cheddar (American) cheese, grated
- 800 g (1 lb 12 oz) skinless white fish fillets (eg. ling, hake), cut into large chunks
- 1½ cups (375 ml/13 fl oz) milk
- 1 onion, finely chopped
- 1 clove garlic, crushed
- 2 tablespoons plain (all-purpose) flour
- 2 tablespoons lemon juice
- 2 teaspoons lemon rind
- 1 tablespoon chopped fresh dill (dill weed)

Preheat the oven to 180°C (350°F/Gas 4). Boil or steam the potatoes until tender (pierce with the point of a small knife – if the potato comes away easily, it is ready) and mash well with the milk or cream, egg and half the butter. Mix in half the Cheddar (American) cheese, then set aside and keep warm.

Put the fish in a shallow frying pan and cover with the milk. Bring to the boil, then reduce the heat and simmer for 2–3 minutes, or until the fish is cooked. Drain the fish well, reserving the milk, and set aside.

Melt the rest of the butter in a pan and cook the onion and garlic over medium heat for 2 minutes. Stir in the flour and cook for 1 minute, or until pale and foaming. Remove from the heat and gradually stir in the reserved milk. Return to the heat and stir constantly until the sauce boils and thickens. Reduce the heat and simmer for 2 minutes. Add the lemon juice, lemon rind and dill (dill weed), and season with plenty of salt and cracked black pepper.

Put the fish in a 1.5 litre (1.6 US qt/1.3 UK qt) capacity ovenproof dish and gently mix in the sauce. Spoon the mashed potato over the fish and top with the remaining Cheddar (American) cheese. Bake for 35 minutes, or until golden brown.

Serves 4

Game Pie

- 1 kg (2 lb 3 oz) rabbit, boned, cut into bite-sized pieces
- 1.25 kg (2 lb 12 oz) venison goulash or diced venison
- ¼ cup (30 g/1 oz) plain (all-purpose) flour
- 2–3 tablespoons oil
- 2 rashers bacon, chopped
- 1 onion, sliced into thin wedges
- 2 cloves garlic, crushed
- 150 g (5¼ oz) button mushrooms, cut in halves
- 1 cup (250 ml/8½ fl oz) red wine
- 1 cup (250 ml/8½ fl oz) beef stock (broth)
- 3 sprigs fresh thyme
- 2 bay leaves
- 1½ × 375 g (13¼ oz) blocks puff pastry, thawed
- 1 egg yolk
- 2 tablespoons milk

Lightly coat the rabbit and venison in seasoned flour. Heat the oil in a large saucepan and cook the bacon over medium heat until golden. Remove. Brown the meats well in batches, remove and set aside. Add the onion and garlic to the saucepan and cook until browned.

Return the bacon and meat to the saucepan and add the mushrooms, wine, stock (broth), thyme and bay leaves. Bring to the boil, then reduce the heat and simmer over low heat, stirring occasionally, for 1½ hours, or until the meat is tender. Transfer to a heatproof bowl. Remove the thyme and bay leaves. Refrigerate until cold.

Preheat the oven to moderately hot 200°C (400°F/Gas 6). Spoon the mixture into a 2 litre (2.1 US qt/1.75 UK qt) ovenproof dish. Roll the half block of pastry on a lightly floured surface to about 5 mm (¼ inch) thick. Cut strips the width of the pie dish rim and secure to the dish with a little water. Reserve the leftover pastry. Roll the other block of pastry on a lightly floured surface until large enough to fit the top of the pie dish. Brush the edges of the pastry strips with a little combined egg yolk and milk. Drape the pastry over the rolling pin and lower it onto the top of the pie. Trim off any excess pastry using a sharp knife. Score the edges of the pastry with the back of a knife to seal. Use any leftover pastry to decorate the top. Cut two slits in the top of the pastry and brush all over with the remaining egg and milk mixture. Bake for 30–40 minutes, or until puffed and golden.

Serves 4–6

Chicken and Sugar Snap Pea Parcels

- 200 g (7 oz) sugar snap peas (snap peas)
- 1 tablespoon oil
- 6 chicken thigh fillets, cut into 1 cm (½ inch) thick strips
- 40 g (1½ oz) butter
- 2 tablespoons plain (all-purpose) flour
- ¾ cup (185 ml/6½ fl oz) chicken stock (broth)
- ⅔ cup (170 ml/5¾ fl oz) dry white wine
- 1 tablespoon wholegrain mustard
- 150 g (5¼ oz) feta cheese, cut into 1 cm (½ inch) cubes
- ⅓ cup (50 g/1¾ oz) sliced sun-dried tomatoes, finely chopped
- 24 sheets filo (phyllo) pastry
- 60 g (2 oz) butter, extra, melted
- sesame and sunflower seeds

Preheat the oven to hot 210°C (415°F/Gas 6–7). Top and tail the sugar snap peas (snap peas), then plunge into boiling water for 1 minute, or until bright in colour but still crunchy. Drain well.

Heat the oil in a heavy-based pan. Cook the chicken quickly, in small batches, over medium heat until well browned. Drain on paper towels.

Melt the butter in a pan and add the flour. Stir over low heat for 2 minutes, or until the flour mixture is light golden and bubbling. Add the stock (broth), wine and mustard, stirring until the mixture is smooth. Stir constantly over medium heat until the mixture boils and thickens. Stir in the chicken, sugar snap peas (snap peas), feta and tomato and mix gently. Remove from the heat and allow to cool. Divide the mixture evenly into eight portions.

Brush three sheets of the pastry with the melted butter. Place the sheets on top of each other. Place one portion of the mixture at one short end of the pastry. Roll and fold the pastry, enclosing the filling to form a parcel. Brush with a little more butter and place seam-side down on a greased baking tray (sheet). Repeat with the remaining pastry, butter and filling. Brush the tops with butter. Sprinkle with the sesame and sunflower seeds. Bake for 20 minutes, or until golden brown and heated through.

Makes 8

Creamy Mushroom Pie

- 2 cups (250 g/8¾ oz) plain (all-purpose) flour
- ½ cup (75 g/2½ oz) fine polenta (cornmeal)
- 125 g (4⅓ oz) butter, chilled and cubed
- ¼ cup (60 ml/2 fl oz) cream
- 2–3 tablespoons iced water

Filling
- 10 g (⅓ oz) dried porcini mushrooms
- 150 g (5¼ oz) oyster mushrooms
- 1 large leek
- 150 g (5¼ oz) butter
- 2 large cloves garlic, crushed
- 200 g (7 oz) shiitake mushrooms, thickly sliced

- 200 g (7 oz) Swiss brown mushrooms, thickly sliced
- 350 g (12¼ oz) field (meadow) mushrooms, sliced
- 100 g (3½ oz) enoki mushrooms
- 2 tablespoons plain (all-purpose) flour
- ½ cup (125 ml/4¼ fl oz) dry white wine
- ½ cup (125 ml/4¼ fl oz) vegetable or chicken stock (broth)
- ¼ cup (60 ml/2 fl oz) thick (double/heavy) cream
- 2 tablespoons chopped fresh thyme
- 1 egg, lightly beaten, to glaze

To make the pastry, sift the flour into a large bowl, then stir in the polenta (cornmeal) and ½ teaspoon of salt. Add the butter and rub into the dry ingredients with your fingertips until the mixture resembles fine breadcrumbs. Make a well in the centre, pour in the cream and mix with a flat-bladed knife, using a cutting action, until the mixture comes together in beads. Add a little water if the mixture is too dry.

Gently gather the dough together and lift out onto a lightly floured work surface. Press together into a ball and then flatten slightly into a disc. Wrap in plastic wrap and refrigerate for 20 minutes.

Soak the porcini mushrooms in 3 tablespoons boiling water for about 15 minutes. Cut any large oyster mushrooms into halves. Thoroughly wash the leek and thinly slice it.

Preheat the oven to hot 210°C (415°F/Gas 6–7). Heat a baking tray (sheet) in the oven. Lightly grease an 18 cm (7 inch) pie dish.

Drain the porcini mushrooms, reserving the soaking liquid, then coarsely chop them. Heat the butter in a large, deep frying pan over medium heat and cook the leek and garlic for 7–8 minutes, or until the leek is soft and golden.

Add all the mushrooms to the pan and cook, stirring, for 5–6 minutes, or until soft. Add the flour to the pan and stir for 1 minute. Pour in the wine and reserved mushroom soaking liquid and bring to the boil for 1 minute, then pour in the stock (broth) and cook for 4–5 minutes, or until the liquid has reduced. Stir in the cream and cook for 1–2 minutes, or until thickened. Stir in the thyme and season. Cool.

Divide the pastry into two portions. Roll out one portion between two sheets of baking paper to 2 mm (⅟₁₆ inch) thick to line the base and side of the pie dish. Line the pie dish, then spoon in the cooled mushroom filling. Lightly brush the edge of the pastry with egg.

Roll out the remaining pastry between the baking paper until about 2 mm (⅟₁₆ inch) thick and cover the pie. Pinch the edges together and pierce the top three times with a fork. Trim the edges. Roll the trimmings and cut into mushroom shapes. Arrange over the pie and lightly brush the top with more egg. Place on the hot tray (sheet) and bake for 35–40 minutes, or until the pastry is golden brown. Set aside for 5 minutes before slicing.

Serves 4–6

Sweet Potato and Fennel Pie

- 2 fennel bulbs (500 g/1 lb 2 oz), thick outer leaves removed, sliced
- 300 g (10½ oz) sweet potato (yam), cut into 1 cm (½ inch) cubes
- 1 tablespoon dried juniper berries, ground
- ¼ cup (60 ml/2 fl oz) olive oil
- 300 g (10½ oz) ricotta
- 1 cup (100 g/3½ oz) grated Parmesan
- 100 g (3½ oz) ground almonds
- 6 sheets ready-rolled shortcrust (pie) pastry
- milk, to glaze
- 3 sheets ready-rolled puff pastry

Preheat the oven to moderate 180°C (350°F/Gas 4). Grease six 11 cm (4⅓ inch) (top) 9.5 cm (3⅔ inch) (base) and 2.5 cm (1 inch) (deep) pie tins. Place the fennel, sweet potato (yam) and juniper berries in a deep roasting tin and toss with the oil. Season, cover with foil and cook for 35 minutes, or until the vegetables have softened. Drain any oil away, transfer to a bowl and chill for 30 minutes, or until cold.

Combine the ricotta, Parmesan and ground almonds in a large bowl. Transfer to a sieve and sit over a bowl for 10 minutes to drain away any liquid from the ricotta.

Cut a 15 cm (6 inch) round from each sheet of shortcrust (pie) pastry and line the pie tins, leaving the excess overhanging. Brush the rims with milk.

Divide the vegetables among the pastry shells, then top with ricotta mixture. Cut six 12 cm (4¾ inch) rounds from the puff pastry, place over the filled shells and trim. Seal the edges with a fork and prick a few holes in the tops. Brush with milk, then bake for 35 minutes, or until golden.

Serves 6

Vegetable Lattice Pie

- 185 g (6½ oz) butter
- 2 cups (250 g/8¾ oz) plain (all-purpose) flour
- 3 tablespoons iced water

Filling
- 1 tablespoon oil
- 1 onion, finely chopped
- 1 small red capsicum (pepper), chopped
- 1 small green capsicum (pepper), chopped
- 150 g (5¼ oz) pumpkin, chopped
- 1 small potato, chopped
- 100 g (3½ oz) broccoli, cut into small florets
- 1 carrot, chopped
- 3 tablespoons plain (all-purpose) flour
- 1 cup (250 ml/8½ fl oz) milk
- 2 egg yolks
- ½ cup (60 g/2 oz) grated Cheddar (American) cheese
- 1 egg, lightly beaten, to glaze

Chop 125 g (4⅓ oz) of the butter. Sift the flour into a large bowl and add the chopped butter. Using your fingertips, rub the butter into the flour until the mixture is fine and crumbly. Add almost all the water and use a knife to mix to a firm dough, adding more water if necessary. Turn onto a lightly floured surface and press together until smooth. Divide the dough in half, roll out one portion and line a deep 20 cm (8 inch) fluted flan tin. Refrigerate for 20 minutes. Roll the remaining pastry out to a 25 cm (10 inch) diameter circle. Cut into strips and lay half of them on a sheet of baking paper, leaving a 2 cm (¾ inch) gap between each strip. Interweave the remaining strips to form a lattice pattern. Cover with plastic wrap and refrigerate, keeping flat, until firm.

Preheat the oven to 180°C (350°F/Gas 4). Cut a sheet of greaseproof paper to cover the pastry-lined tin. Spread a layer of baking beads or dried beans or rice over the paper. Bake for 10 minutes, remove from the oven and discard the paper and beads, beans or rice. Bake for another 10 minutes or until golden. Remove and allow to cool.

Heat the oil in a frying pan. Add the onion and cook for 2 minutes or until soft. Add the caspicum (pepper) and cook, stirring, for another 3 minutes. Steam or boil the remaining vegetables until just tender; drain and cool. Combine the onion, capsicum (pepper) and the other vegetables in a large bowl.

Heat the remaining butter in a small pan. Add the flour and cook, stirring, for 2 minutes. Add the milk gradually, stirring until smooth after each addition. Stir until the sauce boils and thickens. Boil for 1 minute and then remove from the heat.

Add the egg yolks and cheese and stir until smooth. Pour over the vegetables and stir together. Pour into the pastry case and brush the edges with egg. Using the baking paper to help, invert the lattice over the vegetables, trim the edges and brush with a little egg. Press the edges lightly to seal to the cooked pastry. Brush the top with egg and bake for 30 minutes or until the pastry is golden.

Serves 6

Summer Potato Pizza

- 7 g (¼ oz) sachet dry yeast
- 2½ cups (310 g/11 oz) plain (all-purpose) flour
- 2 teaspoons polenta (cornmeal) or semolina
- 2 tablespoons olive oil
- 2 cloves garlic, crushed
- 4–5 potatoes, unpeeled, thinly sliced
- 1 tablespoon fresh rosemary leaves

Preheat the oven to hot 210°C (415°F/Gas 6–7). Combine the yeast, ½ teaspoon of salt and sugar and 1 cup (250 ml/8½ fl oz) of warm water in a bowl. Cover and leave in a warm place for 10 minutes, or until foamy. Sift the flour into a bowl, make a well in the centre, add the yeast mixture and mix to a dough.

Turn the dough out onto a lightly floured surface and knead for 5 minutes, or until smooth and elastic. Roll out to a 30 cm (12 inch) circle. Lightly spray a pizza tray (sheet) with oil and sprinkle with polenta (cornmeal) or semolina.

Place the pizza base on the tray (sheet). Mix 2 teaspoons of the oil with the garlic and brush over the pizza base. Gently toss the remaining olive oil, potato slices, rosemary leaves, 1 teaspoon of salt and some pepper in a bowl.

Arrange the potato slices in overlapping circles over the pizza base and bake for 40 minutes, or until the base is crisp and golden.

Serves 6

Pizzetta Squares

- 2 tablespoons oil
- 4 onions, finely sliced
- 2 sheets frozen puff pastry, thawed
- ⅓ cup (90 g/3¼ oz) sun-dried tomato pesto
- 10 anchovies, finely chopped
- 15 g (½ oz) fresh basil leaves, finely shredded

Preheat the oven to moderately hot 200°C (400°F/Gas 6). Heat the oil in a large pan and cook the onion over medium heat for 20 minutes, or until soft and golden. Cool.

Lay each sheet of pastry on a lightly greased oven tray (sheet), then spread the tomato pesto evenly over the pastry. Scatter the onion over the top.

Sprinkle the anchovies and basil over the top and bake for 20 minutes, or until the squares are puffed and golden. Cool, then cut into squares. Serve warm or at room temperature.

In Advance: Cook the onions 2 days ahead and refrigerate. Bake no earlier than 2 hours ahead.

Makes about 50

Smoked Salmon Pizzas

- **250 g (8¾ oz) low-fat ricotta**
- **6 small oval pitta breads**
- **125 g (4⅓ oz) sliced smoked salmon**
- **1 small red onion, sliced**
- **1 tablespoon baby capers**
- **small dill (dill weed) sprigs, to garnish**
- **1 lemon, cut into thin wedges, for serving**

Preheat the oven to moderate 180°C (350°F/Gas 4). Put the ricotta in a bowl, season well with salt and pepper and stir until smooth. Spread the ricotta over the breads, leaving a clear border around the edge.

Top each pizza with some smoked salmon slices, then some onion pieces. Scatter baby capers over the top and bake on a baking tray (sheet) for 15 minutes, or until the bases are slightly crispy around the edges. Garnish with a few dill (dill weed) sprigs and serve with lemon wedges.

Serves 6

Turkish Pizza

- 1 teaspoon dried yeast
- ½ teaspoon sugar
- 225 g (8 oz) plain (all-purpose) flour
- 4 tablespoons olive oil
- 250 g (8¾ oz) onions, finely chopped
- 500 g (1 lb 2 oz) lamb mince (ground lamb)
- 2 cloves garlic
- 1 teaspoon ground cinnamon
- 1½ teaspoons ground cumin
- ½ teaspoon cayenne (red) pepper
- 3 tablespoons tomato paste (tomato puree)
- 400 g (14 oz) can good-quality crushed tomatoes
- ⅓ cup (50 g/1¾ oz) pine nuts
- 3 tablespoons chopped fresh coriander (cilantro)
- Greek-style natural yoghurt, for serving

Mix the yeast, sugar and ¼ cup (60 ml/2 fl oz) warm water in a bowl. Leave in a warm place for 20 minutes, or until bubbles appear on the surface. The mixture should be frothy and increased in volume.

Sift the flour and 1 teaspoon salt into a bowl, stir in the yeast mixture, 1 tablespoon oil and 100 ml (3½ fl oz) warm water. Mix to form a soft dough, then turn onto a floured board and knead for 10 minutes, or until smooth. Place in an oiled bowl, cover and leave in a warm place for 1 hour, or until doubled in size.

Heat 2 tablespoons oil in a frying pan over low heat and cook the onion for 5 minutes, or until soft but not golden. Add the lamb and cook for 10 minutes, or until brown. Add the garlic and spices, tomato paste (tomato puree) and tomato. Cook for 15 minutes, until quite dry. Add half the pine nuts and 2 tablespoons coriander (cilantro). Season, then leave to cool. Preheat the oven to hot 210°C (415°F/Gas 6–7). Grease two baking trays (sheets).

Knock down the dough, then turn out onto a floured surface. Form into 8 portions and roll each into an 18 × 12 cm (7 × 4¾ inch) oval. Place on the trays (sheets). Divide the lamb among them and spread, leaving a small border. Sprinkle with pine nuts. Brush the edges with oil. Roll the uncovered dough over to cover the outer edges of the filling. Pinch the sides together at each end. Brush with oil. Bake for 15 minutes, or until golden. Sprinkle with coriander (cilantro) and serve with yoghurt.

Makes 8

Mushroom, Ricotta and Olive Pizza

- 4 Roma (egg) tomatoes, quartered
- ¾ teaspoon caster (berry) sugar
- 7 g (¼ oz) dry yeast or 15 g (½ oz) fresh yeast
- ½ cup (125 ml/4¼ fl oz) skim milk
- 1¾ cups (220 g/7¾ oz) plain (all-purpose) flour
- 2 teaspoons olive oil
- 2 cloves garlic, crushed
- 1 onion, thinly sliced
- 750 g (1 lb 10 oz) cap mushrooms, sliced
- 1 cup (250 g/8¾ oz) ricotta cheese
- 2 tablespoons sliced black (ripe) olives
- small fresh basil leaves

Preheat the oven to hot 210°C (415°F/Gas 6–7). Put the tomatoes on a baking tray (sheet) covered with baking paper, sprinkle with salt, cracked black pepper and ½ teaspoon sugar and bake for 20 minutes, or until the edges are starting to darken.

Stir the yeast and remaining sugar with 3 tablespoons warm water until the yeast dissolves. Cover and leave in a warm place until foamy (if the yeast doesn't foam you will have to throw it away and start again). Warm the milk. Sift the flour into a large bowl and stir in the yeast and milk. Mix to a soft dough, then turn onto a lightly floured surface and knead for 5 minutes. Leave, covered, in a lightly oiled bowl in a warm place for 40 minutes, or until doubled in size.

Heat the oil in a pan and fry the garlic and onion until soft. Add the mushrooms and stir until they are soft and the liquid has evaporated. Cool.

Turn the dough out onto a lightly floured surface and knead lightly. Roll out to a 36 cm (14¼ inch) circle and transfer to a lightly greased oven or pizza tray (sheet). Spread with the ricotta, leaving a border to turn over the filling. Top with the mushrooms, leaving a circle in the centre and arrange the tomato and olives in the circle. Fold the dough edge over onto the mushroom and dust the edge with flour. Bake for 25 minutes, or until the crust is golden. Garnish with basil.

Serves 6

Potato and Rosemary Pizzettas

- 1 teaspoon dried yeast
- ½ teaspoon sugar
- 2½ cups (310 g/11 oz) plain (all-purpose) flour
- ⅓ cup (80 ml/2¾ fl oz) olive oil
- 400 g (14 oz) pontiac potatoes (red-skinned, waxy potatoes), unpeeled
- 2 tablespoons olive oil, extra
- 1 tablespoon fresh rosemary leaves

Place the yeast, sugar and ⅓ cup (80 ml/2¾ fl oz) water in a small bowl, cover and leave in a warm place until foamy.

Sift the flour and ¼ teaspoon salt into a large bowl. Make a well in the centre and stir in the yeast mixture, the oil and ⅓ cup (80 ml/2¾ fl oz) water; mix to a soft dough. Turn out onto a lightly floured surface and knead for 5 minutes, or until the dough is smooth and elastic. Place the dough in an oiled bowl, cover and leave in a warm place for about 1 hour, or until the dough has doubled in size.

Preheat the oven to hot 220°C (425°F/Gas 7). Punch down the dough to expel the air. Turn out and knead for 1 minute, or until smooth. Divide into 48 portions and roll each portion to a 5 cm (2 inch) round. Place on lightly greased baking trays (sheets).

Cut the potatoes into slices. Cover each dough round with a slice of potato, leaving a 1 cm (½ inch) border. Brush the pizzettas with the extra olive oil and sprinkle with rosemary leaves and salt. Bake on the highest shelf in the oven for 12–15 minutes, or until the pastry is crisp and lightly browned. Serve immediately.

Makes 48

103

Spanish Pizza

Base
- 7 g (¼ oz) sachet dried yeast
- 1 teaspoon caster (berry) sugar
- 2¼ cups (280 g/9¾ oz) plain (all-purpose) flour
- 1 cup (250 ml/8½ fl oz) warm water

Topping
- 10 English (common) spinach leaves, shredded
- 1 tablespoon olive oil
- 2 cloves garlic, crushed
- 2 onions, chopped
- 440 g (15½ oz) canned tomatoes, drained and crushed
- ¼ teaspoon ground pepper
- 12 pitted black (ripe) olives, chopped

Preheat the oven to hot 210°C (415°F/Gas 6–7). Brush a 30 × 25 cm (12 × 10 inch) Swiss roll tin with melted butter or oil.

To make the Base: Combine the yeast, sugar and flour in a large bowl. Gradually add the warm water and blend until smooth. Knead the dough on a lightly floured surface until smooth and elastic. Place in a lightly oiled basin, cover with a tea towel and leave to rise in a warm position for 15 minutes or until the dough has almost doubled in size.

Put the spinach in a large pan, cover and cook on low heat for 3 minutes. Drain the spinach and cool. Squeeze out the excess moisture and set spinach aside.

Heat the oil in a pan and add the garlic and onions. Cook over low heat for 5–6 minutes. Add the tomatoes and pepper and simmer gently for 5 minutes.

Punch the dough down, remove from the bowl and knead on a lightly floured board for 2–3 minutes. Roll the dough out and fit it in the tin. Spread with spinach, top with the tomato mixture and sprinkle the olives on top.

Bake for 25–30 minutes. Cut into small squares or fingers and serve hot or cold.

Serves 4–6

Quiches

Quiche Lorraine

- 1¼ cups (155 g/5½ oz) plain (all-purpose) flour
- 90 g (3¼ oz) cold butter, chopped
- 2–3 tablespoons iced water
- 4 rashers bacon, rind removed
- 75 g (2½ oz) Gruyère, finely grated
- 3 eggs
- ½ cup (125 ml/4¼ fl oz) cream
- ½ cup (125 ml/4¼ fl oz) milk

Sift the flour into a bowl and rub in the butter with your fingertips until the mixture resembles fine breadcrumbs. Make a well in the centre and add the water. Using a cutting action, mix with a flat-bladed knife until the mixture comes together in beads. Gently gather the dough together and lift onto a floured surface. Press into a ball and flatten it slightly. Wrap in plastic wrap and refrigerate for 15 minutes. Preheat the oven to moderately hot 200°C (400°F/Gas 6).

Roll the dough out between two sheets of baking paper until large enough to line a 23 cm (9 inch) fluted flan tin. Remove the top sheet of paper and invert the pastry into the tin (draping it over the rolling pin may help). Use a small ball of pastry to help press the pastry into the tin, leaving any excess to hang over the side. Roll the rolling pin over the tin to cut off any excess, and then refrigerate for 15 minutes.

Line the pastry shell with enough crumpled greaseproof paper to cover the base and side of the tin. Pour in some baking beads or rice and bake for 15 minutes. Remove the paper and beads or rice and return the pastry to the oven for 10 minutes, or until the base is dry. Cool completely before filling. Reduce the oven to moderate 180°C (350°F/Gas 4).

Cut the bacon into short, thin strips and cook in a frying pan until brown and crisp. Drain, then spread evenly over the pastry base. Sprinkle the cheese over the bacon. In a jug, whisk together the eggs, cream and milk. Stand the tin on a baking tray (sheet), and pour the egg mixture into the pastry shell. Bake for 35–40 minutes, or until set and lightly golden.

Serves 6

Leek and Ham Quiche with Polenta Pastry

- 1 cup (125 g/4⅓ oz) plain (all-purpose) flour
- ½ cup (75 g/2½ oz) polenta (cornmeal)
- 90 g (3¼ oz) butter, chilled and cubed
- 90 g (3¼ oz) cream cheese, chilled and cubed

Leek and Ham Filling
- 50 g (1¾ oz) butter
- 2 leeks, thinly sliced
- 2 eggs, lightly beaten
- 1 cup (250 ml/8½ fl oz) cream
- ½ teaspoon ground nutmeg
- 100 g (3½ oz) ham, chopped
- 75 g (2½ oz) Swiss cheese, grated

Process the flour and polenta (cornmeal) briefly to mix together. Add the butter and cream cheese and process for about 15 seconds until the mixture comes together. Add 1–2 tablespoons of water if needed. Turn out onto a floured surface and gather into a ball. Wrap in plastic wrap and refrigerate for 30 minutes.

To make the filling, heat the butter in a pan and cook the leeks, covered, stirring often, for 10–15 minutes, or until soft but not brown. Cool. Mix together the beaten eggs, cream and nutmeg and season with pepper.

Grease a shallow 21 × 28 cm (8¼ × 11 inch) loose-based tart tin with melted butter. Roll the pastry between two sheets of baking paper until large enough to fit the tin. Trim off any excess pastry and refrigerate for 20 minutes. Preheat the oven to 190°C (375°F/Gas 5). Cover the pastry shell with baking paper and spread with a layer of baking beads or rice. Bake for 15 minutes. Remove the paper and beads or rice and bake for a further 15 minutes, or until the pastry is golden and dry. Reduce the oven to 180°C (350°F/Gas 4).

Spread the leek over the pastry shell and sprinkle with the ham and cheese. Pour in the cream mixture. Bake for 30 minutes, or until golden and set.

Serves 6

Tomato and Bacon Quiche

- 1½ cups (185 g/6½ oz) plain (all-purpose) flour
- pinch of cayenne (red) pepper
- pinch of mustard powder (dry mustard)
- 125 g (4⅓ oz) butter, chilled and cubed
- ⅓ cup (40 g/1½ oz) grated Cheddar (American) cheese
- 1 egg yolk

Filling
- 25 g (¾ oz) butter
- 100 g (3½ oz) lean bacon, chopped
- 1 small onion, finely sliced
- 3 eggs
- ¾ cup (185 ml/6½ fl oz) cream
- ½ teaspoon salt
- 2 tomatoes, peeled, seeded and chopped into chunks
- ¾ cup (90 g/3¼ oz) grated Cheddar (American) cheese

Mix the flour, pepper, mustard and butter in a food processor until crumbly. Add the cheese and egg yolk and process in short bursts until the mixture comes together. Add 1–2 tablespoons of cold water if needed. Turn out onto a floured surface and gather into a ball. Wrap in plastic and refrigerate for 30 minutes. Grease a 23 cm (9 inch) loose-based deep tart tin.

To make the filling, melt the butter in a frying pan and cook the bacon for a few minutes until golden. Add the onion and cook until soft. Remove from the heat. Lightly beat the eggs, cream and salt together. Add the bacon and onion, then fold in the tomato and cheese.

Roll out the pastry on a floured surface until large enough to fit the tin. Trim the excess pastry and refrigerate for 30 minutes. Preheat the oven to 180°C (350°F/ Gas 4). Cover the pastry with baking paper and spread with a layer of baking beads or rice. Bake for 10 minutes. Remove the paper and beads or rice and bake for 10 minutes.

Pour the filling into the pastry shell and bake for 35 minutes until golden.

Serves 6

Corn and Bacon Crustless Quiches

- **4 corn cobs**
- **2 teaspoons olive oil**
- **2 rashers bacon, cut into thin strips**
- **1 small onion, finely chopped**
- **3 eggs, lightly beaten**
- **2 tablespoons chopped chives**
- **2 tablespoons chopped fresh parsley**
- **¾ cup (60 g/2 oz) fresh white breadcrumbs**
- **⅓ cup (80 ml/2¾ fl oz) cream**

Preheat the oven to 180°C (350°F/Gas 4). Lightly grease four ¾ cup (185 ml/6½ fl oz) ramekins. Remove the husks from the corn and, using a coarse grater, grate the corn kernels into a deep bowl – there should be about 1½ cups corn flesh and juice.

Heat the oil in a pan and cook the bacon and onion for 3–4 minutes, or until the onion softens. Transfer to a bowl. Stir in the corn, eggs, chives, parsley, breadcrumbs and cream and season well. Spoon into the ramekins.

Put the ramekins in a large baking dish. Add enough hot water to come halfway up the sides of the ramekins. Lay foil loosely over the top. Bake for 25–30 minutes or until just set.

Makes 4

Mustard Chicken and Asparagus Quiche

- 2 cups (250 g/8¾ oz) plain (all-purpose) flour
- 100 g (3½ oz) cold butter, chopped
- 1 egg yolk

Filling
- 150 g (5¼ oz) asparagus, chopped
- 25 g (¾ oz) butter
- 1 onion, chopped
- ¼ cup (60 g/2 oz) wholegrain mustard
- 200 g (7 oz) soft cream cheese
- ½ cup (125 ml/4¼ fl oz) cream
- 3 eggs, lightly beaten
- 200 g (7 oz) cooked chicken, chopped
- ½ teaspoon black pepper

Process the flour and butter until crumbly. Add the egg yolk and ¼ cup (60 ml/2 fl oz) of water. Process in short bursts until the mixture comes together. Add a little extra water if needed. Turn onto a floured surface and gather into a ball. Cover with plastic wrap and chill for 30 minutes. Grease a deep loose-based flan tin measuring 19 cm (7½ inches) across the base.

Roll out the pastry and line the tin. Trim off any excess with a sharp knife. Place the flan tin on a baking tray (sheet) and chill for 10 minutes. Preheat the oven to moderately hot 200°C (400°F/Gas 6). Cover the pastry with baking paper and fill evenly with baking beads or rice. Bake for 10 minutes. Remove the paper and beads or rice and bake for about 10 minutes, or until the pastry is lightly browned and dry. Cool. Reduce the oven to moderate 180°C (350°F/Gas 4).

To make the filling, boil or steam the asparagus until tender. Drain and pat dry with paper towels. Heat the butter in a pan and cook the onion until translucent. Remove from the heat and add the mustard and cream cheese, stirring until the cheese has melted. Cool. Add the cream, eggs, chicken and asparagus and mix well.

Spoon the filling into the pastry shell and sprinkle with the pepper. Bake for 50 minutes to 1 hour, or until puffed and set. Cool for at least 15 minutes before cutting.

Serves 8

Seafood Quiche

- 2 sheets ready-rolled shortcrust (pie) pastry
- 100 g (3½ oz) scallops
- 30 g (1 oz) butter
- 100 g (3½ oz) raw prawn (shrimp) meat
- 100 g (3½ oz) canned, fresh or frozen crab meat
- 90 g (3¼ oz) Cheddar (American) cheese, grated
- 3 eggs
- 1 tablespoon plain (all-purpose) flour
- ½ cup (125 ml/4¼ fl oz) cream
- ½ cup (125 ml/4¼ fl oz) milk
- 1 small fennel bulb, finely sliced
- 1 tablespoon grated Parmesan

Lightly grease a 23 cm (9 inch) diameter loose-based flan tin. Place the 2 sheets of pastry slightly overlapping, on a work bench, and roll out until large enough to fit the prepared tin. Press the pastry into the base and side of the tin and trim off any excess with a sharp knife. Refrigerate for 20 minutes.

Slice off any vein or hard white muscle from the scallops, leaving any roe attached. Preheat the oven to 190°C (375°F/Gas 5).

Cover the pastry with baking paper, fill evenly with baking beads or uncooked rice and bake for 10 minutes. Remove the paper and beads or rice and bake for another 10 minutes, or until lightly golden. Cool on a wire rack. If the pastry puffs up, press down lightly with a tea towel.

Melt the butter in a frying pan and fry the prawns and scallops for 2–3 minutes, or until cooked. Allow to cool, then arrange all the seafood over the base of the pastry shell. Sprinkle with the cheese.

Beat the eggs in a small jug, whisk in the flour, cream and milk, and season with salt and pepper. Pour over the filling. Sprinkle with fennel and Parmesan. Bake for 30–35 minutes, or until set and golden brown. Cool slightly before serving.

Serves 4–6

Crab and Lime Quiches

- 2 sheets frozen puff pastry, thawed
- 2 eggs
- ¾ cup (185 ml/6½ fl oz) coconut cream
- finely grated rind of 1 small lime
- 2 teaspoons lime juice
- 200 g (7 oz) can crab meat, drained
- 1 tablespoon chopped fresh chives

Preheat the oven to hot 210°C (415°F/Gas 6–7). Using two 12-hole round-based patty (bun) tins, lightly grease 18 of the holes. Cut 18 rounds of pastry, using an 8 cm (3 inch) cutter.

Beat the eggs lightly in a small bowl and add the remaining ingredients. Season with salt and white pepper. Spoon about 1 tablespoon of filling into each pastry case.

Bake for 20 minutes, or until golden. The quiches will rise during cooking, then deflate slightly. Serve warm.

Makes 18

Mini Salmon and Camembert Quiches

Pastry
- 2 cups (250 g/8¾ oz) plain (all-purpose) flour
- 150 g (5¼ oz) butter, chopped
- 2 egg yolks, lightly beaten
- ½ teaspoon paprika

Filling
- 1 tablespoon olive oil
- 2 small leeks, finely sliced
- 75 g (2½ oz) smoked salmon, thinly sliced
- 80 g (2¾ oz) Camembert, chopped
- 2 eggs, lightly beaten
- ½ cup (125 ml/4¼ fl oz) cream
- 2 teaspoons grated lemon rind
- 1 teaspoon chopped fresh dill (dill weed)
- 1 tablespoon finely chopped fresh chives, for serving

Sift the flour into a large bowl and rub in the butter with your fingertips until the mixture resembles fine breadcrumbs. Make a well, add the egg yolk, paprika and 1 teaspoon water and mix with a flat-bladed knife, using a cutting action, until the mixture comes together in beads. Gently gather together and lift onto a lightly floured work surface. Press together into a ball, wrap in plastic wrap and refrigerate for 30 minutes.

Grease two 12-hole patty (bun) tins. Divide the pastry into 4 pieces. Roll each between 2 sheets of baking paper to 2 mm (¹⁄₁₆ inch) thick. Cut 24 rounds using a 7 cm (2¾ inch) fluted cutter. Lift the rounds into the patty (bun) tins, pressing into shape but being careful not to stretch the pastry. Chill for 30 minutes.

Preheat the oven to moderate 180°C (350°F/Gas 4). Bake the pastry for 5 minutes, or until lightly golden. If the pastry has puffed up, press down lightly with a tea towel.

For the filling, heat the oil in a frying pan and cook the leek for 2–3 minutes, or until soft. Remove from the pan and cool. Divide the leek, salmon and Camembert pieces among the pastries.

Whisk the egg, cream, lemon rind and dill (dill weed) together in a jug, then pour some into each pastry. Bake for 15–20 minutes, or until lightly golden and set. Serve sprinkled with chives.

Note: You can substitute crab meat or small prawns (shrimps) for the salmon.

Makes 24

Prawn, Crab and Cheese Quiches

- 2 cups (250 g/8¾ oz) plain (all-purpose) flour
- 125 g (4⅓ oz) butter, chilled and cubed
- 2 egg yolks
- 3–4 tablespoons iced water

Filling
- 170 g (6 oz) can crab meat, drained and squeezed dry
- 4 spring (green) onions, chopped
- 2 eggs, lightly beaten
- 1 cup (250 ml/8½ fl oz) cream
- 1 cup (125 g/4⅓ oz) finely grated Cheddar (American) cheese
- 2 tablespoons chopped fresh dill (dill weed)
- 1 teaspoon grated lemon rind
- 200 g (7 oz) small prawns (shrimps), cooked and peeled

Process the flour and butter for 15 seconds, or until the mixture resembles fine breadcrumbs. Add the egg yolks and water. Process in short bursts until the mixture comes together. Add a little more water if needed. Turn out onto a floured surface and gather into a ball. Cover with plastic wrap and refrigerate for at least 15 minutes.

Grease eight 8 cm (3 inch) loose-based tart tins. Divide the pastry into eight equal pieces and roll out until large enough to fit the tins. Trim off any excess pastry. Cover and refrigerate for 15 minutes. Preheat the oven to 190°C (375°F/Gas 5). Cover the pastry shells with baking paper and spread with a layer of baking beads or rice. Bake for 10 minutes. Remove the paper and beads or rice and bake for a further 10 minutes.

To make the filling, mix together the crab meat, spring (green) onions, beaten eggs, cream, cheese, dill (dill weed) and lemon rind. Divide the prawns (shrimps) among the pastry shells. The crab filling will be quite thick, so use a fork to spread it over the prawns (shrimps). Bake for 15–20 minutes, or until the filling is golden brown.

Serves 4

Potato, Leek and Spinach Quiche

- 2 cups (250 g/8¾ oz) plain (all-purpose) flour
- 125 g (4⅓ oz) cold butter, chopped

Filling
- 3 potatoes
- 30 g (1 oz) butter
- 2 tablespoons oil
- 2 cloves garlic, crushed

- 2 leeks, sliced
- 500 g (1 lb 2 oz) English (common) spinach, trimmed
- 1 cup (125 g/4⅓ oz) grated Cheddar (American) cheese
- 4 eggs
- ½ cup (125 ml/4¼ fl oz) cream
- ½ cup (125 ml/4¼ fl oz) milk

Place the flour in a food processor, add the butter and process for about 15 seconds until the mixture is crumbly. Add 2–3 tablespoons of water and process in short bursts until the mixture just comes together when you squeeze a little between your fingers. Add a little extra water if you think the dough is too dry. Turn out onto a floured surface and quickly bring the mixture together into a ball. Cover the pastry with plastic wrap and refrigerate for at least 30 minutes. Roll the pastry out between two sheets of baking paper until it is large enough to line a deep loose-based fluted flan tin measuring 21 cm (8¼ inches) across the base. Place on a baking tray (sheet) and refrigerate for 20 minutes.

Peel and thinly slice the potatoes. Melt the butter and oil together in a frying pan and add the garlic and sliced potatoes. Gently turn the potatoes until they are coated, then cover and cook for 5 minutes over low heat. Remove the potatoes with a slotted spoon, drain on paper towels and set aside. Add the leeks to the pan and cook until they are softened, then remove from the heat.

Wash the spinach and put in a large saucepan with just the water clinging to the leaves. Cover the pan and cook for 2 minutes, or until it has just wilted. Cool the spinach and squeeze out any excess water, then spread the leaves out on a paper towel or a tea towel to allow to dry.

Preheat the oven to moderate 180°C (350°F/Gas 4). Cover the pastry shell with baking paper and fill evenly with baking beads or rice. Bake for 15 minutes. Remove the paper and beads or rice and bake for a further 15 minutes.

Spread half the cheese over the bottom of the pastry base and top with half the potatoes, half the spinach and half the leeks. Repeat these layers again. In a large jug, mix together the eggs, cream and milk and pour over the layered mixture. Bake for 1 hour 20 minutes, or until the filling is firm. Serve warm or cold.

Note: Spinach can be kept in a plastic bag and stored for up to 3 days in the refrigerator. It can often be very gritty, so wash thoroughly in a few changes of water. When cooking the spinach, you don't need to add any extra water, just heat it with the water still clinging to the leaves.

Serves 6–8

Roast Vegetable Quiche

- cooking oil spray
- 1 large potato
- 400 g (14 oz) pumpkin
- 200 g (7 oz) orange sweet potato (yam)
- 2 large parsnips
- 1 red capsicum (pepper)
- 2 onions, cut into wedges
- 6 cloves garlic, halved
- 2 teaspoons olive oil

- 1¼ cups (150 g/5¼ oz) plain (all-purpose) flour
- 40 g (1½ oz) butter
- 45 g (1⅔ oz) ricotta
- 1 cup (250 ml/8½ fl oz) skim milk
- 3 eggs, lightly beaten
- ¼ cup (30 g/1 oz) grated reduced-fat Cheddar (American) cheese
- 2 tablespoons chopped fresh basil

Preheat the oven to moderate 180°C (350°F/Gas 4). Lightly spray a 3.5 cm (1⅓ inch) deep, 23 cm (9 inch) diameter loose-based flan tin with oil. Cut the potato, pumpkin, sweet potato (yam), parsnips and capsicum (pepper) into bite-sized chunks, place in a baking dish with the onion and garlic and drizzle with the oil. Season and bake for 1 hour, or until the vegetables are tender. Leave to cool.

Mix the flour, butter and ricotta in a food processor, then gradually add up to 3 tablespoons of the milk, enough to form a soft dough. Turn out onto a lightly floured surface and gather together into a smooth ball. Cover and refrigerate for 15 minutes.

Roll the pastry out on a lightly floured surface, then ease into the tin, bringing it gently up the side. Trim the edge and refrigerate for another 10 minutes. Increase the oven to moderately hot 200°C (400°F/Gas 6). Cover the pastry with crumpled baking paper and fill with baking beads or uncooked rice. Bake for 10 minutes, remove the beads or rice and paper, then bake for another 10 minutes, or until golden brown.

Place the vegetables in the pastry base and pour in the combined remaining milk, eggs, cheese and basil. Reduce the oven temperature to moderate 180°C (350°F/Gas 4) and bake for 1 hour 10 minutes, or until set in the centre. Leave for 5 minutes before removing from the tin to serve.

Serves 6

Mushroom Quiche with Parsley Pastry

- 1¼ cups (155 g/5½ oz) plain (all-purpose) flour
- ¼ cup (15 g/½ oz) chopped fresh parsley
- 90 g (3¼ oz) butter, chilled and cubed
- 1 egg yolk
- 2 tablespoons iced water

Filling
- 30 g (1 oz) butter
- 1 red onion, chopped

- 175 g (6¼ oz) button mushrooms, sliced
- 1 teaspoon lemon juice
- ⅓ cup (20 g/⅔ oz) chopped fresh parsley
- ⅓ cup (20 g/⅔ oz) chopped chives
- 1 egg, lightly beaten
- ⅓ cup (80 ml/2¾ oz) cream

Process the flour, parsley and butter for 15 seconds, or until crumbly. Add the egg yolk and water. Process in short bursts until the mixture comes together. Add a little more water if needed. Turn out onto a floured surface and gather into a ball. Cover with plastic wrap and refrigerate for at least 30 minutes.

Roll out the pastry between two sheets of baking paper until large enough to fit a 35 × 10 cm (14 × 4 inch) loose-based tart tin. Trim away the excess pastry. Refrigerate for 20 minutes. Preheat the oven to 190°C (375°F/Gas 5). Cover the pastry with baking paper and spread with a layer of baking beads or rice. Bake for 15 minutes. Remove the paper and beads or rice and bake for 10 minutes, or until the pastry is dry. Reduce the oven to 180°C (350°F/Gas 4).

To make the mushroom filling, melt the butter in a pan and cook the onion for 2–3 minutes until soft. Add the mushrooms and cook, stirring, for 2–3 minutes until soft. Stir in the lemon juice and herbs. Mix the egg and cream together and season.

Spread the mushroom filling into the pastry shell and pour over the egg and cream. Bake for 25–30 minutes, or until the filling has set.

Serves 4–6

Tarts

Vegetable Tart with Salsa Verde

- 1¾ cups (215 g/7½ oz) plain (all-purpose) flour
- 120 g (4¼ oz) chilled butter, cubed
- ¼ cup (60 ml/2 fl oz) cream
- 1–2 tablespoons chilled water
- 1 large (250 g/8¾ oz) Desiree potato (red-skinned potato with yellow flesh), cut into 2 cm (¾ inch) cubes
- 1 tablespoon olive oil
- 2 cloves garlic, crushed
- 1 red capsicum (pepper), cut into cubes
- 1 red onion, sliced into rings
- 2 zucchini (courgettes), sliced
- 2 tablespoons chopped fresh dill (dill weed)
- 1 tablespoon chopped fresh thyme
- 1 tablespoon drained baby capers

- 150 g (5¼ oz) marinated quartered artichoke hearts, drained
- ⅔ cup (30 g/1 oz) baby English (common) spinach leaves

Salsa Verde
- 1 clove garlic
- 2 cups (40 g/1½ oz) fresh flat-leaf parsley
- ⅓ cup (80 ml/2¾ fl oz) extra virgin olive oil
- 3 tablespoons chopped fresh dill (dill weed)
- 1½ tablespoons Dijon mustard
- 1 tablespoon red wine vinegar
- 1 tablespoon drained baby capers

Sift the flour and ½ teaspoon salt into a large bowl. Add the butter and rub it into the flour with your fingertips until it resembles fine breadcrumbs. Add the cream and water and mix with a flat-bladed knife until the mixture comes together in beads. Gather together and lift onto a lightly floured work surface. Press into a ball, then flatten into a disc, wrap in plastic wrap and refrigerate for 30 minutes.

Preheat the oven to moderately hot 200°C (400°F/Gas 6). Grease a 28 cm (11 inch) loose-bottomed flan tin. Roll the dough out between two sheets of baking paper large enough to line the tin. Remove the paper and invert the pastry into the tin. Use a small pastry ball to press the pastry into the tin, allowing any excess to hang over the side. Roll a rolling pin over the tin, cutting off any excess. Cover the pastry with a piece of crumpled baking paper, then add baking beads or rice. Place the tin on a baking tray and bake for 15–20 minutes. Remove the paper and beads or rice, reduce the heat to moderate 180°C (350°F/Gas 4) and bake for 20 minutes, or until golden.

To make the salsa verde, combine all the ingredients in a food processor and process until almost smooth.

Boil the potato until just tender. Drain. Heat the oil in a large frying pan and cook the garlic, capsicum (pepper) and onion over medium heat for 3 minutes, stirring frequently. Add the zucchini (courgettes), dill (dill weed), thyme and capers and cook for 3 minutes. Reduce the heat to low, add the potato and artichokes, and heat through. Season to taste.

To assemble, spread 3 tablespoons of the salsa over the pastry. Spoon the vegetable mixture into the case and drizzle with half the remaining salsa. Pile the spinach in the centre and drizzle with the remaining salsa.

Serves 6

Herbed Fish Tartlets

- 1¼ cups (155 g/5½ oz) plain (all-purpose) flour
- 90 g (3¼ oz) butter, chopped
- 1 tablespoon chopped fresh thyme
- 1 tablespoon chopped fresh dill (dill weed)
- 2 tablespoons chopped fresh parsley
- 90 g (3¼ oz) Cheddar (American) cheese, finely grated
- 3–4 tablespoons iced water

Filling
- 400 g (14 oz) skinless white fish fillets (eg. blue-eye, warehou, cod, jewfish)
- 2 spring (green) onions, finely chopped
- 2 tablespoons chopped fresh parsley
- 60 g (2 oz) Cheddar (American) cheese, finely grated
- 2 eggs
- ½ cup (125 ml/4¼ fl oz) cream

Lightly grease eight 10 cm (4 inch) round fluted flan tins. Sift the flour into a large bowl. Rub the butter into the flour with your fingertips until it resembles fine breadcrumbs. Stir in the herbs and cheese. Make a well in the centre. Add almost all the water and mix with a flat-bladed knife, using a cutting action, until the mixture comes together in beads. Gather together and form into a ball, adding more water if necessary. Wrap in plastic and refrigerate for 15 minutes.

Preheat the oven to hot 210°C (415°F/Gas 6–7). Divide the pastry into 8 portions. Roll each on a lightly floured surface, large enough to fit the tins. Ease into the tins, pressing into the sides. Trim the edges with a sharp knife or rolling pin. Place the tins on a baking tray (sheet). Cover each piece of pastry with a sheet of crumpled baking paper. Spread a single layer of dried beans or uncooked rice evenly over the base. Bake for 10 minutes. Remove the paper and beans or rice and bake for 10 minutes, or until lightly browned. Cool.

Place the fish in a frying pan and add water to cover. Bring to the boil, reduce the heat and simmer gently for 3 minutes. Remove from the pan with a slotted spoon and drain on crumpled paper towel. Allow to cool, then flake with a fork. Divide among the cases and sprinkle with the combined spring (green) onion, parsley and cheese. In a jug, whisk together the eggs and cream, then pour over the fish. Bake for 25 minutes, or until set and golden brown. Serve immediately.

Note: Smoked fish can be used. You can make the recipe in a 23 cm (9 inch) flan tin. Cooking time may be longer but check after 25 minutes.

Makes 8

Mediterranean Ricotta Tarts

- ⅓ cup (35 g/1¼ oz) dry breadcrumbs
- 2 tablespoons virgin olive oil
- 1 clove garlic, crushed
- ½ red capsicum (pepper), quartered and cut into 5 mm (¼ inch) wide strips
- 1 zucchini (courgette), cut into 5 cm × 5 mm (2 inch × ¼ inch) strips
- 2 slices prosciutto, chopped
- 375 g (13¼ oz) firm ricotta (see Note)
- ⅓ cup (40 g/1½ oz) grated Cheddar (American) cheese
- ⅓ cup (35 g/1¼ oz) grated Parmesan
- 2 tablespoons shredded fresh basil
- 4 black (ripe) olives, pitted and sliced

Preheat the oven to moderate 180°C (350°F/Gas 4). Lightly grease four 8 cm × 2.5 cm deep (3 inch × 1 inch deep) fluted tart tins. Lightly sprinkle 1 teaspoon of the breadcrumbs on the base and side of each tin.

To make the topping, heat half the oil in a frying pan, add the garlic, capsicum (pepper) and zucchini (courgette) and cook, stirring, over medium heat for 5 minutes, or until the vegetables are soft. Remove from the heat and add the prosciutto. Season to taste.

Combine the ricotta with the cheeses and remaining breadcrumbs. Season. Press the mixture into the tins and smooth the surface. Sprinkle with basil.

Scatter the topping over the ricotta mixture, top with the olives, then drizzle with the remaining oil.

Bake for 20 minutes, or until the tarts are slightly puffed and golden around the edges. Cool completely (the tarts will deflate on cooling) and carefully remove from the tins. Do not refrigerate.

Note: Use firm ricotta or very well-drained ricotta, or the tarts will be difficult to remove from the tins.

Serves 4

Ratatouille Tarte Tatin

- 1½ cups (185 g/6½ oz) plain (all-purpose) flour
- 90 g (3¼ oz) butter, chopped
- 1 egg
- 1 tablespoon oil
- 30 g (1 oz) butter, extra
- 2 zucchini (courgettes), halved lengthways and sliced
- 250 g (8¾ oz) eggplant (aubergine), diced
- 1 red capsicum (pepper), diced
- 1 green capsicum (pepper), diced
- 1 large red onion, diced
- 250 g (8¾ oz) cherry tomatoes, halved
- 2 tablespoons balsamic vinegar
- ½ cup (60 g/2 oz) grated Cheddar (American) cheese
- 300 g (10½ oz) sour cream
- 3 tablespoons good-quality pesto

Sift the flour into a bowl and add the butter. Rub the butter into the flour with your fingertips until it resembles fine breadcrumbs. Make a well in the centre and add the egg (and 2 tablespoons water if the mixture is too dry). Mix with a flat-bladed knife, using a cutting action, until the mixture comes together in beads. Gather the dough together and lift onto a floured work surface. Press into a ball, flatten slightly into a disc, then wrap in plastic wrap and refrigerate for 20 minutes.

Preheat the oven to moderately hot 200°C (400°F/Gas 6). Grease a 25 cm (12 inch) springform tin and line with baking paper. Heat the oil and extra butter in a large frying pan and cook the zucchini (courgettes), eggplant (aubergine), capsicums (peppers) and onion over high heat for 8 minutes, or until just soft. Add the tomatoes and vinegar and cook for 3–4 minutes.

Place the tin on a baking tray (sheet) and neatly lay the vegetables in the tin, then sprinkle with cheese. Roll the dough out between two sheets of baking paper to a 28 cm (11 inch) circle. Remove the paper and invert the pastry into the tin over the filling. Use a spoon handle to tuck the edge of the pastry down the side of the tin. Bake for 30–35 minutes (some liquid will leak out), then leave to stand for 1–2 minutes. Remove from the tin and place on a serving plate, pastry-side-down. Mix the sour cream and pesto together in a small bowl. Serve with the tarte tatin.

Serves 6

Roast Vegetable Tart

- 2 slender eggplants (aubergines), halved and cut into thick slices
- 350 g (12¼ oz) pumpkin, chopped
- 2 zucchini (courgettes), halved and cut into thick slices
- 1–2 tablespoons olive oil
- 1 large red capsicum (pepper), chopped
- 1 teaspoon olive oil, extra
- 1 red onion, cut into thin wedges
- 1 tablespoon Korma curry paste
- plain yoghurt, to serve

Pastry
- 1½ cups (185 g/6½ oz) plain (all-purpose) flour
- 125 g (4⅓ oz) butter, chopped
- ⅔ cup (100 g/3½ oz) roasted cashews, finely chopped
- 1 teaspoon cumin seeds
- 2–3 tablespoons chilled water

Preheat the oven to moderately hot 200°C (400°F/Gas 6). Put the eggplant (aubergine), pumpkin and zucchini (courgette) on a lined oven tray (sheet), then brush with oil and bake for 30 minutes. Turn, add the capsicum (pepper) and bake for 30 minutes. Cool.

Meanwhile, heat the extra oil in a frying pan and cook the onion for 2–3 minutes, or until soft. Add the curry paste and cook, stirring, for 1 minute, or until fragrant and well mixed. Cool. Reduce the oven to moderate 180°C (350°F/Gas 4).

To make the pastry, sift the flour into a large bowl and add the butter. Rub the butter into the flour with your fingertips until it resembles fine breadcrumbs. Stir in the cashews and cumin seeds. Make a well in the centre and add the water. Mix with a flat-bladed knife, using a cutting action, until the mixture comes together in beads. Gather the dough together and lift out onto a sheet of baking paper. Flatten to a disc, then roll out to a 35 cm (14 inch) circle.

Lift onto an oven tray (sheet) and spread the onion mixture over the pastry, leaving a wide border. Arrange the other vegetables over the onion, piling them slightly higher in the centre. Working your way around, fold the edge of the pastry in pleats over the vegetables. Bake for 45 minutes, or until the pastry is golden. Serve immediately with plain yoghurt.

Serves 4–6

125

Tomato and Onion Tart

- 1 cup (125 g/4⅓ oz) plain (all-purpose) flour
- ½ cup (75 g/2½ oz) wholemeal (whole wheat) flour
- 100 g (3½ oz) butter, chilled and cubed
- 1 tablespoon sesame seeds
- 1 egg, lightly beaten

Filling
- 500 g (1 lb 2 oz) tomatoes, finely chopped
- 2 tablespoons tomato paste (tomato puree)
- 1 teaspoon dried oregano
- ½ teaspoon sugar
- 1 tablespoon olive oil
- 3 red onions, sliced
- 1 teaspoon chopped fresh thyme
- 3 red capsicums (peppers)
- ⅓ cup (35 g/1¼ oz) grated Parmesan

Process the flours, butter and sesame seeds for about 15 seconds, or until the mixture resembles fine breadcrumbs. Add the egg and process in short bursts until the mixture just comes together. Add a little cold water if necessary. Turn out onto a lightly floured surface and gather into a ball. Wrap in plastic and refrigerate for at least 20 minutes. Preheat the oven to 200°C (400°F/Gas 6) and grease a shallow 19 × 28 cm (7½ × 11 inch) loose-based fluted tart tin.

Roll out the pastry on a sheet of baking paper until large enough to line the tin. Press well into the sides and trim away the excess. Prick the pastry all over with a fork and bake for 12 minutes, or until just brown and dry. Allow to cool.

Heat the tomatoes, tomato paste (tomato puree), oregano and sugar in a pan. Bring to the boil, then reduce the heat and simmer for 15–20 minutes, or until thick. Allow to cool. Season well.

Heat the oil in a pan and add the onion and thyme. Cook until the onion is soft and transparent.

Quarter the capsicums (peppers) and remove the seeds and membrane. Grill, skin-side-up, until the skins have blistered. Cool in a plastic bag. Remove the skins and cut into quarters.

Spread the onion evenly over the base of the pastry shell and top with the tomato sauce. Sprinkle with cheese then top with the capsicum (peppers). Bake for 30 minutes, or until heated through and the pastry is crisp. Serve hot.

Storage: The pastry can be made in advance and kept in the freezer for up to 3 months; or in the fridge for a day. Make sure it is well covered. Allow enough time to bring the pastry to room temperature before rolling it out.

Serves 6

Spicy Chicken Tarts

- 2 large onions, finely chopped
- 400 g (14 oz) eggplant (aubergine), cubed
- 2 cloves garlic, crushed
- 2 × 410 g (14½ oz) cans chopped tomatoes
- 1 tablespoon tomato paste (tomato puree)
- 3 teaspoons soft brown sugar
- 1 tablespoon red wine vinegar
- ¼ cup (15 g/½ oz) chopped fresh parsley
- 4 sheets ready-rolled shortcrust (pie) pastry
- 2 teaspoons ground cumin seeds
- 2 teaspoons ground coriander
- 1 teaspoon paprika
- 400 g (14 oz) chicken breast fillets
- oil, for cooking
- sour cream, to serve
- fresh coriander (cilantro) leaves, to serve

Fry the onion in a little oil until golden. Add the eggplant (aubergine) and garlic and cook for a few minutes. Stir in the tomato, tomato paste (tomato puree), sugar and vinegar. Bring to the boil, then reduce the heat, cover and simmer for 20 minutes. Uncover and simmer for 10 minutes, or until thick. Add the parsley and season. Preheat the oven to moderately hot 190°C (375°F/Gas 5).

Grease 8 small pie tins measuring 7.5 cm (3 inches) across the base, line with the pastry and decorate the edges. Prick the bases using a fork. Bake for 15 minutes, or until golden.

Mix the cumin, coriander and paprika together. Coat the chicken pieces in the spices. Heat some oil in a frying pan and cook the chicken until brown and cooked through. Cut diagonally. Fill the pie shells with the eggplant mixture and add the chicken, sour cream and coriander leaves (cilantro).

Makes 8

Caramelised Onion, Rocket and Blue Cheese Tarts

Pastry
- 2 cups (250 g/8¾ oz) plain (all-purpose) flour
- 125 g (4⅓ oz) butter, chilled and cut into cubes
- ¼ cup (25 g/¾ oz) finely grated Parmesan
- 1 egg, lightly beaten
- ¼ cup (60 ml/2 fl oz) chilled water

Filling
- 2 tablespoons olive oil
- 3 onions, thinly sliced
- 100 g (3½ oz) baby rocket (arugula) leaves
- 100 g (3½ oz) blue cheese, lightly crumbled
- 3 eggs, lightly beaten
- ¼ cup (60 ml/2 fl oz) cream
- ½ cup (50 g/1¾ oz) finely grated Parmesan
- pinch grated fresh nutmeg

To make the pastry, sift the flour into a large bowl and add the butter. Rub the butter into the flour with your fingertips until it resembles fine breadcrumbs. Stir in the Parmesan.

Make a well in the centre of the dry ingredients, add the egg and water and mix with a flat-bladed knife, using a cutting action, until the mixture comes together in beads.

Gently gather the dough together and lift out onto a lightly floured work surface. Press into a ball and flatten it slightly into a disc, wrap in plastic wrap and refrigerate for 30 minutes.

Preheat the oven to moderately hot 200°C (400°F/Gas 6). Divide the pastry into six. Roll the dough out between two sheets of baking paper to fit six round 8 cm × 3 cm deep (3 inch × 1¼ inch deep) fluted loose-bottomed tart tins, remove the top sheet of paper and invert the pastry into the tins. Use a small ball of pastry to help press the pastry into the tins, allowing any excess to hang over the sides. Roll the rolling pin over the tins to cut off any excess.

Line the pastry shells with a piece of crumpled baking paper and pour in some baking beads or uncooked rice. Bake for 10 minutes, then remove the paper and beads or rice and return the pastry to the oven for 10 minutes, or until the base is dry and golden. Cool slightly. Reduce the oven to moderate 180°C (350°F/Gas 4).

Heat the oil in a large frying pan, add the onion and cook over medium heat for 20 minutes, or until the onion is caramelised and golden. (Don't rush this step.)

Add the rocket (arugula) and stir until wilted. Remove from the pan and cool.

Divide the onion mixture among the tart bases, then sprinkle with the blue cheese. Whisk together the eggs, cream, Parmesan and nutmeg and pour over each of the tarts. Place on a baking tray (sheet) and bake for 25 minutes. Serve hot or cold with a green salad.

Serves 6

Chocolate Tarts

- 1¼ cups (155 g/5½ oz) plain (all-purpose) flour
- 75 g (2½ oz) butter, chopped
- ¼ cup (60 g/2 oz) caster (berry) sugar
- 2 egg yolks
- 250 g (8¾ oz) dark chocolate, finely chopped
- 1 cup (250 ml/8 fl oz) cream
- 1 tablespoon orange-flavoured liqueur
- 1 orange
- ½ cup (125 g/4⅓ oz) caster (berry) sugar, extra

Lightly grease two 12-hole tartlet tins. Sift the flour into a large bowl and add the butter. Rub in with your fingertips until the mixture resembles fine breadcrumbs. Stir in the sugar. Make a well and add the egg yolks and up to 2 tablespoons water. Mix with a flat-bladed knife using a cutting action, until the mixture comes together in beads. Gather together and lift out onto a lightly floured work surface. Press into a ball and flatten slightly into a disc. Wrap in plastic and refrigerate for 20 minutes.

Preheat the oven to moderate 180°C (350°F/Gas 4). Roll the dough between two sheets of baking paper and cut rounds with a 5 cm (2 inch) cutter. Press into the tins.

Bake for about 10 minutes, or until lightly browned. Remove from the tins and cool. Repeat to use all the pastry. Allow to cool.

Put the chocolate in a heatproof bowl. Bring the cream to the boil in a small pan and pour over the chocolate. Leave for 1 minute, then stir until the chocolate has melted. Stir in the liqueur. Allow to set, stirring occasionally until thick.

Meanwhile, thinly peel the orange, avoiding the bitter white pith, and cut into short thin strips. Combine the extra sugar, rind and ½ cup (125 ml/4¼ fl oz) water in a small pan, stir over heat until the sugar has dissolved, then simmer for about 5–10 minutes, or until thick and syrupy. Remove the rind with tongs and drain on baking paper; allow to cool.

Spoon the chocolate mixture into a piping bag fitted with a 1 cm (½ inch) plain piping nozzle. Pipe three small blobs of ganache into the pastry case, pulling up as you pipe so the ganache forms a point. Dust with cocoa, decorate with the orange rind and refrigerate until ready to serve.

Makes about 45

Chocolate Ricotta Tart

- 1½ cups (185 g/6½ oz) plain (all-purpose) flour
- 100 g (3½ oz) unsalted butter, chopped
- 2 tablespoons caster (berry) sugar

Filling
- 1.25 kg (2 lb 12 oz) ricotta
- ½ cup (125 g/4⅓ oz) caster (berry) sugar

- 2 tablespoons plain (all-purpose) flour
- 1 teaspoon instant coffee
- 125 g (4⅓ oz) chocolate, finely chopped
- 4 egg yolks
- 40 g (1½ oz) chocolate, extra
- ½ teaspoon vegetable oil

Sift the flour into a large bowl and add the butter. Rub the butter into the flour with your fingertips, until fine and crumbly. Stir in the sugar. Add 3 tablespoons cold water and cut with a knife to form a dough, adding a little more water if necessary. Turn out onto a lightly floured surface and gather together into a ball. Lightly grease a 25 cm (10 inch) diameter springform tin. Roll out the dough, then line the tin so that the pastry comes about two-thirds of the way up the side. Cover and refrigerate while making the filling.

To make the filling, mix together the ricotta, sugar, flour and a pinch of salt until smooth. Dissolve the coffee in 2 teaspoons hot water. Stir into the ricotta mixture, with the chocolate and egg yolks, until mixed. Spoon into the pastry shell and smooth. Chill for 30 minutes, or until firm. Preheat the oven to moderate 180°C (350°F/Gas 4).

Put the springform tin on a baking tray (sheet). Bake for 1 hour, or until firm. Turn off the oven and leave to cool with the door ajar – the tart may crack slightly but this will not be noticeable when it has been decorated. To decorate, melt the extra chocolate and stir in the oil. With a fork, flick thin drizzles of melted chocolate over the tart. Cool completely before serving.

Serves 8–10

Honey and Pine Nut Tart

- 1½ cups (235 g/8⅓ oz) pine nuts
- ½ cup (175 g/6¼ oz) honey
- 115 g (4 oz) unsalted butter, softened
- ½ cup (125 g/4⅓ oz) caster (berry) sugar
- 3 eggs, lightly beaten
- ¼ teaspoon vanilla essence
- 1 tablespoon almond liqueur
- 1 teaspoon finely grated lemon rind
- 1 tablespoon lemon juice
- icing (powdered) sugar, for dusting

- crème fraîche or mascarpone, to serve

Pastry
- 2 cups (250 g/8¾ oz) plain (all-purpose) flour
- 1½ tablespoons icing (powdered) sugar
- 115 g (4 oz) chilled unsalted butter, chopped
- 1 egg, lightly beaten

Preheat the oven to moderately hot 190°C (375°F/Gas 5) and place a baking tray (sheet) on the middle shelf. Lightly grease a 23 cm (9 inch), 3.5 cm (1⅜ inch) deep loose-based tart tin. To make the pastry, sift the flour and icing (powdered) sugar into a large bowl and add the butter. Rub the butter into the flour with your fingertips until it resembles fine breadcrumbs. Make a well in the centre and add the egg and 2 tablespoons cold water. Mix with a flat-bladed knife, using a cutting action, until the mixture comes together in beads.

Gather the dough together and lift out onto a lightly floured work surface. Press together into a ball, roll out to a circle 3 mm (⅛ inch) thick and invert into the tin. Use a small ball of pastry to press the pastry into the tin, allowing any excess to hang over the sides. Roll a rolling pin over the tin, cutting off any excess pastry. Prick the base all over with a fork and chill for 15 minutes. Roll out the pastry scraps and cut out 3 leaves for decoration. Cover and refrigerate for 15 minutes.

Line the pastry with baking paper and fill with baking beads or uncooked rice. Bake on the heated tray (sheet) for 10 minutes, then remove the tart tin, leaving the tray (sheet) in the oven. Reduce the oven to moderate 180°C (350°F/Gas 4).

To make the filling, spread the pine nuts on a baking tray (sheet) and roast in the oven for 3 minutes, or until golden. Heat the honey in a small saucepan until runny, then allow to cool.

Cream the butter and sugar in a bowl until smooth and pale. Gradually add the eggs, beating well after each addition. Mix in the honey, vanilla, liqueur, lemon rind and juice and a pinch of salt. Stir in the pine nuts, spoon into the pastry case and smooth the surface. Arrange the reserved pastry leaves in the centre.

Place the tin on the hot tray (sheet) and bake for 40 minutes, or until golden and set. Cover the top with foil after 25 minutes. Serve warm or at room temperature, dusted with icing (powdered) sugar. Serve with crème fraîche or mascarpone.

Serves 6

Banana and Blueberry Tart

- cooking oil spray
- 1 cup (125 g/4⅓ oz) plain (all-purpose) flour
- ½ cup (60 g/2 oz) self-raising flour
- 1 teaspoon cinnamon
- 1 teaspoon ground ginger
- 40 g (1½ oz) butter, chopped

- ½ cup (95 g/3⅓ oz) soft brown sugar
- ½ cup (125 ml/4¼ fl oz) buttermilk
- 200 g (7 oz) blueberries
- 2 bananas
- 2 teaspoons lemon juice
- 1 tablespoon demerara sugar

Preheat the oven to moderately hot 200°C (400°F/Gas 6). Spray a baking tray (sheet) or pizza tray (sheet) lightly with oil. Sift both the flours and the spices into a bowl. Add the butter and brown sugar, and rub in with your fingertips until the butter is combined well with the flour. Make a well in the centre and add enough buttermilk to mix to a soft dough.

Roll the dough out on a lightly floured surface to a 23 cm (9 inch) diameter round. Place on the tray (sheet) and roll the edge to form a lip to hold the fruit in.

Spread the blueberries over the dough, keeping them within the lip. Slice the bananas and toss the slices in the lemon juice. Arrange the banana evenly over the top of the blueberries, then sprinkle with the demerara sugar and bake for 25 minutes, or until the base is browned. Serve immediately.

Note: The dough for this tart can be made in a food processor if you wish. The fruit topping can be varied by using raspberries. Other soft or stoned fruit also work very well.

Serves 6

Little Lemon Tarts

- **2 cups (250 g/8¾ oz) plain (all-purpose) flour**
- **125 g (4⅓ oz) butter, chopped**
- **2 teaspoons caster (berry) sugar**
- **1 teaspoon grated lemon rind**
- **1 egg yolk**

Filling
- **125 g (4⅓ oz) cream cheese, softened**
- **½ cup (125 g/4⅓ oz) caster (berry) sugar**
- **2 egg yolks**
- **2 tablespoons lemon juice**
- **½ cup (160 g/5⅔ oz) sweetened condensed milk**

Preheat oven to moderate 180°C (350°F/Gas 4). Brush two 12-cup shallow patty (bun) tins with oil. Sift flour and a pinch of salt into a bowl; rub in butter. Add sugar, rind, egg yolk and 2–3 tablespoons iced water; mix with a knife. Gently knead on lightly floured surface until smooth. Cover in plastic wrap and chill for 10 minutes.

To make filling: Using electric beaters, beat combined cream cheese, sugar and egg yolks until smooth and thickened. Add lemon juice and condensed milk; beat until well combined.

Roll out the dough between sheets of baking paper to 3 mm (about ⅛ inch) thickness. Using a 7 cm (2¾ inch) fluted, round cutter, cut rounds from pastry. Gently press into patty (bun) tins. Lightly prick each round 3 times with a fork, bake for 10 minutes or until just starting to turn golden. Remove from oven and spoon 2 teaspoons of filling into each case. Return to oven for another 5 minutes or until filling has set. Cool slightly before removing from tins. Garnish with strips of candied lemon peel, if desired.

Makes 24

Date and Mascarpone Tart

Coconut Pastry
- ½ cup (90 g/3¼ oz) rice flour
- ½ cup (60 g/2 oz) plain (all-purpose) flour
- 100 g (3½ oz) chilled unsalted butter, chopped
- 2 tablespoons icing (powdered) sugar
- ¼ cup (25 g/¾ oz) desiccated (fine) coconut
- 100 g (3½ oz) marzipan, grated

Filling
- 8 fresh dates (about 200 g/7 oz), pitted
- 2 eggs
- 2 teaspoons custard powder
- 125 g (4⅓ oz) mascarpone
- 2 tablespoons caster (berry) sugar
- ⅓ cup (80 ml/2¾ fl oz) cream
- 2 tablespoons flaked almonds

Preheat the oven to moderate 180°C (350°F/Gas 4). Grease a shallow, 10 × 34 cm (4 × 13½ inch) fluted loose-bottomed flan tin. Sift the flours into a large bowl. Using just your fingertips, rub in the butter until the mixture resembles breadcrumbs, then press the mixture together gently. Stir in the icing (powdered) sugar, coconut and marzipan. Turn out onto a lightly floured surface and gather together into a ball. Flatten slightly, cover with plastic wrap and refrigerate for 15 minutes.

Roll out the pastry between two sheets of baking paper until large enough to line the tin. Ease the pastry into the tin and trim the edge. Refrigerate for 5–10 minutes. Line the pastry-lined tin with a crumpled sheet of baking paper and spread a layer of baking beads or rice evenly over the paper. Place the tin on a baking tray (sheet) and bake for 10 minutes. Remove the paper and beads or rice, bake for another 5 minutes, or until just golden, then allow to cool.

Cut the dates into quarters lengthways and arrange over the pastry. Whisk together the eggs, custard powder, mascarpone, caster (berry) sugar and cream until smooth. Pour the mixture over the dates, then sprinkle with the flaked almonds. Bake for 25–30 minutes, or until golden and just set, then allow to cool slightly. Serve warm. The tart can be decorated if you wish.

Serves 6–8

Passionfruit Tart

- ¾ cup (90 g/3¼ oz) plain (all-purpose) flour
- 2 tablespoons icing (powdered) sugar
- 2 tablespoons custard powder
- 30 g (1 oz) butter
- 3 tablespoons light evaporated milk

Filling
- ½ cup (125 g/4⅓ oz) ricotta
- 1 teaspoon vanilla essence
- ¼ cup (30 g/1 oz) icing (powdered) sugar
- 2 eggs, lightly beaten
- 4 tablespoons passionfruit pulp (about 8 passionfruit)
- ¾ cup (185 ml/6½ fl oz) light evaporated milk

Preheat the oven to 200°C (400°F/Gas 6). Lightly spray a 23 cm (9 inch) loose-based flan tin with oil. Sift the flour, icing (powdered) sugar and custard powder into a bowl and rub in the butter until crumbs form. Add enough evaporated milk to form a soft dough. Bring together on a floured surface until just smooth. Gather into a ball, wrap in plastic and chill for 15 minutes.

Roll the pastry out on a floured surface to fit the tin, then refrigerate for 15 minutes. Cover with baking paper and fill with rice or dried beans. Bake for 10 minutes, remove the rice or beans and paper and bake for another 5–8 minutes, or until golden. Allow to cool. Reduce the oven to warm 160°C (315°F/Gas 2–3).

Beat the ricotta with the vanilla essence and icing (powdered) sugar until smooth. Add the eggs, passionfruit pulp and milk, then beat well. Put the tin with the pastry case on a baking tray (sheet) and pour in the filling. Bake for 40 minutes, or until set. Cool in the tin. Dust with icing (powdered) sugar to serve.

Serves 8

Prune and Almond Tart

- 375 g (13¼ oz) pitted prunes (dried plums)
- ⅔ cup (170 ml/5¾ fl oz) brandy
- ⅓ cup (105 g/3⅔ oz) redcurrant jelly

- ¼ cup (60 g/2 oz) caster (berry) sugar
- 1 egg yolk
- 2–3 tablespoons chilled water
- 50 g (1¾ oz) marzipan, grated

Almond Pastry
- 1½ cups (185 g/6½ oz) plain (all-purpose) flour
- 125 g (4⅓ oz) chilled unsalted butter, chopped
- ⅓ cup (60 g/2 oz) ground almonds

Custard Cream
- ¼ cup (30 g/1 oz) custard powder
- 1⅔ cups (410 ml/13¾ fl oz) milk
- 1 tablespoon caster (berry) sugar
- ½ cup (125 g/4⅓ oz) sour cream
- 2 teaspoons vanilla essence

Put the prunes (dried plums) in a pan with the brandy, leave to soak for 1 hour, then simmer over very low heat for 10 minutes, or until the prunes (dried plums) are tender but not mushy. Remove the prunes (dried plums) with a slotted spoon and leave to cool. Add the redcurrant jelly to the pan and stir over low heat until dissolved. Cover and set aside.

To make the almond pastry, sift the flour into a large bowl. Rub in the butter with just your fingertips, until the mixture resembles breadcrumbs. Stir in the almonds and sugar using a flat-bladed knife. Add the egg yolk and water, until the dough just comes together. Turn out onto a lightly floured surface and gather together into a ball. Flatten slightly, cover with plastic wrap and refrigerate for 15 minutes. Preheat the oven to moderate 180°C (350°F/Gas 4) and heat a baking tray (sheet).

Roll out the chilled pastry between 2 sheets of baking paper until large enough to line the base and side of a lightly greased 23 cm (9 inch) loose-bottomed flan tin. Ease the pastry into the tin and trim the edge. Refrigerate for 15 minutes. Line the pastry with a sheet of crumpled baking paper and spread a layer of baking beads or rice evenly over the paper, then bake on the heated baking tray for 15 minutes.

Remove the paper and beads or rice and bake the pastry for another 5 minutes. Reduce the heat to warm 160°C (315°F/Gas 2–3). Sprinkle marzipan over the pastry base, then bake for another 5–10 minutes, or until golden. Leave in the tin to cool.

To make the custard cream, in a small bowl, mix the custard powder with a little milk until smooth. Transfer to a pan and add the remaining milk and sugar. Stir over medium heat for 5 minutes, or until the mixture boils and thickens. Stir in the sour cream and vanilla essence, remove from the heat and cover the surface with plastic wrap to prevent a skin forming. Allow to cool slightly.

Spread the custard cream, while it is still warm, evenly over the pastry case. Cut the prunes (dried plums) in half lengthways and arrange over the custard. Warm the redcurrant mixture and carefully spoon over the tart to cover it completely. Refrigerate for at least 2 hours to allow the custard to firm before serving.

Serves 6–8

Tarte Tatin

- 100 g (3½ oz) unsalted butter
- ¾ cup (185 g/6½ oz) sugar
- 6 large sweet apples, peeled, cored and quartered (see Note)
- 1 sheet puff pastry

Preheat the oven to 220°C (425°F/Gas 7). Lightly grease a 23 cm (9 inch) shallow cake tin. Melt the butter in a frying pan, add the sugar and cook, stirring, over medium heat for 4–5 minutes, or until the sugar starts to caramelise and turn brown. Continue to cook, stirring, until the caramel turns golden brown.

Add the apple to the pan and cook over low heat for 20–25 minutes, or until it starts to turn golden brown. Carefully turn the apple over and cook the other side until evenly coloured. If much liquid comes out of the apple, increase the heat until it has evaporated – the caramel should be sticky rather than runny. Remove from the heat. Using tongs, arrange the hot apple in circles in the tin and pour the sauce over the top.

Place the pastry over the apple, tucking the edge down firmly with the end of a spoon. Bake for 30–35 minutes, or until the pastry is cooked. Leave for 15 minutes before inverting onto a serving plate. Remove the paper before serving.

Note: The moisture content of the different apples varies quite a lot, which affects the cooking time. Golden delicious, pink lady or fuji are good to use because they don't break down during cooking.

Serves 6

Tarte au Citron

- 3 eggs
- 2 egg yolks
- ¾ cup (185 g/6½ oz) caster (berry) sugar
- ½ cup (125 ml/4¼ fl oz) cream
- ¾ cup (185 ml/6½ fl oz) lemon juice
- 1½ tablespoons finely grated lemon rind
- 3 small lemons, washed and scrubbed
- ⅔ cup (160 g/5⅔ oz) sugar

Pastry
- 1 cup (125 g/4⅓ oz) plain (all-purpose) flour
- 75 g (2½ oz) unsalted butter, softened
- 1 egg yolk
- 2 tablespoons icing (powdered) sugar, sifted

For the pastry, sift the flour and a pinch of salt into a large bowl. Make a well and add the butter, egg yolk and icing (powdered) sugar. Work together the butter, yolk and sugar with your fingertips, then slowly incorporate the flour. Bring together into a ball – you may need to add a few drops of cold water. Flatten the ball slightly, cover with plastic wrap and refrigerate for 20 minutes.

Preheat the oven to moderately hot 200°C (400°F/Gas 6). Lightly grease a shallow loose-based flan tin, about 2 cm (¾ inch) deep and 21 cm (8¼ inches) across the base.

Roll out the pastry between two sheets of baking paper until 3 mm (⅛ inch) thick, to fit the base and side of the tin. Trim the edge. Chill for 10 minutes. Line the pastry with baking paper, fill with baking beads or rice and bake for 10 minutes, or until cooked. Remove the paper and beads or rice and bake for 6–8 minutes, until the pastry looks dry all over. Cool the pastry and reduce the oven to slow 150°C (300°F/Gas 2).

Whisk the eggs, yolks and sugar together, add the cream and juice and mix. Strain into a jug and add the rind. Place the flan tin on a baking tray (sheet) in the centre of the oven and pour in the filling right to the top. Bake for 40 minutes, or until just set – it should wobble in the middle when the tin is tapped. Cool before removing from the tin.

Cut the lemons into very thin (about 2 mm/¹⁄₁₆ inch) slices. Blanch in simmering water for 5 minutes. Combine the sugar and 200 ml (6¾ fl oz) water in a small frying pan and stir over low heat until the sugar has dissolved.

Add the lemon slices and simmer over low heat for 40 minutes, or until the peel is very tender and the pith looks transparent. Lift out of the syrup using a slotted spoon and drain on baking paper. If serving immediately, cover the surface with the lemon. If not, keep the slices covered and decorate the tart when ready to serve. Serve warm or chilled.

Serves 6–8

Fruit Tart

Shortcrust (Pie) Pastry
- 1¼ cups (155 g/5½ oz) plain (all-purpose) flour
- 2 tablespoons caster (berry) sugar
- 90 g (3¼ oz) chilled unsalted butter, chopped
- 1 egg yolk
- 1 tablespoon chilled water

Filling
- 1 cup (250 ml/8½ fl oz) milk
- 3 egg yolks
- ¼ cup (60 g/2 oz) caster (berry) sugar
- 2 tablespoons plain (all-purpose) flour
- 1 teaspoon vanilla essence
- strawberries, kiwi fruit and blueberries
- apricot jam (jelly), to glaze

Sift the flour into a bowl and stir in the sugar. Add the butter and using just your fingertips, rub into the flour until the mixture resembles breadcrumbs. Make a well in the centre, add the egg yolk and water. Using a knife, mix to a dough. Turn out onto a lightly floured surface and gather together into a ball. Press together gently until smooth, and then roll out to fit a 34 × 10 cm (13½ × 4 inch) loose-bottomed, fluted flan tin. Line the tin with pastry and trim away any excess. Refrigerate for 20 minutes. Preheat the oven to moderately hot 190°C (375°F/Gas 5).

Line the pastry-lined tin with a sheet of crumpled baking paper and spread a layer of baking beads or rice evenly over the paper. Bake for 15 minutes, remove the paper and beads or rice and bake for another 20 minutes, until cooked on the base and golden brown around the edge. Set aside to cool completely.

To make the filling, put the milk into a small pan and bring to the boil. Set aside while quickly whisking the egg yolks and sugar together in a bowl, until light and creamy. Whisk in the flour. Pour the hot milk slowly onto the egg mixture, whisking constantly. Wash out the pan, return the milk mixture and bring to the boil over medium heat, stirring with a wire whisk. Boil for 2 minutes, stirring occasionally. Transfer to a bowl, stir in the vanilla essence, and leave to cool, stirring frequently to avoid a skin forming. When cooled to room temperature, cover the surface with plastic wrap and refrigerate until cold.

Cut the strawberries in half and peel and slice the kiwi fruit. Spoon the cold custard into the cold pastry shell, then arrange the fruit over the custard, pressing in slightly. Heat the jam (jelly) in the microwave or in a small pan until liquid, sieve to remove any lumps, then, using a pastry brush, glaze the fruit. Serve the tart on the same day, at room temperature. If it is to be left for a while on a hot day, refrigerate it.

Note: If you don't have a rectangular tin, this tart may be made in a 23 cm (9 inch) flan tin. You can use different fruits to top the tart, according to taste and season.

Serves 6

Egg Tarts

Outer Dough
- 1⅓ cups (165 g/5¾ oz) plain (all-purpose) flour
- 2 tablespoons icing (berry) sugar
- ⅓ cup (80 ml/2¾ oz) water
- 2 tablespoons oil

Inner Dough
- 1 cup (125 g/4⅓ oz) plain (all-purpose) flour
- 100 g (3½ oz) lard, chopped

Custard
- ⅓ cup (80 ml/2¾ oz) water
- ¼ cup (60 g/2 oz) caster (berry) sugar
- 2 eggs

To make Outer Dough: Sift the flour and icing (berry) sugar into a medium bowl. Make a well in the centre. Pour in the combined water and oil. Mix with a knife to form a rough dough. (If the flour is very dry, add a little extra water.) Turn out onto a lightly floured surface and gather together in a smooth ball. Cover and set aside for 15 minutes.

To make Inner Dough: Sift the flour into a medium bowl. Using your fingertips, rub the lard into the flour until the mixture resembles coarse breadcrumbs. Press the dough together into a ball, cover and set aside for 15 minutes.

On a lightly floured surface, roll the Outer Dough into a rectangle about 10 × 20 cm (4 × 8 inches). On a lightly floured surface, roll the Inner Dough into a smaller rectangle, one-third the size of the Outer Dough. Place the Inner Dough in the centre of the Outer Dough. Fold the Outer Dough over the Inner Dough so the short edges overlap and the Inner Dough is enclosed. Pinch the edges together to seal.

On a lightly floured surface, roll the dough away from you in one direction into a long rectangle, until it is about half as thick as it was previously. Turn the dough 90 degrees so that the long edges are now horizontal to you. Fold the pastry into 3 layers by taking the left-hand edge over first, and then folding the right-hand edge on top. Wrap the dough in plastic wrap and refrigerate for 30 minutes.

Preheat the oven to hot 210°C (415°F/Gas 6–7). Brush 2 shallow 12-cup patty (bun) tins with melted butter or oil.

To make Custard: Place the water and sugar in a pan and stir without boiling until the sugar dissolves. Bring to the boil and simmer without stirring for 1 minute. Cool the mixture for 5 minutes. Place the eggs in a bowl and beat lightly with a fork. Whisk the sugar syrup into the eggs until just combined. Strain into a jug.

Place the pastry on a lightly floured surface. With one open end towards you, roll the pastry out to a rectangle about 3 mm (⅛ inch) thick. Cut out rounds of pastry using a 7 cm (2¾ inch) fluted cutter. Carefully place the pastry rounds into the prepared patty (bun) tins. Fill each pastry case two-thirds full with the egg custard mixture. Bake for 15 minutes, or until just set. Take care not to overcook the custard.

Leave the egg tarts for 3 minutes before removing them from the tin. Slip a flat-bladed knife down the side of each tart to help lift it out. Cool the tarts on a wire rack, and serve warm or cold.

Makes 18

Sweet
Pies

Real Lemon Pie

Lemon Filling
- 4 thin-skinned lemons
- 2 cups (500 g/1 lb 2 oz) caster (berry) sugar
- 4 eggs

Shortcrust (Pie) Pastry
- 1¾ cups (220 g/7¾ oz) plain (all-purpose) flour
- 150 g (5¼ oz) chilled unsalted butter, chopped
- 2 tablespoons caster (berry) sugar
- milk, for glazing

Wash the lemons. Slice 2 unpeeled lemons very thinly and remove the seeds. Peel the other lemons, removing all the pith, and slice the flesh very thinly. Remove the seeds. Put all the lemons in a bowl with the sugar and stir until all the slices are coated. Cover and leave overnight.

Preheat the oven to moderate 180°C (350°F/Gas 4). Sift the flour and a pinch of salt into a bowl. Use your fingertips to rub in the butter until crumbly. Stir in the sugar. Gradually add 1–2 tablespoons water, mixing with a knife. Gather the dough together, divide in half and roll each portion into a 25 cm (10 inch) circle. Lightly grease a 23 cm (9 inch) pie dish and line with pastry. Cover and chill the other circle.

Beat the eggs and add to the lemon slices, mixing gently but thoroughly. Spoon into the pastry shell and cover with the pastry circle, crimping the edges to seal. Decorate the top with pastry scraps, brush with milk and bake for 50–55 minutes, or until golden brown.

Note: To use this pastry for a delicious apple pie, peel, core and slice 5 apples into thin slices, toss the apple slices in 3 tablespoons caster (berry) sugar and a large pinch of cinnamon and fill the pie. Cover with the pastry lid and press the edges together to seal. Trim the edges and make two or three slashes in the top of the the pie. Dust with 1 tablespoon caster (berry) sugar and bake in a preheated moderate 180°C (350°F/Gas 4) oven for 50 minutes.

Serves 8–10

Apple Pie

Filling
- 6 large Granny Smith apples
- 2 tablespoons caster (berry) sugar
- 1 teaspoon finely grated lemon rind
- pinch ground cloves

Pastry
- 2 cups (250 g/8¾ oz) plain (all-purpose) flour
- 3 tablespoons self-raising flour
- 150 g (5¼ oz) cold butter, chopped
- 2 tablespoons caster (berry) sugar
- 4–5 tablespoons iced water
- 2 tablespoons apricot jam (jelly)
- 1 egg, lightly beaten
- 1 tablespoon sugar

Peel, core and cut the apples into wedges. Place in a heavy-based pan with the sugar, lemon rind, cloves and 2 tablespoons water. Cover and cook gently for 8 minutes, or until the apple is just tender, shaking the pan occasionally. Drain and allow to cool completely.

Sift the flours into a bowl and add the butter. Rub the butter into the flour using your fingertips until it resembles fine breadcrumbs. Add the sugar, mix well, and then make a well in the centre. Add the water and mix with a flat-bladed knife, using a cutting action, until the mixture comes together in beads. Gather the pastry together on a floured surface. Divide into two, making one half a little bigger. Cover with plastic wrap and refrigerate for 20 minutes.

Preheat the oven to moderately hot 200°C (400°F/Gas 6). Roll out the larger piece of pastry between two sheets of baking paper to line the base and side of a 23 cm (9 inch) pie plate. Peel off the top piece of paper and invert the pastry into the dish. Peel off the other baking sheet and trim off the excess pastry. Brush the jam (jelly) over the base and spoon the apple filling into the shell. Roll out the remaining piece of pastry between the baking paper until large enough to cover the pie. Brush a little water around the rim, then place the top on, inverting the pastry off the baking paper. Trim off the excess pastry, pinch the edges together and cut a couple of steam slits in the top.

Bring together the excess pastry bits, gently re-roll and cut into leaves to decorate the top. Brush the top lightly with egg then sprinkle on the sugar. Bake for 20 minutes, then reduce the temperature to moderate 180°C (350°F/Gas 4) and bake for a further 15–20 minutes, or until golden.

Serves 6

Blueberry Pie

- 1½ cups (185 g/6½ oz) plain (all-purpose) flour
- 125 g (4⅓ oz) butter, chopped
- ½ cup (60 g/2 oz) icing (powdered) sugar
- ¼ cup (60 ml/2 fl oz) lemon juice

- 500 g (1 lb 2 oz) fresh blueberries
- 3 tablespoons icing (powdered) sugar, extra
- 1 teaspoon finely grated lemon rind
- ½ teaspoon ground cinnamon
- 1 egg white, lightly beaten

Preheat the oven to moderate 180°C (350°F/Gas 4). Place the flour, butter and icing (powdered) sugar in a food processor. Process for 15 seconds or until fine and crumbly. Add almost all the juice and process briefly until the mixture comes together, adding more juice if necessary.

Turn the dough out onto a sheet of baking paper and press together until smooth. Roll out to a circle about 30 cm (12 inches) in diameter and cover with plastic wrap. Refrigerate for 10 minutes. Place blueberries in a bowl and sprinkle sugar, rind and cinnamon over the top.

Place the dough (still on baking paper) onto an oven tray (sheet). Brush the centre lightly with egg white. Pile blueberry mixture onto dough in a circle 20 cm (8 inches) in diameter; fold edges of the pastry over the filling. Bake for 30–35 minutes or until golden. Dust the top with icing (powdered) sugar and serve.

Serves 4

Shaker Lemon Pie

* 2 lemons
* ½ cup (60 g/2 oz) plain (all-purpose) flour
* 2 cups (500 g/1 lb 2 oz) caster (berry) sugar
* 40 g (1½ oz) unsalted butter, melted
* 4 eggs, lightly beaten
* 1 egg, extra, lightly beaten, to glaze

Pastry
* 3 cups (375 g/13¼ oz) plain (all-purpose) flour
* 185 g (6½ oz) unsalted butter, chilled and cubed
* 2 tablespoons caster (berry) sugar
* 4–5 tablespoons iced water

Finely grate 1 lemon to give 2 teaspoons of rind. Place this in a large bowl. Cut the pith off both lemons and discard. Thinly slice the lemon flesh, discarding the seeds.

Sift the flour into the bowl with the rind, then stir in the sugar and a pinch of salt. Add the butter and egg and stir until smooth. Gently fold in the lemon slices.

Preheat the oven to 200°C (400°F/Gas 6) and heat a baking tray (sheet). Grease a 20 cm (8 inch) pie dish.

To make the pastry, sift the flour and ¼ teaspoon salt into a large bowl and rub in the butter with your fingertips until the mixture resembles fine breadcrumbs. Mix in the sugar. Make a well, add almost all the water and mix with a flat-bladed knife, using a cutting action, until the mixture comes together in beads, adding more water if necessary. Gather together on a lightly floured surface and press into a disc. Wrap in plastic and refrigerate for 20 minutes.

Roll out two-thirds of the pastry until large enough to fit the dish. Spoon the filling into the pastry shell. Roll out the remaining pastry until large enough to cover the pie. Using a sharp knife, cut out three small triangles in a row across the centre of the lid. Brush the rim of the pastry base with beaten egg, then press the lid in place. Trim off any excess. Scallop the edges with your fingers, then go around the open scallops and mark with the tines of a narrow fork. Brush the top with egg glaze.

Bake on the hot tray (sheet) for 20 minutes. Reduce the temperature to 180°C (350°F/Gas 4), cover the pie with foil and bake for 30 minutes, or until the filling is set and the pastry golden.

Serves 6–8

Tourte de Blettes

- 60 g (2 oz) sultanas (golden raisins)
- 2 tablespoons brandy
- 400 g (14 oz) plain (all-purpose) flour
- 100 g (3½ oz) icing (powdered) sugar
- 250 g (8¾ oz) unsalted butter, softened and chopped
- 3 eggs
- 800 g (1 lb 12 oz) silverbeet (Swiss chard), stalks removed
- 100 g (3½ oz) pine nuts, toasted
- 3 green cooking apples
- 1 teaspoon grated lemon rind
- 115 g (4 oz) mild goat's cheese
- 1 egg yolk, extra, for glazing
- icing (powdered) sugar, extra, for dusting

Soak the sultanas (golden raisins) in the brandy. Sift the flour and 1 tablespoon icing (powdered) sugar into a large bowl and rub in the butter with your fingertips until the mixture resembles fine breadcrumbs. Make a well, add 1 egg and mix with a flat-bladed knife, using a cutting action, until the mixture comes together in beads. Add 1 tablespoon water if the mixture is a little dry. Gather together and lift onto a lightly floured work surface. Press into a ball and flatten to a disc. Wrap in plastic wrap and refrigerate for 30 minutes.

Preheat the oven to moderate 180°C (350°F/Gas 4). Heat a baking tray (sheet) in the oven.

Wash the silverbeet (swiss chard) and pat dry. Place in a food processor with 2 eggs and the remaining icing (powdered) sugar. Process to chop the silverbeet (swiss chard) and combine, but don't overprocess. Transfer to a bowl. Drain the sultanas (golden raisins) and add to the bowl with the pine nuts. Season with salt and pepper.

Bring the pastry to room temperature, then break into two portions. Roll one half and use to line a 26 cm (10½ inch) loose-based tart tin.

Peel the apples, slice thinly and toss with the lemon rind. Place the silverbeet (swiss chard) on the pastry and top with the crumbled goat's cheese. Spiral the apples on top, making one or two layers.

Roll out the remaining pastry and cover the pie. Trim off the excess pastry and seal the edges with a little water. Crimp the edges.

Brush the pie with the egg yolk and bake for 45–50 minutes, until golden. Cool slightly. Dust with icing (powdered) sugar. Serve warm.

Serves 6–8

Pecan Pie

- 1½ cups (185 g/6½ oz) plain (all-purpose) flour
- 100 g (3½ oz) cold butter, chopped
- 2 tablespoons iced water

Filling
- 2 cups (200 g/7 oz) whole pecans
- 3 eggs
- 60 g (2 oz) butter, melted
- ⅔ cup (155 g/5½ oz) soft brown sugar
- ⅔ cup (170 ml/5¾ fl oz) glucose (corn) syrup
- 1 teaspoon vanilla essence

Sift the flour into a bowl and rub in the butter with your fingertips until the mixture resembles fine breadcrumbs. Add the water and mix it in with a flat-bladed knife, using a cutting action, until the mixture comes together in beads. Gather the dough together, cover with plastic wrap and refrigerate for 20 minutes.

Transfer the dough to a sheet of baking paper and roll it out to a 3 mm (⅛ inch) thickness. It should be large enough to line a 23 cm (9 inch) pie dish, with some pastry left over to decorate the edge. Invert the pastry into the dish and remove the baking paper. Line the dish with the pastry, and remove the excess. Gather the dough scraps together and roll them out to a 3 mm (⅛ inch) thickness. Using small cutters, cut shapes from the pastry (if you are making leaves, score veins into the leaves with a small sharp knife). Brush the pastry rim with water, and attach the pastry shapes. Chill for 20 minutes. Preheat the oven to moderate 180°C (350°F/Gas 4).

Cover the decorative edge of the pastry with wide strips of foil to prevent burning. Line the pastry shell with a sheet of crumpled greaseproof paper and fill with baking beads or rice. Bake for 15 minutes, then remove the beads or rice and paper and bake for 15 minutes more, until the base is lightly golden and dry. Remove the foil and set aside to cool before filling.

Place the pecans on the pastry base. Whisk together the eggs, butter, sugar, syrup, vanilla and a good pinch of salt. Pour over the pecans. Place the pie dish on a baking tray (sheet), and bake for 45 minutes. Cool completely.

Note: Use any decorative shape you like for the edge. Simple leaf shapes can be cut free-hand from the pastry, if you do not have small cutters.

Serves 6

Apple Crumble

- 1 kg (2 lb 3 oz) green apples, peeled, cored and thinly sliced
- 2 tablespoons caster (berry) sugar
- ¾ cup (90 g/3¼ oz) plain (all-purpose) flour
- 1 teaspoon ground cinnamon
- 100 g (3½ oz) cold butter, chopped
- ½ cup (115 g/4 oz) firmly packed soft brown sugar
- ½ cup (50 g/1¾ oz) rolled oats

Preheat the oven to moderately hot 190°C (375°F/Gas 5). Brush a 1.25 litre (1.3 US qt/1.1 UK qt) shallow heatproof dish with melted butter. Put the apple in a large bowl and add the caster (berry) sugar and 3 tablespoons water. Mix to combine.

Sift the flour and cinnamon into a bowl. With your fingertips, rub in the butter until the mixture resembles coarse breadcrumbs. Add the brown sugar and rolled oats, and mix together well.

Spoon the apple into the prepared dish and sprinkle on the topping. Bake for 40 minutes, or until the apple is tender and the crumble topping is golden. Serve hot with custard or cream and a sprinkling of cinnamon.

Serves 6

Pumpkin Pie

- 1¼ cups (155 g/5½ oz) plain (all-purpose) flour
- 100 g (3½ oz) butter, chopped
- 2 teaspoons caster (berry) sugar
- 4 tablespoons chilled water
- 1 egg yolk, lightly beaten, mixed with 1 tablespoon milk, for glazing

Filling
- 2 eggs, lightly beaten
- ¾ cup (140 g/5 oz) soft brown sugar
- 500 g (1 lb 2 oz) pumpkin, cooked, mashed and cooled
- ⅓ cup (80 ml/2¾ fl oz) cream
- 1 tablespoon sweet sherry
- 1 teaspoon ground cinnamon
- ½ teaspoon ground nutmeg
- ½ teaspoon ground ginger

Sift the flour into a large bowl and add chopped butter. Using your fingertips, rub the butter into the flour for 2 minutes or until the mixture is fine and crumbly. Stir in the caster (berry) sugar. Add almost all the liquid and mix to a firm dough, adding more liquid if necessary. Turn onto a lightly floured surface and press together for 1 minute or until smooth.

Roll out the pastry, on a sheet of baking paper, until it is large enough to cover the base and side of a 23 cm (9 inch) diameter pie dish. Line the dish with pastry, trim away excess and crimp the edges. Roll out the pastry trimmings to a thickness of 2 mm (¹⁄₁₆ inch). Using a sharp knife, cut out leaf shapes of different sizes. Score vein markings onto the leaves. Refrigerate the pastry-lined dish and the leaf shapes for about 20 minutes.

Cut a sheet of greaseproof paper to cover the pastry-lined dish. Spread a layer of dried beans or rice over the paper. Bake for 10 minutes, remove from oven and discard paper and beans or rice. Return the pastry to the oven for 10 minutes or until lightly golden. Meanwhile, place the leaves on an oven tray (sheet) lined with baking paper, brush with egg glaze and bake for 10–15 minutes, until golden; set aside to cool.

To make Filling: Preheat the oven to moderate 180°C (350°F/Gas 4). Whisk the eggs and sugar in a large bowl. Add the cooled pumpkin, cream, sweet sherry and spices and stir to combine thoroughly. Pour the mixture into the pastry shell, smooth the surface with the back of a spoon and bake for 40 minutes or until set.

If the pastry edge begins to brown too much during cooking, cover the edge with foil. Allow the pie to cool to room temperature and place the leaves on top of the filling. Serve with cream or ice cream, if desired.

Note: As an alternative to using the pastry trimmings to make the decoration, you can use a sheet of ready-rolled puff pastry. Cut out some leaf shapes, brush with egg white and bake on a tray (sheet), in a moderate 180°C (350°F/Gas 4) oven, until puffed and golden, about 10–15 minutes.

Serves 8

Lemon Meringue Pie

- 1½ cups (185 g/6½ oz) plain (all-purpose) flour
- 2 tablespoons icing (powdered) sugar
- 125 g (4⅓ oz) chilled unsalted butter, chopped
- 3 tablespoons iced water

Filling and Topping
- ¼ cup (30 g/1 oz) cornflour (cornstarch)
- ¼ cup (30 g/1 oz) plain (all-purpose) flour

- 1 cup (250 g/8¾ oz) caster (berry) sugar
- ¾ cup (185 ml/6½ fl oz) lemon juice
- 3 teaspoons grated lemon rind
- 40 g (1½ oz) unsalted butter, chopped
- 6 eggs, separated
- 1½ cups (375 g/13¼ oz) caster (berry) sugar, extra
- ½ teaspoon cornflour (cornstarch), extra

Sift the flour and icing (powdered) sugar into a large bowl. Rub the butter into the flour with your fingertips until the mixture resembles breadcrumbs. Add almost all the water and mix to a firm dough, adding more liquid if necessary. Turn onto a lightly floured surface and gather together into a ball. Roll between two sheets of baking paper until large enough to fit a 23 cm (9 inch) pie plate. Line the pie plate with the pastry, trim the edge and chill for 20 minutes. Preheat the oven to moderate 180°C (350°F/Gas 4).

Line the pastry with a sheet of crumpled baking paper and spread a layer of baking beads or rice evenly over the paper. Bake for 10 minutes, then remove the paper and beads or rice. Bake for another 10 minutes, or until the pastry is lightly golden. Leave to cool.

To make the filling, place the flours and sugar in a medium pan. Whisk in the lemon juice, rind and 1½ cups (375 ml/13 oz) water. Whisk continually over medium heat until the mixture boils and thickens. Reduce the heat and cook for another minute, then whisk in the butter and egg yolks, one at a time. Transfer to a bowl, cover the surface with plastic wrap and allow to cool completely.

To make the topping, preheat the oven to hot 220°C (425°F/Gas 7). Beat the egg whites in a small, dry bowl with electric beaters, until soft peaks form. Add the extra sugar gradually, beating constantly until the meringue is thick and glossy. Beat in the extra cornflour (cornstarch). Pour the cold filling into the cold pastry shell. Spread with meringue to cover, forming peaks. Bake for 5–10 minutes, or until lightly browned. Serve hot or cold.

Serves 6

Mango and Passionfruit Pies

- **750 g (1 lb 10 oz) sweet shortcrust (pie) pastry**
- **3 ripe mangoes, peeled and sliced or chopped, or 400 g (14 oz) can mango slices, drained**
- **¼ cup (60 g/2 oz) passionfruit pulp**
- **1 tablespoon custard powder**
- **⅓ cup (90 g/3¼ oz) caster (berry) sugar**
- **1 egg, lightly beaten**
- **icing (powdered) sugar, to dust**

Preheat the oven to 190°C (375°F/Gas 5). Grease six 8 cm (3 inch) fluted tart tins. Roll out two-thirds of the pastry between two sheets of baking paper until 3 mm (⅛ inch) thick. Cut out six 13 cm (5 inch) circles. Line the tins with the circles and trim the edges. Refrigerate while you make the filling.

Mix together the mango, passionfruit, custard powder and sugar.

Roll out the remaining pastry between two sheets of baking paper to a thickness of 3 mm (⅛ inch). Cut out six 11 cm (4⅓ inch) circles. Re-roll the trimmings and cut out small shapes for decorations.

Fill the pastry cases with the mango mixture and brush the edges with egg. Top with the pastry circles and press the edges to seal. Trim the edges and decorate with the shapes. Brush the tops with beaten egg and dust with icing (powdered) sugar. Bake for 20–25 minutes, or until the pastry is golden brown.

Makes 6

Cherry Pie

- **500 g (1 lb 2 oz) sweet shortcrust (pie) pastry**
- **2 × 425 g (15 oz) cans seedless black cherries, drained well**
- **⅓ cup (60 g/2 oz) soft brown sugar**
- **1½ teaspoons ground cinnamon**
- **1 teaspoon finely grated lemon rind**
- **1 teaspoon finely grated orange rind**
- **1–2 drops almond essence**
- **¼ cup (25 g/¾ oz) ground almonds**
- **1 egg, lightly beaten**

Preheat the oven to moderately hot 190°C (375°F/Gas 5). Roll out two-thirds of the dough between two sheets of baking paper to form a circle large enough to fit a 23 cm (9 inch) (top) 20 cm (8 inch) (base) 2 cm (¾ inch) (deep) pie plate. Remove the top sheet of baking paper and invert the pastry into the pie plate. Cut away the excess pastry with a small sharp knife. Roll out the remaining pastry large enough to cover the pie. Refrigerate, covered in plastic wrap, for 20 minutes.

Place the cherries, sugar, cinnamon, rinds and almond essence in a bowl and mix to coat the cherries.

Line the pastry base with ground almonds. Spoon in the filling, brush the pastry edges with beaten egg, and cover with the pastry lid. Use a fork to seal the edges of the pastry. Cut four slits in the top of the pie to allow steam to escape, then brush the pastry with beaten egg. Bake for 1 hour, or until the pastry is golden and the juices are bubbling through the slits in the pastry. Serve warm.

Serves 6

Rhubarb and Pear Crumble

- **600 g (1 lb 5 oz) rhubarb**
- **2 strips lemon rind**
- **1 tablespoon honey, or to taste**
- **2 firm, ripe pears**
- **½ cup (50 g/1¾ oz) rolled oats**

- **⅓ cup (60 g/2 oz) soft brown sugar**
- **¼ cup (35 g/1¼ oz) wholemeal (whole wheat) flour**
- **50 g (1¾ oz) butter**

Trim the rhubarb, wash and cut into 3 cm (1¼ inch) pieces. Place in a medium pan with the lemon rind and 1 tablespoon water. Cook, covered, over low heat for 10 minutes, or until tender. Cool a little. Stir in the honey and remove the lemon rind.

Preheat the oven to moderate 180°C (350°F/Gas 4). Peel, core and cut the pears into 2 cm (¾ inch) cubes and combine with the rhubarb. Pour into a 1.25 litre (1.3 US qt/1.1 UK qt) dish and smooth the surface.

To make the topping, combine the oats, flour and brown sugar in a bowl. Rub in the butter with your fingertips until the mixture is crumbly. Spread over the fruit. Bake for 15 minutes, or until cooked and golden.

Serves 6

Nutty Fig Pie

- **375 g (13¼ oz) sweet shortcrust (pie) pastry**
- **200 g (7 oz) hazelnuts**
- **100 g (3½ oz) pine nuts**
- **100 g (3½ oz) flaked almonds**
- **100 g (3½ oz) blanched almonds**
- **150 ml (5 fl oz) cream**
- **60 g (2 oz) unsalted butter**
- **¼ cup (90 g/3¼ oz) honey**
- **½ cup (90 g/3¼ oz) soft brown sugar**
- **150 g (5¼ oz) dessert figs, quartered**

Preheat the oven to 200°C (400°F/Gas 6) and grease an 18 cm (7 inch) pie tin. Roll the pastry out between two sheets of baking paper until large enough to line the tin, trimming away the excess. Prick the base several times with a fork. Score the edge with a fork. Refrigerate for 20 minutes, then bake for 15 minutes, or until dry and lightly golden. Allow to cool.

Meanwhile, bake the hazelnuts on a baking tray (sheet) for 8 minutes, or until the skins start to peel away. Tip into a tea towel and rub to remove the skins. Place the pine nuts, flaked almonds and blanched almonds on a baking tray (sheet) and bake for 5–6 minutes, or until lightly golden.

Place the cream, butter, honey and brown sugar in a saucepan and stir over medium heat until the sugar dissolves and the butter melts. Remove from the heat and stir in the nuts and figs. Spoon into the pastry case and bake for 30 minutes. Remove and cool until firm before slicing.

Serves 8

162

Cookies

Choc-Mint Swirls

- **65 g (2⅓ oz) unsalted butter**
- **¼ cup (60 g/2 oz) caster (berry) sugar**
- **½ cup (60 g/2 oz) plain (all-purpose) flour**
- **⅓ cup (40 g/1½ oz) self-raising flour**
- **2 tablespoons cocoa powder**
- **1–2 tablespoons milk**
- **22 choc chips (bits/morsels)**

Filling
- **100 g (3½ oz) unsalted butter, extra**
- **1⅓ cups (165 g/5¾ oz) icing (powdered) sugar**
- **few drops peppermint essence**

Preheat the oven to 180°C (350°F/Gas 4). Line two 32 × 28 cm (12½ × 11 inch) baking trays (sheets) with baking paper. Using electric beaters, beat the butter and sugar in a small mixing bowl until light and creamy. Add the sifted flours, cocoa and milk. Stir with a flat-bladed knife until the mixture forms a soft dough. Turn out onto a piece of baking paper and knead for 1 minute or until smooth.

Roll the dough out to 5 mm (¼ inch) thickness. Cut into rounds, using a 4 cm (1½ inch) plain biscuit (cookie) cutter. Place on the prepared tray (sheet) and bake for 15 minutes. Transfer to a wire rack to cool completely before decorating.

To make the filling, beat the butter with electric beaters until soft. Add the icing (powdered) sugar and beat until smooth, creamy and light. Add the peppermint essence and beat until combined. Using a piping bag fitted with a large fluted nozzle, carefully pipe a flower of peppermint cream onto each biscuit (cookie). Place a choc chip (bit/morsel) in the centre of each flower.

Storage: Store for up to 2 days in an airtight container.

Variation: Dust the biscuits with one teaspoon each of icing (powdered) sugar and cocoa powder, sifted together.

Makes 22

Sweet Twists

- 1 egg
- 1½ tablespoons sugar
- ½ cup (125 ml/4¼ fl oz) milk
- 2 cups (250 g/8¾ oz) plain (all-purpose) flour

- oil, for deep-frying
- 1¾ cups (215 g/7½ oz) icing (powdered) sugar

Beat the egg with the sugar in a bowl, then stir in the milk. Sift the flour with ½ teaspoon salt and mix in to form a stiff dough, adding more milk if necessary. Roll out on a lightly floured work surface. Cut into strips about 10 cm (4 inches) long and 3 cm (1¼ inches) wide. Make a slit along the length, like a buttonhole. Tuck one end through the slit and pull through to make a twist.

Fill a deep heavy-based pan one third full of oil and heat the oil to 180°C (350°F). The oil is ready when a cube of bread dropped into the oil turns golden brown in 15 seconds. Fry 3 or 4 khvorst (fried cookies) at a time, until golden brown on both sides. Drain on crumpled paper towel. Sift icing (powdered) sugar over the pastry after it is fried but before it gets cold.

In Advance: These will keep for up to 2 weeks in a dry airtight container.

Makes 45

Melting Moments with Jam and Cream

- **125 g (4⅓ oz) unsalted butter**
- **½ cup (125 g/4⅓ oz) caster (berry) sugar**
- **2 egg yolks**
- **1 teaspoon vanilla essence**
- **¼ cup (30 g/1 oz) custard powder**
- **¾ cup (90 g/3¼ oz) plain (all-purpose) flour**

- **¾ cup (90 g/3¼ oz) self-raising flour**
- **½ cup (160 g/5⅔ oz) strawberry jam (jelly)**
- **¾ cup (185 ml/6½ fl oz) thick cream, whipped**

Preheat oven to moderate 180°C (350°F/Gas 4). Line two biscuit trays (cookie sheets) with baking paper. Using electric beaters, beat the butter and sugar until light and creamy. Add the egg yolks one at a time, beating thoroughly after each addition. Add the vanilla; beat until combined.

Transfer the mixture to a large bowl. Using a flat-bladed knife, incorporate the custard powder and sifted flours. Stir until ingredients are just combined. Gather the mixture together with fingertips to form a soft dough.

Roll 1 level teaspoonful of mixture at a time into balls. Arrange about 5 cm (2 inches) apart on prepared trays (sheets). Flatten slightly with a fork. Bake 12 minutes or until golden. Stand biscuits (cookies) on trays for 5 minutes before putting a wire rack to cool. Spread half the biscuits (cookies) with ¼ teaspoon of jam (jelly) on each. Spoon or pipe cream over jam (jelly), sandwich with remaining biscuits (cookies).

Makes 20

Vanilla Almond Biscotti with Geranium Cream

- ½ cup (125 g/4⅓ oz) caster (berry) sugar
- 2 tablespoons caster (berry) sugar, extra
- 1 vanilla bean, split in half
- 3 rose-scented geranium leaves

Biscotti
- 125 g (4⅓ oz) blanched almonds
- 3 egg whites
- ¾ cup (90 g/3¼ oz) plain (all-purpose) flour

Geranium Cream
- 1 cup (250 ml/8½ fl oz) cream
- ½ cup (125 ml/4¼ fl oz) thick (double/heavy) cream
- selection of fruits in season: grapes, kiwi fruit, strawberries, blueberries, blackberries, raspberries or mulberries

Preheat oven to moderate 180°C (350°F/Gas 4). Place each measure of caster (berry) sugar into a separate screw-top jar. Add vanilla bean to the ½ cup of sugar and geranium leaves to the 2 tablespoons of sugar. Shake each jar for 10 seconds, then set aside for at least 2 hours to allow flavours to develop.

To make Biscotti: Brush a 26 × 8 × 4.5 cm (10½ × 3 × 1¾ inch) bar tin with oil or melted butter; line the base and sides with baking paper. Spread the blanched almonds on a baking tray (sheet) and bake in the oven for 4 minutes or until the nuts are lightly golden; cool.

Place the egg whites in a clean, dry bowl. Using electric beaters, beat until stiff peaks form. Gradually add the vanilla-scented sugar, beating constantly until the mixture is thick and glossy and the sugar has dissolved.

Transfer the mixture to a large bowl. Add the sifted flour and almonds. Using a metal spoon, gently fold the ingredients together. Spread into the prepared tin and smooth the surface. Bake for 25 minutes; remove from oven and allow to cool completely in the tin. Turn the loaf out and then wrap in aluminium foil. Refrigerate overnight.

Preheat the oven to warm 160°C (315°F/Gas 2–3). Brush two baking trays (sheets) with oil or melted butter. Using a sharp serrated knife, cut the cooked loaf into 5 mm (¼ inch) slices. Arrange the slices on the baking trays (sheets); bake for 30 minutes or until lightly golden and crisp.

To make Geranium Cream: Using electric beaters, beat the geranium-flavoured sugar with cream until firm peaks form. Using a metal spoon, fold into thick cream. Trim fruits and serve with biscotti and cream. Vanilla Almond Biscotti will keep for up to 2 weeks in an airtight container. Fruits and cream are best prepared on the day of serving. Vanilla and geranium sugars can be prepared up to 2 weeks in advance.

Note: This dessert can be served on individual plates but would make an attractive platter for a party or buffet. Vanilla Almond Biscotti are also delicious served plain, as an accompaniment to coffee. As a variation, other nuts can be used instead of almonds. Roasted hazelnuts or pistachios are particularly delicious.

Serves 6–8

Ginger Pecan Biscotti

- 1 cup (100 g/3½ oz) pecans
- 2 eggs
- ⅔ cup (155 g/5½ oz) soft brown sugar
- 1 cup (125 g/4⅓ oz) self-raising flour
- ¾ cup (90 g/3¼ oz) plain (all-purpose) flour
- 100 g (3½ oz) glacé (glazed) ginger, finely chopped

Preheat the oven to warm 160°C (315°F/Gas 2–3). Spread the pecans on a baking tray (sheet) and bake for 10–12 minutes, or until fragrant. Tip onto a chopping board to cool, then roughly chop. Cover the baking tray (sheet) with baking paper.

Put the eggs and sugar in a bowl and beat with electric beaters until pale and creamy. Sift the flours into the bowl and add the nuts and ginger. Mix to a soft dough, then place on the tray and shape into a 9 × 23 cm (3½ × 9 inch) loaf.

Bake for 45 minutes, or until lightly golden. Transfer to a wire rack to cool for about 20 minutes, then carefully cut into 1 cm (½ inch) slices with a large serrated bread knife. It will be crumbly on the edges, so work slowly and, if possible, try to hold the sides as you cut. Arrange the slices on baking trays (sheets) and bake again for about 10 minutes each side. Don't worry if they don't seem fully dry as they will become crisp on cooling. Cool completely before storing in an airtight container.

Makes about 20

Viennese Fingers

- 100 g (3½ oz) unsalted butter, softened
- ⅓ cup (40 g/1½ oz) icing (powdered) sugar
- 2 egg yolks
- 1½ teaspoons vanilla essence
- 1 cup (125 g/4⅓ oz) plain (all-purpose) flour
- 100 g (3½ oz) dark (semi-sweet) cooking chocolate, chopped
- 30 g (1 oz) unsalted butter, extra, for icing

Preheat the oven to 180°C (350°F/Gas 4). Line two baking trays (sheets) with baking paper.

Using electric beaters, cream the butter and icing (powdered) sugar in a small mixing bowl until light and fluffy. Gradually add the egg yolks and vanilla essence and beat thoroughly. Transfer the mixture to a large mixing bowl, then sift in the flour. Using a flat-bladed knife, mix until just combined and the mixture is smooth.

Spoon the mixture into a piping bag fitted with a fluted 1 cm (½ inch) piping nozzle and pipe the mixture into wavy 6 cm (2½ inch) lengths on the prepared trays (sheets).

Bake the cookies for 12 minutes, or until golden brown. Allow to cool slightly on the trays (sheets), then transfer to a wire rack to cool completely.

Place the chocolate and extra butter in a small heatproof bowl. Half-fill a saucepan with water and bring to the boil, then remove from the heat. Sit the bowl over the pan, making sure the base of the bowl does not sit in the water. Stir occasionally until the chocolate and butter have melted together and the mixture is smooth. Dip half of each biscuit (cookie) into the melted chocolate mixture and leave to set on greaseproof paper or foil.

Storage: Store in an airtight container for up to 2 days.

Note: To make piping easier, fold down the bag by 5 cm (2 inches) before adding the mixture, then unfold. The top will be clean and easy to twist, stopping any mixture from squirting out the top.

Makes 20

Honey Biscuits

- 1⅔ cups (210 g/7⅓ oz) plain (all-purpose) flour
- 1 teaspoon baking powder
- 1 tablespoon finely grated orange rind
- 1 teaspoon ground cinnamon
- ½ cup (60 g/2 oz) walnuts, finely chopped
- 60 g (2 oz) unsalted butter, softened
- ¼ cup (60 g/2 oz) caster (berry) sugar
- ¼ cup (60 ml/2 fl oz) olive oil
- ¼ cup (60 ml/2 fl oz) orange juice

Syrup
- 75 g (2½ oz) caster (berry) sugar
- 2 tablespoons runny honey
- 1 teaspoon ground cinnamon
- 2 tablespoons orange juice

Preheat the oven to moderate 180°C (350°F/Gas 4). Line a baking tray (sheet) with baking paper. Sift the flour and baking powder into a bowl. Mix in the rind, cinnamon and half the walnuts.

Cream the butter and sugar in another bowl with electric beaters until pale and fluffy. Mix the oil and orange juice in a jug and add a little at a time to the butter and sugar mixture, whisking constantly.

Mix the flour in two batches into the butter mixture, then bring the dough together with your hands. Shape tablespoons of dough into balls and place on the tray (sheet). Flatten slightly and bake for 20–25 minutes, until golden. Cool on the tray (sheet).

Make the syrup by mixing all the ingredients with ¼ cup (60 ml/2 fl oz) water and the remaining walnuts in a small saucepan. Bring to the boil over medium heat until the sugar dissolves, then reduce the heat to low and simmer for 10 minutes. The syrup will thicken.

Using a slotted spoon, dip a few biscuits (cookies) at a time in the hot syrup. Use another spoon to baste them, then transfer to a plate.

Makes 20

Brazil Nut and Coffee Biscotti

- **3 teaspoons instant coffee powder**
- **1 tablespoon dark rum, warmed**
- **2 eggs**
- **½ cup (125 g/4⅓ oz) caster (berry) sugar**
- **1¼ cups (155 g/5½ oz) plain (all-purpose) flour**
- **½ cup (60 g/2 oz) self-raising flour**
- **1 teaspoon ground cinnamon**
- **¾ cup (105 g/3⅔ oz) brazil nuts, roughly chopped**
- **1 tablespoon caster (berry) sugar, extra**

Preheat the oven to 180°C (350°F/Gas 4). Dissolve the coffee in the rum. Beat the eggs and sugar until thick and creamy, then beat in the coffee. Sift the flours and cinnamon into a bowl, then stir in the nuts. Mix in the egg mixture.

Divide the mixture into two rolls, each about 28 cm (11 inches) long. Line a baking tray (sheet) with baking paper, put the rolls on it and press lightly to flatten to about 6 cm (2½ inches) across. Brush lightly with water and sprinkle with the extra sugar. Bake for 25 minutes, or until firm and light brown. Cool until warm on the tray (sheet). Reduce the oven temperature to warm 160°C (315°F/Gas 2–3).

Cut into 1 cm (½ inch) thick diagonal slices. Bake in a single layer on the lined tray (sheet) for 20 minutes, or until dry, turning once. Cool on a rack. When cold, store in an airtight container for 2–3 weeks.

Makes 40 pieces

Coffee Kisses

- 3 cups (375 g/13¼ oz) self-raising flour
- 160 g (5⅔ oz) butter, chopped
- ½ cup (125 g/4⅓ oz) caster (berry) sugar
- 1 egg, lightly beaten
- 1 tablespoon instant coffee powder
- 1–2 tablespoons iced water

Coffee Butter Cream
- 80 g (2¾ oz) butter
- 1 cup (125 g/4⅓ oz) icing (powdered) sugar, sifted
- 2 teaspoons water
- 2 teaspoons instant coffee powder
- 100 g (3½ oz) white chocolate, melted

Preheat oven to moderate 180°C (350°F/Gas 4). Brush two biscuit trays (cookie sheets) with oil. Line with baking paper. Sift flour into a bowl. Add butter and rub into flour, using your fingertips, until mixture resembles fine breadcrumbs. Add combined sugar, egg and coffee powder, dissolved in the water, all at once. Mix with a knife until the ingredients come together to form a soft dough. Lightly knead until smooth.

Roll out between two sheets of baking paper to 5 mm (¼ inch) thickness. Cut into 5 cm (2 inch) rounds, using a fluted biscuit (cookie) cutter. Place on prepared trays (sheets). Bake for 10 minutes or until lightly golden. Transfer to a wire rack.

To make Coffee Butter Cream: Using electric beaters, beat butter and icing (powdered) sugar until light and creamy. Add combined water and coffee powder and beat until mixed. Place in a piping bag fitted with a fluted nozzle and pipe onto half of the biscuits (cookies). Top with another biscuit (cookie); sandwich together. Drizzle or pipe with melted chocolate. Top each with a chocolate-coated coffee bean, if desired.

Makes 30

Passionfruit Shortbread

- 250 g (8¾ oz) butter
- ⅓ cup (90 g/3¼ oz) caster (berry) sugar
- 2¼ cups (280 g/9¾ oz) plain (all-purpose) flour
- ¼ cup (45 g/1⅔ oz) rice flour
- 40 g (1½ oz) white choc melts, melted

Passionfruit Icing
- 1¼ cups (155 g/5½ oz) icing (powdered) sugar, sifted
- 2 tablespoons passionfruit pulp
- 20 g (⅔ oz) softened butter
- 1 tablespoon water

Preheat the oven to 160°C (315°F/Gas 2–3). Line two baking trays (sheets) with baking paper. Using electric beaters, beat the butter and sugar in a small mixing bowl until light and creamy. Fold in the sifted flours and mix until a soft dough forms. Turn out onto a lightly floured surface. Knead gently for 1 minute or until smooth.

Roll out the dough between two sheets of baking paper to 5 mm (¼ inch) thickness. Using a sharp knife, cut into 4 × 4 cm (1½ × 1½ inch) diamonds. Place on the prepared trays (sheets), allowing room for spreading. Re-roll the pastry and cut out diamonds in the same way. Bake for 15 minutes, or until the biscuits (cookies) are lightly brown. Stand for 5 minutes before transferring onto a wire rack to cool.

To make the passionfruit icing, combine the icing (powdered) sugar, passionfruit pulp, butter and water in a bowl to form a smooth paste. Stand the bowl in pan of simmering water, stirring until the icing is smooth and glossy. Remove the pan from heat but leave the bowl of icing to stand in the warm water while icing the biscuits (cookies). Using a flat-bladed knife, spread each diamond with ½ teaspoon of icing.

Leave the biscuits (cookies) to stand for 15 minutes to set, then drizzle or pipe a decorative pattern on top with the melted white chocolate.

Storage: These biscuits (cookies) can be stored in an airtight container for up to 2 days.

Note: Overheating the icing will make it dull and grainy. Try to work as quickly as possible and dip the knife into hot water occasionally to give the icing a smooth finish. If fresh passionfruit is out of season, substitute canned pulp.

Makes about 40

Amaretti

- 1 tablespoon plain (all-purpose) flour
- 1 tablespoon cornflour (cornstarch)
- 1 teaspoon ground cinnamon
- ⅔ cup (160 g/5⅔ oz) caster (berry) sugar
- 1 teaspoon grated lemon rind
- 1 cup (185 g/6½ oz) ground almonds
- 2 egg whites
- ¼ cup (30 g/1 oz) icing (powdered) sugar

Line two baking trays (sheets) with baking paper. Sift the plain (all-purpose) flour, cornflour (cornstarch), cinnamon and half the caster (berry) sugar into a large bowl; add the lemon rind and ground almonds.

Place the egg whites in a small, dry bowl. With electric beaters, beat the egg whites until soft peaks form. Add the remaining caster (berry) sugar gradually, beating constantly until the mixture is thick and glossy, stiff peaks form and all the sugar has dissolved. Using a metal spoon, fold the egg white into the dry ingredients. Stir until the ingredients are just combined and the mixture forms a soft dough.

With oiled or wetted hands, roll 2 level teaspoons of mixture at a time into a ball. Arrange on the prepared tray (sheet), allowing room for spreading. Set the tray (sheet) aside, uncovered, for 1 hour before baking.

Heat the oven to moderate 180°C (350°F/Gas 4). Sift the icing (powdered) sugar liberally over the biscuits (cookies). Bake for 15–20 minutes, or until crisp and lightly browned. Transfer to a wire rack to cool.

In Advance: The biscuits (cookies) can be stored in an airtight container for up to 2 days.

Note: You can use orange rind instead of lemon rind. These biscuits (cookies) have a chewy texture and are perfect served with coffee.

Makes 40

Stained-Glass Window Delights

- 150 g (5¼ oz) unsalted butter, cubed, softened
- ½ cup (60 g/2 oz) icing (powdered) sugar
- 1 egg
- 1 teaspoon vanilla essence
- ⅓ cup (40 g/1½ oz) custard powder
- 2 cups (250 g/8¾ oz) plain (all-purpose) flour
- ¼ cup (30 g/1 oz) self-raising flour
- 200 g (7 oz) assorted boiled lollies (candies/sweets)
- beaten egg, to glaze

Line two baking trays (sheets) with baking paper. Beat the butter and icing (powdered) sugar until light and creamy. Add the egg and vanilla and beat until fluffy, then beat in the custard powder. Fold in the combined sifted flours.

Turn onto a lightly floured surface and knead until smooth. Roll between 2 sheets of baking paper to 3 mm (⅛ inch) thick. Refrigerate for 15 minutes, or until firm.

Preheat the oven to moderately hot 200°C (400°F/Gas 6). Separate the lollies (candies/sweets) into their different colours and crush using a rolling pin. Cut out the dough with a 9.5 cm (3⅔ inch) fluted round cutter. Lay on the trays (sheets). Use small cutters to cut shapes from inside the circles.

Glaze the biscuits (cookies) with the beaten egg and bake for 5 minutes. Don't let the glaze drip into the cutout sections of the biscuits (cookies) or the stained glass will be cloudy. Fill each cut-out section with a different-coloured lolly (candy/sweet). Bake for 5–6 minutes, or until the lollies (candies/sweets) melt. Leave for 10 minutes, then cool on a wire rack.

Makes about 20

Lemon and Lime Treats

- 150 g (5¼ oz) butter, softened
- ¾ cup (185 g/6½ oz) caster (berry) sugar
- 1 egg, lightly beaten
- 1 tablespoon lime juice
- 2 teaspoons grated lime rind
- 2 teaspoons grated lemon rind
- 1 cup (125 g/4⅓ oz) plain (all-purpose) flour
- ½ cup (60 g/2 oz) self-raising flour
- 60 g (2 oz) marzipan, grated

Lime Icing
- 1 cup (125 g/4⅓ oz) icing (powdered) sugar, sifted
- 1 teaspoon finely grated lime rind
- 1 tablespoon lime juice
- 2 teaspoons water

Line two oven trays (sheets) with baking paper. Using electric beaters, beat the butter and sugar in a bowl until light and creamy. Add the egg, juice and rinds, beating until well combined.

Transfer the mixture to a large bowl. Using a flat-bladed knife, mix the flours and marzipan until a soft dough forms. Divide the mixture in two. Turn one portion out onto a lightly floured surface and press together until smooth.

Form the biscuit (cookie) dough into a log shape about 4 cm (1½ inches) in diameter. Wrap the log in plastic wrap and refrigerate for 1 hour. Repeat the process with the remaining dough. Preheat the oven to 180°C (350°F/Gas 4). Cut the dough into 1 cm (½ inch) slices. Place the slices on the prepared trays (sheets) and bake for 10–15 minutes or until the biscuits (cookies) are lightly golden. Leave on the trays (sheets) until cool. Dip the biscuits (cookies) in the icing. Decorate if you like.

To make the icing, place the icing (powdered) sugar, lime rind, lime juice and water in a bowl. Stir. Beat the mixture until smooth. If the mixture is too thick, add a little extra water.

Makes 30

Cinnamon Stars

- **2 egg whites**
- **2¼ cups (280 g/9¾ oz) icing (powdered) sugar**
- **1½ cups (145 g/5 oz) ground almonds**
- **1½ tablespoons ground cinnamon**

Beat the egg whites lightly with a wooden spoon in a large bowl. Gradually stir in the sifted icing (powdered) sugar to form a smooth paste. Remove ⅓ cup (100 g/ 3½ oz), cover and set aside. Add the almonds and cinnamon to the remaining icing and gently press together with your hands. Add 1 teaspoon water if the mixture is too dry. Press together well before adding any water as the warmth of your hands will soften the mixture.

Lightly dust a work surface with icing (powdered) sugar and roll out the mixture to about 3 mm (⅛ inch) thick. Spread with a thin layer of the reserved icing. Leave, uncovered, at room temperature for 30–35 minutes, or until the icing has set. Preheat the oven to slow 150°C (300°F/Gas 2).

Cut out shapes using a star cutter (about 5 cm/2 inches across from point to point). Dip the cutter in icing (powdered) sugar to help prevent sticking. Place the stars on a baking tray (sheet) covered with baking paper and cook for 10 minutes, or until just firm. Turn the tray (sheet) around after 5 minutes. Cool on the tray (sheet). Store in an airtight container up to 2 weeks.

Makes about 30

Afghans

- 150 g (5¼ oz) unsalted butter, softened
- ⅓ cup (60 g/2 oz) lightly packed soft brown sugar
- 1 egg, lightly beaten
- 1 teaspoon vanilla essence
- 1 cup (125 g/4⅓ oz) plain (all-purpose) flour
- 2 tablespoons cocoa powder
- ⅓ cup (30 g/1 oz) desiccated (fine) coconut
- 1½ cups (45 g/1⅔ oz) lightly crushed cornflakes
- ½ cup (90 g/3⅓ oz) dark (semi-sweet) choc chips (bits/morsels)

Preheat the oven to 180°C (350°F/Gas 4). Line two baking trays (sheets) with baking paper.

Using electic beaters, cream the butter and sugar in a large mixing bowl until light and fluffy. Add the egg and vanilla and beat well.

Add the sifted flour and cocoa powder to the bowl with the coconut and cornflakes. Stir with a metal spoon until the ingredients are just combined. Put level tablespoons of mixture on the prepared trays (sheets), allowing room for spreading. Bake for 20 minutes, or until lightly browned, then leave on the tray (sheet) to cool completely.

Place the choc chips (bits/morsels) in a small heatproof bowl. Bring a saucepan of water to the boil, then remove the pan from the heat. Sit the bowl over the pan, making sure the base of the bowl does not sit in the water. Stir until the chocolate has melted and the mixture is smooth. Spread the top of each biscuit (cookie) thickly with the melted chocolate and allow to set.

Makes 25

Crackle Cookies

- 125 g (4⅓ oz) unsalted butter, softened
- 2 cups (370 g/13 oz) soft brown sugar
- 1 teaspoon vanilla essence
- 2 eggs
- 60 g (2 oz) dark (semi-sweet) chocolate, melted
- ⅓ cup (80 ml/2¾ fl oz) milk
- 2¾ cups (340 g/12 oz) plain (all-purpose) flour
- 2 tablespoons cocoa powder
- 2 teaspoons baking powder
- ¼ teaspoon ground allspice
- ⅔ cup (85 g/3 oz) chopped pecans
- icing (powdered) sugar, to coat

Lightly grease two baking trays (sheets). Beat the butter, sugar and vanilla until light and creamy. Beat in the eggs, one at a time. Stir the chocolate and milk into the butter mixture.

Sift the flour, cocoa, baking powder, allspice and a pinch of salt into the butter mixture and mix well. Stir the pecans through. Refrigerate for at least 3 hours, or overnight.

Preheat the oven to moderate 180°C (350°F/Gas 4). Roll tablespoons of the mixture into balls and roll each in sifted icing (powdered) sugar to coat.

Place well apart on the trays (sheets) to allow for spreading. Bake for 20–25 minutes, or until lightly browned and just firm. Leave on the trays (sheets) for 3–4 minutes, then cool on a wire rack.

Makes about 60

Muffins
and
Cupcakes

Corn Muffins

- 1 cup (125 g/4⅓ oz) plain (all-purpose) flour
- ¼ teaspoon salt
- 1 tablespoon baking powder
- 1 cup (150 g/5¼ oz) fine polenta (cornmeal)
- 1 tablespoon caster (berry) sugar
- 1 egg
- ⅔ cup (170 ml/5¾ fl oz) milk
- ¼ teaspoon hot chilli (pepper) sauce (optional)
- ¼ cup (60 ml/2 fl oz) oil
- ½ red capsicum (pepper), finely chopped
- 440 g (15½ oz) canned corn kernels, drained
- 3 tablespoons finely chopped fresh parsley

Preheat the oven to hot 210°C (415°F/Gas 6–7). Brush a 12-hole muffin tin with oil or melted butter. Sift flour, salt and baking powder into a large bowl. Add the polenta (cornmeal) and sugar. Stir thoroughly until all the ingredients are well mixed. Make a well in the centre of the mixture.

Combine egg, milk, hot chilli (pepper) sauce and oil in a separate bowl. Add egg mixture, capsicum (pepper), corn and parsley all at once to dry ingredients. Stir quickly with a wooden spoon or rubber spatula until all ingredients are just moistened. (Do not over-mix – batter should be quite lumpy.)

Spoon into tin. Bake 20 minutes or until golden. Remove from oven, loosen with a knife but leave in tin 2 minutes; cool on a wire rack.

Makes 12

Spicy Vegetable Muffins

- 2 cups (250 g/8¾ oz) self-raising flour
- 3 teaspoons curry powder
- salt and freshly ground black pepper
- ½ cup (80 g/2¾ oz) grated carrot
- ½ cup (60 g/2 oz) grated orange sweet potato (yam)
- 1 cup (125 g/4⅓ oz) grated Cheddar (American) cheese
- 90 g (3¼ oz) butter, melted
- 1 egg, lightly beaten
- ¾ cup (185 ml/6½ fl oz) milk

Preheat oven to moderate 180°C (350°F/Gas 4). Brush a 12-hole muffin tin with oil or melted butter. Sift the flour, curry powder, salt and pepper into a bowl. Add the carrot, sweet potato (yam) and cheese and mix through with your fingertips until ingredients are evenly combined. Make a well in the centre.

Add the combined butter, egg and milk all at once. Using a wooden spoon, stir until the ingredients are just combined. (Do not over-mix – batter should be quite lumpy.)

Spoon batter into tin. Bake for 25 minutes or until puffed and golden, then loosen with a knife and leave in the tin for 2 minutes before turning out onto a wire rack to cool.

Makes 12

Carrot Muffins

- 2 carrots, peeled
- 2 medium zucchinis (courgettes)
- 2 cups (250 g/8¾ oz) self-raising flour
- pinch salt
- 1 teaspoon ground cinnamon
- ½ teaspoon ground nutmeg
- ½ cup (60 g/2 oz) chopped pecans
- 2 eggs
- 1 cup (250 ml/8½ fl oz) milk
- 90 g (3¼ oz) butter, melted

Preheat the oven to hot 210°C (415°F/Gas 6–7). Brush a 12-hole muffin tin with melted butter or oil. Grate the zucchinis (courgettes) and carrots. Sift the flour, salt, cinnamon and nutmeg into a large bowl. Add the carrot, zucchini (courgette) and chopped pecans. Stir thoroughly until all the ingredients are well combined.

Combine the eggs, milk and melted butter in a separate bowl and whisk well until combined.

Make a well in the centre of the flour mixture; add the egg mixture all at once. Mix quickly with a fork or rubber spatula until all the ingredients are just moistened. (Do not over-mix; the batter should be quite lumpy.)

Spoon the batter evenly into the prepared tin. Bake for 15–20 minutes or until golden. Loosen the muffins with a flat-bladed knife or spatula and leave in the tin for 2 minutes, before turning out onto a wire rack to cool.

Makes 12

Chocolate-Coffee Cups

- **200 g (7 oz) dark (semi-sweet) chocolate melts**
- **20 foil cups**
- **1 tablespoon cream**
- **50 g (1¾ oz) white chocolate, chopped**
- **1 tablespoon coffee liqueur**
- **10 coffee beans, halved**

Put the dark (semi-sweet) chocolate in a heatproof bowl. Bring a pan of water to the boil, remove from the heat and sit the bowl over the pan, making sure the base of the bowl does not sit in the water. Stir occasionally until the chocolate has melted. Cool slightly.

Working with one foil cup at a time, put 1 teaspoon of chocolate in each. Use a small new paintbrush to coat the inside with chocolate, making sure it is thick and there are no gaps. Turn the cups upside down on a wire rack and leave until firm. Set the remaining chocolate aside.

Combine the cream, white chocolate and coffee liqueur in a heatproof bowl. Stir over a pan of simmering water until smooth. Cool slightly, then spoon into the chocolate cups. Press half a coffee bean into each cup. Allow to set.

Remelt the reserved chocolate. Spoon it over the filling and tap to level, then leave to set.

Makes 20

Chocolate Cups with Caramel

- **150 g (5¼ oz) dark (semi-sweet) chocolate melts**
- **24 small foil confectionery cups**
- **80 g (2¾ oz) nougat, caramel and chocolate bar, chopped**
- **¼ cup (60 ml/2 fl oz) cream**
- **50 g (1¾ oz) white chocolate melts**

Place the dark (semi-sweet) chocolate in a small heatproof bowl. Bring a small pan of water to the boil and remove from the heat. Sit the bowl over the pan, making sure the bowl does not touch the water. Stir occasionally until the chocolate has melted and the mixture is smooth.

Using a small new paintbrush, brush a thin layer of chocolate inside the foil cases. Stand the cases upside-down on a wire rack to set. (Return the remaining chocolate to the pan of steaming water for later use.)

Combine the nougat, caramel and chocolate bar and cream in a small pan and stir over low heat until the chocolate has melted and the mixture is smooth. Transfer to a bowl and leave until just starting to set, then spoon into each cup leaving about 3 mm (about ⅛ inch) of space at the top.

Spoon the reserved melted chocolate into the caramel cases and allow the chocolate to set. Melt the white chocolate in the same way as the dark (semi-sweet) chocolate. Place in a small paper piping bag and drizzle patterns over the cups. Carefully peel away the foil when the chocolate has set.

Note: Ensure the chocolate is set before piping the white chocolate on the top.

In Advance: Caramel cups can be made up to 3 days ahead.

Makes 24

Blueberry Muffins

- **3 cups (375 g/13¼ oz) plain (all-purpose) flour**
- **1 tablespoon baking powder**
- **¾ cup (140 g/5 oz) soft brown sugar**
- **125 g (4⅓ oz) butter, melted**

- **2 eggs, lightly beaten**
- **1 cup (250 ml/8½ fl oz) milk**
- **1 cup (155 g/5½ oz) blueberries**
- **icing (powdered) sugar, for sprinkling**

Preheat oven to hot 210°C (415°F/Gas 6–7). Brush a 6-hole large muffin tin with melted butter or oil. Sift flour and baking powder into a large bowl. Stir in sugar; make a well in centre.

Add combined melted butter, eggs and milk all at once; stir until just blended. (Do not overmix; the batter should look quite lumpy.)

Fold in blueberries thoroughly but lightly. Spoon batter into tin. Bake 20 minutes or until golden brown. Loosen with a knife and transfer to a wire rack to cool. Sprinkle with icing (powdered) sugar.

Makes 6 large muffins

Banana Muffins

- **2 cups (250 g/8¾ oz) self-raising flour**
- **1 cup (75 g/2½ oz) oat bran**
- **¾ cup (185 g/6½ oz) caster (berry) sugar**

- **60 g (2 oz) butter, melted**
- **¾ cup (185 ml/6½ fl oz) milk**
- **2 eggs, lightly beaten**
- **1 cup (240 g/8½ oz) mashed, ripe banana (2 medium bananas)**

Preheat the oven to 210°C (415°F/Gas 6–7). Lightly grease a 12-hole muffin tin. Sift the flour into a large bowl and add the oat bran and the sugar. Make a well in the centre of the dry ingredients.

Combine the butter, milk, eggs and banana in a separate mixing bowl and add to the flour mixture all at once. Using a wooden spoon, stir until just mixed. (Do not overbeat; the batter should remain lumpy.)

Spoon the mixture into the prepared tin. Bake for 15 minutes, or until puffed and brown. Transfer the muffins to a wire rack to cool completely.

Topping Suggestion: For muffins with a difference, beat 100 g (3½ oz) cream cheese, 2 tablespoons icing (powdered) sugar and 2 teaspoons lemon juice with electric beaters until light and creamy. Spread over the muffins and top with dried banana slices.

Makes 12

Double Choc Muffins

- 2 cups (250 g/8¾ oz) plain (all-purpose) flour
- 2½ teaspoons baking powder
- ¼ cup (30 g/1 oz) cocoa powder
- 2 tablespoons caster (berry) sugar
- 1 cup (175 g/6¼ oz) dark (semi-sweet) choc chips (bits or morsels)

- 1 egg, lightly beaten
- ½ cup (125 g/4⅓ oz) sour cream
- ¾ cup (185 ml/6½ fl oz) milk
- 90 g (3¼ oz) butter, melted

Preheat the oven to moderate 180°C (350°F/Gas 4). Brush a 6-hole large muffin tin with melted butter or oil. Sift the flour, baking powder and cocoa into a large mixing bowl. Add the sugar and the choc bits and stir to mix through. Make a well in the centre of the mixture. Add the combined egg, sour cream, milk and melted butter all at once and stir with a fork until just combined. (Do not overbeat – batter should look quite lumpy.)

Spoon the mixture into the tin. Bake for 12–15 minutes or until firm. Loosen the muffins with a knife before turning out onto a wire rack to cool.

Note: For a delicious topping, combine 50 g (1¾ oz) chocolate, 1 tablespoon cream and 10 g (⅓ oz) butter in a pan; stir over low heat until smooth. Refrigerate until firm, then pipe or spoon over muffins. Sprinkle with icing (powdered) sugar.

Makes 6 large muffins

Mini Coffee and Walnut Sour Cream Cakes

- ¾ cup (75 g/2½ oz) walnuts
- ⅔ cup (155 g/5½ oz) firmly packed soft brown sugar
- 125 g (4⅓ oz) unsalted butter, softened

- 2 eggs, lightly beaten
- 1 cup (125 g/4⅓ oz) self-raising flour
- ⅓ cup (80 g/2¾ oz) sour cream
- 1 tablespoon coffee and chicory essence

Preheat the oven to 160°C (315°F/Gas 2–3). Lightly grease two 12-hole ¼-cup (60 ml/2 fl oz) mini muffin tins. Process the walnuts and ¼ cup (45 g/1⅓ oz) of the brown sugar in a food processor until the walnuts are roughly chopped into small pieces. Transfer to a mixing bowl.

Cream the butter and remaining sugar together in the food processor until pale and creamy. With the motor running, gradually add the egg and process until smooth. Add the flour and blend until well mixed. Add the sour cream and essence and process until thoroughly mixed.

Spoon ½ teaspoon of the walnut and sugar mixture into the base of each muffin hole, followed by a teaspoon of the cake mixture. Sprinkle a little more walnut mixture over the top, a little more cake mixture and top with the remaining walnut mixture. Bake for 20 minutes, or until risen and springy to the touch. Leave in the tins for 5 minutes. Remove the cakes using a flat-bladed knife to loosen the side and base, then transfer to a wire rack to cool completely.

Makes 24

Individual White Chocolate Chip Cakes

- 125 g (4⅓ oz) unsalted butter, softened
- ¾ cup (185 g/6½ oz) caster (berry) sugar
- 2 eggs, lightly beaten
- 1 teaspoon vanilla essence
- 2 cups (250 g/8¾ oz) self-raising flour, sifted
- ½ cup (125 ml/4¼ fl oz) buttermilk
- 1¼ cups (280 g/9¾ oz) white chocolate chips (bits/morsels)

Preheat the oven to 170°C (325°F/Gas 3). Lightly grease a 12-hole ½-cup (125 ml/4¼ fl oz) muffin tin.

Place the butter and sugar in a large mixing bowl. Using electric beaters, beat until pale and creamy. Gradually add the beaten eggs, beating well after each addition. Add the vanilla essence and beat until well combined. Fold in the flour alternately with the buttermilk, then fold in the chocolate chips (bits/morsels).

Fill each muffin hole three-quarters full with the mixture and bake for 20 minutes, or until a skewer comes out clean when inserted into the centre of each cake. Leave in the tin for 5 minutes before turning out onto a wire rack to cool completely. Use a flat-bladed knife to loosen around the edges of the cakes if they stick.

Makes 12

Butterfly Cupcakes

- 125 g (4⅓ oz) unsalted butter, softened
- ⅔ cup (160 g/5⅔ oz) caster (berry) sugar
- 1½ cups (185 g/6½ oz) self-raising flour
- ½ cup (125 ml/4¼ fl oz) milk
- 2 eggs
- ½ cup (125 ml/4¼ fl oz) thick (double/heavy) cream
- ¼ cup (80 g/2¾ oz) strawberry jam (jelly)
- icing (powdered) sugar, to dust

Preheat the oven to 180°C (350°F/Gas 4). Line a flat-bottomed 12-hole cupcake tray with cupcake papers. Place the butter, sugar, flour, milk and eggs in a large mixing bowl. Using electric beaters, beat on low speed then increase the speed and beat until the mixture is smooth and pale. Divide the mixture evenly among the papers and bake for 30 minutes, or until cooked and golden. Transfer to a wire rack to cool.

Cut shallow rounds from the centre of each cake using the point of a sharp knife, then cut in half. Spoon 2 teaspoons cream into each cavity, top with 1 teaspoon jam (jelly) and position two halves of the cake tops in the jam (jelly) to resemble butterfly wings. Dust with icing (powdered) sugar.

Note: If using foil cases instead of the standard cupcake papers as suggested, the size and number of butterfly cakes may vary.

Makes 12

Strawberry and Passionfruit Muffins

- 1¾ cups (215 g/7½ oz) self-raising flour
- pinch salt
- 1 teaspoon baking powder
- ½ teaspoon bicarbonate of soda (baking soda)
- ¼ cup (60 g/2 oz) caster (berry) sugar
- 1 cup (175 g/6¼ oz) chopped fresh strawberries
- ½ cup (125 g/4⅓ oz) canned (or fresh) passionfruit pulp
- 1 egg
- ¾ cup (185 ml/6½ fl oz) milk
- 60 g (2 oz) butter, melted

Preheat the oven to hot 210°C (415°F/Gas 6–7). Brush a 12-hole muffin tin with melted butter or oil.

Sift the flour, salt, baking powder, bicarbonate of soda (baking soda) and sugar into a bowl. Add the strawberries and stir to combine. Make a well in the centre.

Add the passionfruit pulp and the combined egg and milk. Pour the melted butter into the flour mixture all at once and lightly stir with a fork until just combined. (Do not overbeat; the batter should be quite lumpy.)

Spoon the mixture into the prepared tins and bake for 10–15 minutes, or until golden brown. Loosen the muffins with a flat-bladed knife or spatula and turn out onto a wire rack to cool. Top with softened, sweetened cream cheese or whipped cream and fresh strawberry halves and sprinkle with icing (powdered) sugar, if desired.

Makes 12

Orange Poppyseed Muffins

- 1¾ cups (215 g/7½ oz) self-raising flour
- 1 tablespoon caster (berry) sugar
- 1 teaspoon baking powder
- ¼ teaspoon bicarbonate of soda (baking soda)
- 1 tablespoon poppy seeds

- 90 g (3¼ oz) butter
- ½ cup (160 g/5⅔ oz) orange marmalade
- 1 egg, lightly beaten
- ¾ cup (185 ml/6½ fl oz) milk
- icing (powdered) sugar, to dust

Preheat the oven to 210°C (415°F/Gas 6–7). Lightly grease a 12-hole muffin tin. Sift the flour, sugar, baking powder and bicarbonate of soda (baking soda) into a mixing bowl. Add the poppy seeds and stir. Make a well in the centre.

Combine the butter and marmalade in a small saucepan and stir over low heat until marmalade becomes runny and butter has melted. Add the butter mixture and combined egg and milk to flour mixture; stir until just combined. (Do not overmix, the batter should be quite lumpy.)

Spoon the batter into the prepared tin and cook for 10–12 minutes or until golden. Loosen the muffins with a flat-bladed knife and transfer to a wire rack. Dust with the icing (powdered) sugar.

Topping Suggestion: Beat 60 g (2 oz) soft butter, 2 tablespoons icing (powdered) sugar and 1 teaspoon orange rind until light and creamy. Cut a small section from the top of the muffin, fill with mixture and replace the tops.

Makes 12

Fruity
Desserts

Creamy Fresh Strawberry Rolls

- 250 g (8¾ oz) strawberries, hulled
- 60 g (2 oz) butter
- 2 egg yolks
- ⅓ cup (80 ml/2¾ fl oz) cream
- ⅓ cup (90 g/3¼ oz) sugar
- 1 teaspoon lemon juice
- 6 fresh lasagne sheets (noodles), 16 cm × 21 cm (6⅓ × 8¼ inches)
- ⅓ cup (40 g/1½ oz) toasted slivered almonds, plus 1 tablespoon for decoration
- icing (powdered) sugar, for dusting

Preheat the oven to moderate 180°C (350°F/Gas 4) and grease a gratin dish. Halve the strawberries, slicing from top to bottom. Melt 20 g (⅔ oz) of butter in a pan and lightly toss the strawberries for 20 seconds. Remove from the pan. Melt another 20 g (⅔ oz) of butter in the pan. Mix the egg yolks with the cream, then add to the pan with the sugar and lemon juice. Cook, stirring often, until very thick. Remove from the heat and stir in the strawberries. Cool.

Cook the fresh lasagne sheets (noodles), two at a time, in plenty of boiling water for 3 minutes, or until al dente. Transfer to a bowl of cold water and leave for 1 minute before placing on tea towels to dry.

Divide the strawberry mixture and the almonds among the pasta sheets, leaving a 3 cm (1¼ inch) border all around. Fold in the long edges first, then carefully fold up the end closest to you and roll. As the mixture begins to ooze, bring the top end over and towards you. Carefully place, seam-side-down, in the prepared dish. Position the rolls closely side-by-side.

Dot the top with pieces of the remaining butter. Sprinkle with extra almonds and 2 teaspoons of sifted icing (powdered) sugar. Bake for 15 minutes, then place under a preheated grill (broiler) for 5 minutes or until lightly browned.

Note: This dessert is delicious accompanied by vanilla ice cream and a strawberry coulis. For a change, you can use fresh raspberries when they are in season. They will not need to be cooked, so just add them to the prepared cream mixture. Blueberries can also be used and should be prepared the same way as the strawberries, but not sliced. You can use dry lasagne sheets (noodles) instead of fresh, but they are often thicker, less pliable and slippery to handle. If you use them, cook them as they come from the packet, then trim to the dimensions above.

Serves 6

Trifle

- ½ cup (45 g/1⅔ oz) flaked almonds
- 250 g (8¾ oz) packet jam (jelly) rollettes (mini jam/jelly Swiss rolls)
- ⅓ cup (80 ml/2¾ fl oz) dry sherry
- 2 fresh mangoes or 2 fresh peaches, chopped
- 2½ cups (600 ml/20 fl oz) ready-made custard
- 300 ml (10 fl oz) cream

Preheat the oven to moderate 180°C (350°F/Gas 4). Scatter the flaked almonds over a baking tray (sheet) and cook in the oven for 6–8 minutes, or until golden. Cut the jam (jelly) rollettes into 1 cm (½ inch) slices and place half on the base of a 2.5 litre (2.6 US qt/2.2 UK qt) glass serving bowl.

Sprinkle with half the sherry and half the mango or peach. Cover with half the custard. Repeat with the remaining ingredients, then refrigerate until cold.

Whisk the cream until stiff peaks form, then spread over the custard and scatter with the toasted almonds.

Note: If possible, use fresh fruit. If you can't buy fresh, ripe fruit, use a 425 g (15 oz) can of drained peach or mango slices.

Serves 6

Pear Dumplings

- 1 cup (250 g/8¾ oz) caster (berry) sugar
- 2 cinnamon sticks
- 2 cloves
- 4 pears
- 2 cups (250 g/8¾ oz) plain (all-purpose) flour
- 150 g (5¼ oz) chilled unsalted butter, chopped
- ⅔ cup (85 g/3 oz) icing (powdered) sugar
- ⅓ cup (80 ml/2¾ fl oz) lemon juice
- 1 egg, lightly beaten

Stir the sugar with 1.5 litres (1.6 US qt/1.3 UK qt) water in a large pan over low heat until the sugar has completely dissolved. Add the cinnamon sticks and cloves and bring to the boil.

Peel the pears, leaving the stems intact. Add to the pan, cover and simmer for about 10 minutes, until just tender when tested with the point of a sharp knife. Remove the pears, drain thoroughly and cool completely. Remove the pear cores using a melon baller – leave the stem attached.

Sift the flour into a large bowl and rub in the butter until it resembles fine breadcrumbs. Stir in the icing (powdered) sugar. Add almost all the juice and mix with a flat-bladed knife until the mixture comes together, adding more juice if necessary. Turn onto a lightly floured work surface and gather together into a ball. Chill for 20 minutes.

Preheat the oven to moderate 180°C (350°F/Gas 4). Line a flat baking tray (sheet) with baking paper. Divide the dough into 4 equal portions and roll one portion out to a 23 cm (9 inches) diameter circle. Place a pear in the centre of the pastry, cut the pastry into a wide cross and set cut-out sections aside. Carefully fold one section of pastry at a time up the side of the pear, trimming and pressing the edges together to neatly cover. Repeat with the remaining pears.

Cut leaf shapes from the leftover pastry. Brush the pears all over with egg and attach the leaves, then brush the leaves with egg. Put the pears on the tray (sheet) and bake for 30 minutes, or until golden brown. Serve warm with custard or cream.

Serves 4

Meringue Baskets with Fruit

- 2 egg whites
- small pinch of cream of tartar
- ½ cup (125 g/4⅓ oz) caster (berry) sugar
- 2 tablespoons custard powder
- 2 cups (500 ml/17 fl oz) skim milk
- 1 teaspoon vanilla essence
- 1 peach, cut into thin wedges
- 1 kiwi fruit, cut into thin wedges
- 2 strawberries, cut in half
- 2 tablespoons apricot jam (jelly)

Preheat the oven to slow 150°C (300°F/Gas 2) and line a baking tray (sheet) with baking paper. Beat the egg whites and cream of tartar with electric beaters until soft peaks form. Gradually add the sugar and beat until it is dissolved and the mixture is stiff and glossy.

Fit a piping bag with a medium star nozzle and pipe coiled spirals of the meringue (about 8 cm/3 inches) onto the tray (sheet). Pipe an extra ring around the top edge to make baskets. Bake for 30 minutes, then reduce the heat to very slow 120°C (250°F/Gas ½). Bake for 45 minutes, turn the oven off and cool with the oven door ajar.

Mix the custard powder with a little of the milk to form a smooth paste. Transfer to a pan with the remaining milk and the vanilla. Stir over medium heat until the mixture boils and thickens. Remove from the heat and place plastic wrap over the surface to stop a skin forming. Set aside and, when cool, stir until smooth. Spoon some of the cold custard into each basket. Top with fruit. Heat the jam (jelly) until liquid, then brush over the fruit to glaze.

Serves 6

199

Spiced Apple Sponge

- 850 g (1 lb 14 oz) Granny Smith apples
- 30 g (1 oz) butter
- ⅓ cup (40 g/1½ oz) raisins (dark raisins)
- 2 tablespoons lemon juice
- 4 cloves
- 1 cinnamon stick
- pinch nutmeg
- ⅔ cup (160 g/5⅔ oz) caster (berry) sugar
- 2 eggs
- finely grated zest of 1 lemon
- ¼ cup (30 g/1 oz) self-raising flour
- ¼ cup (30 g/1 oz) cornflour (cornstarch)
- sifted icing (powdered) sugar, to serve

Preheat the oven to moderate 180°C (350°F/Gas 4). Peel, core and slice the apples into eighths. Melt the butter in a large frying pan, add the apple and cook, stirring occasionally, over high heat for 7 minutes, or until browned. Add the raisins, lemon juice, cloves, cinnamon, nutmeg, half the sugar and ½ cup (125 ml/4¼ fl oz) water. Bring to the boil, then lower the heat and simmer for 3 minutes, or until the apple is tender. Remove the cinnamon stick and cloves. Spoon the apple mixture into a deep 2 litre (2.1 US qt/1.75 UK qt) round ovenproof dish.

To make the sponge topping, beat the eggs, remaining sugar and lemon zest in a small bowl with electric beaters for 7–8 minutes, or until the mixture is light and creamy. Fold in the sifted flours with a metal spoon.

Spoon the sponge topping over the apples. Bake in the oven for 30 minutes, or until the sponge is well risen and golden. Dust with icing (powdered) sugar before serving. Suggested accompaniments include ice cream, whipped cream, hot or cold custard, sweetened ricotta cheese, and spiced mascarpone.

Storage Time: The apple mixture can be prepared several hours ahead and reheated before spooning on the sponge topping. This dish is best eaten immediately.

Serves 4

Baked Apples

- **4 Granny Smith apples**
- **50 g (1¾ oz) dried apricots, finely chopped**
- **50 g (1¾ oz) dates, finely chopped**
- **1 tablespoon dry breadcrumbs**
- **½ teaspoon ground cinnamon**
- **1 tablespoon honey, warmed**
- **2 teaspoons apricot jam (jelly), warmed**
- **20 g (⅔ oz) firm butter**
- **ground nutmeg, to serve**

Preheat the oven to moderate 180°C (350°F/Gas 4) and lightly grease an ovenproof dish.

Core the apples and, using a small sharp knife, run a small slit around the circumference of each apple (this will stop it splitting during baking).

Combine the dried apricots, dates, breadcrumbs, cinnamon, honey and jam (jelly) in a bowl. Divide the mixture into four, and push it into the apples using two teaspoons or your fingers. Dot the top of each apple with the butter, and put the apples in the prepared dish.

Bake for about 45–50 minutes, or until the apples are tender all the way through – test with a skewer to be absolutely sure. Serve hot with cream or ice cream. Sprinkle some nutmeg over the top before serving.

Serves 4

Poached Pears with Chocolate Shortbread Flowers

- 6 medium pears
- 1½ cups (375 ml/13 fl oz) sweet dessert wine
- 1 vanilla bean, split lengthways

Cardamom Custard
- 1 cup (250 ml/8½ fl oz) milk
- ½ cup (125 ml/4¼ fl oz) cream
- 6 cardamom pods, crushed
- 3 egg yolks
- 2 tablespoons caster (berry) sugar

Chocolate Shortbread Flowers
- 60 g (2 oz) unsalted butter, chopped
- 2 tablespoons soft brown sugar
- 1 egg yolk
- 1 tablespoon cocoa powder
- ½ cup (60 g/2 oz) plain (all-purpose) flour
- ¼ cup (30 g/1 oz) cornflour (cornstarch)
- icing (powdered) sugar, for dusting

Toffee Fingers
- 1 cup (250 g/8¾ oz) caster (berry) sugar

Peel the pears and remove the cores with a melon baller. Place in a saucepan large enough to hold all the pears. Add the wine and vanilla bean, cover and simmer for 20–25 minutes, or until soft (cooking time will depend on the ripeness of the pears). Remove the pan from the heat and allow the pears to cool in the syrup.

To make the cardamom custard, combine the milk, cream and cardamom pods in a small pan, bring to the boil and remove from the heat. Beat the egg yolks and sugar in a heatproof bowl for about 5 minutes, or until light and fluffy, then gradually pour in the hot milk mixture. Place the bowl over a pan of simmering water and stir with a wooden spoon for 10–15 minutes, or until the mixture coats the back of a wooden spoon. Strain and cool.

To make the chocolate shortbread flowers, preheat the oven to moderate 180°C (350°F/Gas 4). Beat the butter and sugar in a small bowl with electric beaters until light and creamy. Add the egg yolk, then the sifted cocoa and flours. Press together to form a soft dough. Wrap in plastic wrap and refrigerate for 30 minutes. Roll the dough out between two sheets of baking paper to 5 mm (¼ inch) thick. Cut 42 rounds from the pastry, using a 3 cm (1¼ inch) round cutter. Cut the remaining pastry into 12 small leaves. For each flower, use 7 rounds, slightly overlapping, to form a flower on a baking tray (sheet) lined with baking paper. Decorate with the leaves. Bake for 10–15 minutes, or until the pastry is firm to touch. Remove from the tray (sheet) and cool on a wire rack.

To make the toffee fingers, line two or three baking trays (sheets) with baking paper. Sprinkle the sugar over the base of a heavy-based frying pan, then stir gently until the sugar has dissolved and is light golden brown. Remove from the heat (the toffee will continue to darken away from the heat). Use a spoon to drizzle 13 cm (5 inch) lengths of toffee onto the prepared trays (sheets), about 5 mm (¼ inch) wide, and allow to set until cold.

To assemble for serving, dust the shortbread flowers very lightly with icing (powdered) sugar, place in the centre of a serving plate and position a well-drained pear on top. Spoon cardamom custard around the outside of the shortbread. Stand the toffee strips up around the outside of the pear like a tepee.

Note: The cardamom custard can be made three days ahead. Pears and shortbread rounds can be made a day ahead and the shortbread can be frozen.

Serves 6

Fruit Covered with Meringue

- **4 ripe peaches or nectarines**
- **40 g (1½ oz) marzipan**
- **3 egg whites**
- **⅔ cup (160 g/5⅔ oz) caster (berry) sugar**
- **demerara sugar, to sprinkle**

Preheat the oven to moderately hot 200°C (400°F/Gas 6). Cut the peaches in half and remove the stone. To remove the skin, place the peaches cut-side-down on a plate, put the plate in the sink and pour boiling water over, followed by cold water. Drain immediately and peel. Roll the marzipan into 4 small balls, put them in the gaps left by the peach stones, then put the halves back together. Stand the peaches in a shallow ovenproof dish.

Whisk the egg whites in a large, clean, dry bowl until stiff peaks form, gradually add the sugar and whisk until thick and glossy. Cover the fruit with a layer of meringue, making sure there are no gaps. Using a fork, rough up the surface of the meringue. Sprinkle with demerara sugar and bake for 15–20 minutes, until the meringue is lightly browned. Gently lift out. These can be served with cream or ice cream.

Serves 4

Panforte

- ⅔ cup (100 g/3½ oz) blanched almonds
- ¾ cup (105 g/3⅔ oz) roasted, skinned hazelnuts
- ½ cup (95 g/3⅓ oz) crystallised (candied) peel, chopped
- ½ cup (100 g/3½ oz) chopped crystallised (candied) pineapple
- ¼ cup (30 g/1 oz) cocoa powder
- ½ cup (60 g/2 oz) plain (all-purpose) flour
- ½ teaspoon ground cinnamon
- ¼ teaspoon mixed spice
- ⅓ cup (90 g/3¼ oz) sugar
- ⅓ cup (115 g/4 oz) honey
- icing (powdered) sugar, for dusting

Line a 20 cm (8 inch) springform tin with baking paper and grease well with butter. Toast the almonds under a hot grill (broiler) until brown, then leave to cool. Put the nuts in a bowl with the peel, pineapple, cocoa powder, flour and spices and toss them all together. Preheat the oven to slow 150°C (300°F/Gas 2).

Put the sugar and honey in a saucepan and melt them together over low heat. Cook the syrup until a little of it dropped into cold water forms a soft ball when moulded between your finger and thumb. The colour will turn from golden to brown.

Pour the syrup into the nut mixture and mix well, working fast before it stiffens too much. Spoon straight into the tin, press firmly and smooth the surface. Bake for 35 minutes. Unlike other cakes this will neither firm up nor colour as it cooks at all so you need to time it carefully.

Cool in the tin until the cake firms enough to enable you to remove the side of the tin. Peel off the paper, turn the cake over onto another piece of paper and leave to cool completely. Dust the top heavily with icing (powdered) sugar before serving.

Makes 1

Cherry Cheese Strudel

- 500 g (1 lb 2 oz) ricotta
- 2 teaspoons lemon or orange rind
- ¼ cup (60 g/2 oz) sugar
- ½ cup (40 g/1½ oz) fresh breadcrumbs
- 2 tablespoons ground almonds
- 2 eggs
- 425 g (15 oz) can pitted black cherries
- 2 teaspoons cornflour (cornstarch)
- 8 sheets filo (phyllo) pastry
- 60 g (2 oz) unsalted butter, melted
- 2 tablespoons dry breadcrumbs
- icing (powdered) sugar, to dust

Preheat the oven to moderate 180°C (350°F/Gas 4). Lightly grease a baking tray (sheet) with melted butter. Combine the ricotta, rind, sugar, breadcrumbs and almonds in a bowl. Add the eggs and mix well. Drain the cherries, reserving half the juice. Blend the cornflour (cornstarch) with the reserved cherry juice in a small pan. Stir over heat until the mixture boils and thickens, then cool slightly.

Layer the pastry sheets, brushing between each sheet with melted butter and sprinkling with a few breadcrumbs. Form a large square by placing the second sheet halfway down the first sheet. Alternate layers, brushing with melted butter and sprinkling with breadcrumbs.

Place the ricotta mixture along one long edge of the pastry. Shape into a log and top with cherries and cooled syrup. Roll the pastry around the ricotta filling, folding in the edges as you roll. Finish with a pastry edge underneath. Place on the prepared tray (sheet) and bake for 35–40 minutes, or until the pastry is golden. Serve in slices, warm or cold, heavily dusted with icing (powdered) sugar. Can be served with cream.

Serves 8–10

Strawberry Swiss Roll

- 3 eggs, separated
- ½ cup (125 g/4⅓ oz) caster (berry) sugar, plus 1 tablespoon, extra
- ¾ cup (90 g/3¼ oz) self-raising flour, sifted
- ½ cup (160 g/5⅔ oz) strawberry jam (jelly)
- ¾ cup (185 ml/6½ fl oz) cream
- 250 g (8¾ oz) strawberries, quartered

Preheat the oven to moderately hot 200°C (400°F/Gas 6). Sprinkle a tablespoon of sugar over a piece of baking paper 30 × 35 cm (12 × 14 inch), resting on a tea towel. Brush a 25 × 30 cm (10 × 12 inch) Swiss roll tin with oil or melted butter and line with baking paper.

Beat the egg whites until soft peaks form. Gradually add the sugar and beat until dissolved. Beat in the lightly beaten egg yolks until thick.

Fold in the flour and 2 tablespoons hot water. Spread into the tin and bake for 8–10 minutes, or until firm and golden. Turn out onto the sugared paper and peel the paper from the base. Using the tea towel as a guide, roll up loosely from the narrow end. Leave for 20 minutes, or until cooled, then unroll. (This prevents the sponge cracking when rolled with filling.)

Beat the cream and extra sugar until soft peaks form. Spread the roll with jam (jelly) and top with cream and strawberries. Re-roll and chill.

Serves 6–8

Figs in Honey Syrup

- 100 g (3½ oz) blanched whole almonds
- 12 whole fresh figs (about 750 g/1 lb 10 oz)
- ½ cup (125 g/4⅓ oz) sugar
- ⅓ cup (115 g/4 oz) honey
- 2 tablespoons lemon juice
- 6 cm (2½ inch) sliver of lemon rind
- 1 cinnamon stick
- 1 cup (250 g/8¾ oz) Greek-style natural yoghurt

Preheat the oven to moderate 180°C (350°F/Gas 4). Place the almonds on a baking tray (sheet) and bake for 5 minutes, or until golden. Leave to cool. Cut the stems off the figs and make a small crossways incision 5 mm (¼ inch) deep on top of each. Push a blanched almond into the base of each fig. Roughly chop the remaining almonds.

Place 3 cups (750 ml/26 fl oz) water in a large saucepan, add the sugar and stir over medium heat until the sugar dissolves. Increase the heat and bring to the boil. Stir in the honey, lemon juice, lemon rind and cinnamon stick. Reduce the heat to medium, place the figs in the pan and simmer gently for 30 minutes. Remove with a slotted spoon and place on a large serving dish.

Boil the liquid over high heat for about 15–20 minutes, or until thick and syrupy. Remove the cinnamon and rind. Cool the syrup slightly and pour over the figs. Sprinkle with almonds and serve warm or cold with yoghurt.

Serves 4

Hot Fruit Soufflé

- unsalted butter, melted, for greasing
- caster (berry) sugar, for sprinkling
- 60 g (2 oz) unsalted butter, extra
- ½ cup (60 g/2 oz) plain (all-purpose) flour
- 1½ cups (375 ml/13 fl oz) pureed fruit (see Note)
- ¼ cup (60 g/2 oz) caster (berry) sugar, extra
- 4 egg whites
- icing (powdered) sugar, to dust

Prepare a 1.25 litre (1.3 US qt/1.1 UK qt) soufflé dish by brushing melted butter evenly and generously over the dish, especially at the rim. Sprinkle with caster (berry) sugar, shake to coat evenly, then tip out any excess. Preheat the oven to moderately hot 200°C (400°F/Gas 6) and put a baking tray (sheet) on the top shelf to heat.

Melt the extra butter in a saucepan, add the flour and mix well. Remove from the heat, stir until smooth, then stir in the fruit puree. Return the saucepan to the heat, bring the mixture to the boil and simmer for 2 minutes. Add the extra sugar a little at a time, tasting for sweetness as you go. Add a little extra sugar if necessary. Leave to cool.

Whisk the egg whites in a large clean bowl until soft peaks form, add 1 tablespoon to the fruit mixture and mix well. Fold in the remaining whites, being careful not to lose too much volume. Fill the soufflé dish to three-quarters full.

Put the soufflé dish on the hot baking tray (sheet) and bake for 20–25 minutes, until risen well and golden. Serve immediately, dusted with icing (powdered) sugar.

Note: To ensure success when making soufflés, make sure you fold the egg whites into the basic soufflé mixture as gently as possible. It is better to leave a few pieces of egg white unmixed than to end up with a flat soufflé.

Suitable fruits to use are those that make a good puree, such as raspberries, strawberries, mangoes, peaches, apricots and passionfruit. Bananas are a little too heavy. You could use apples or plums, or dried fruit, but you'd have to cook them into a puree first.

Serves 4

Hot Passionfruit Soufflé

- 2 egg yolks
- ½ cup (125 g/4⅓ oz) passionfruit pulp (about 6 passionfruit)
- 2 tablespoons lemon juice
- ¾ cup (90 g/3¼ oz) icing (powdered) sugar
- 6 egg whites
- icing (powdered) sugar, for decorating

Preheat oven to hot 210°C (415°F/Gas 6–7). Place a collar of baking paper to come about 3 cm (1¼ inches) above the sides of 4 small ramekins. Tie securely with string. Lightly grease base and side of ramekins (including the paper) and sprinkle with caster (berry) sugar; shake out excess.

Combine yolks, pulp, lemon juice and half the icing (powdered) sugar in a large bowl. Whisk until well combined. With electric beaters, beat egg whites in a large bowl until soft peaks form. Gradually add the remaining icing (powdered) sugar, beating well after each addition.

Using a large metal spoon, fold the egg white mixture in batches through the passionfruit mixture. Spoon into dishes. Using a flat-bladed knife, cut through the mixture in a circular motion 2 cm (¾ inch) from the edge. Place the dish on a large oven tray (sheet) and bake for 20–25 minutes or until the soufflé is well-risen and cooked through. Cut the collars from the dishes and serve the soufflés immediately, sprinkled with sifted icing (powdered) sugar.

Serves 4

Peach Charlottes with Melba Sauce

- 1 cup (250 g/8¾ oz) sugar
- 4 cups (1 litre (1.1 US qt/ 1.75 UK qt) water
- 6 medium peaches
- ⅓ cup (80 ml/2¾ fl oz) peach liqueur
- 2 loaves brioche
- 100 g (3½ oz) butter, melted

- ½ cup (160 g/5⅔ oz) apricot jam (jelly), warmed and sieved

Melba Sauce
- 315 g (11¼ oz) fresh or thawed frozen raspberries
- 2 tablespoons icing (powdered) sugar

Preheat the oven to moderate 180°C (350°F/Gas 4). Brush four 1-cup capacity ovenproof ramekins or moulds with melted butter. Combine the sugar and water in large, heavy-based pan. Stir over medium heat until the sugar completely dissolves. Bring to the boil, reduce heat slightly and add the whole peaches. Simmer, covered for 20 minutes. Drain and cool. Peel the skins and slice the flesh thickly. Place in a bowl, sprinkle with liqueur and set aside for 20 minutes.

Cut the brioche into 1 cm (½ inch) thick slices; remove the crusts. With a scone-cutter, cut rounds to fit the tops and bases of each dish. Cut the remaining slices into 2 cm (¾ inch) wide fingers and trim to fit the height of the dish. Dip the first round into melted butter and place in the base of the dish. Dip brioche fingers into melted butter and press around the sides of dish, overlapping slightly. Line all the dishes in this manner.

Fill the lined dishes evenly with peach slices and top with the last round of brioche dipped in melted butter. Press to seal. Place the dishes on a baking tray (sheet) and bake for 20 minutes. Turn onto serving plates, brush with jam (jelly) and pour Melba Sauce alongside. Serve with fresh berries, if desired.

To make Melba Sauce: Process the berries in a food processor and add icing (powdered) sugar, to taste. Push through a fine sieve.

Note: The peaches can be cooked, the dishes lined with brioche and the sauce made, up to 6 hours ahead. Refrigerate the charlottes, then fill and bake them close to serving time.

Serves 4

Cranberry Kisel

- 2 lemons
- 1½ cups (375 g/13¼ oz) caster (berry) sugar
- 2 cinnamon sticks
- 600 g (1 lb 5 oz) cranberries (fresh or frozen)
- 2 teaspoons cornflour (cornstarch)
- 2 teaspoons orange juice

Yoghurt Cream
- 1 cup (250 ml/8½ fl oz) cream
- ½ cup (125 ml/4¼ fl oz) natural yoghurt
- ½ cup (115 g/4 oz) soft brown sugar

Remove the peel from the lemons in large strips with a vegetable peeler, avoiding the white pith. Place the peel, sugar, cinnamon sticks and 1½ cups (375 ml/13 fl oz) water into a saucepan and stir over low heat until the sugar has dissolved. Bring to the boil, reduce the heat and simmer for 5 minutes.

Rinse the cranberries (not necessary if frozen) and remove any stems. Add the cranberries to the hot syrup, return to the boil and simmer for 10 minutes, or until the skins have split. Remove from the heat and set aside to cool.

When cool, remove and discard the peel and cinnamon sticks. Remove about ½ cup of the berries and reserve. Blend or process the remaining mixture until smooth, return to the saucepan and add the reserved whole berries. Blend the cornflour (cornstarch) and orange juice in a small bowl, add to the puree then stir over medium heat for 5 minutes, or until the mixture boils and thickens. Serve cold or warm with yoghurt cream.

For the yoghurt cream, beat the cream in a bowl until soft peaks form, then fold the yoghurt through. Transfer to a small bowl and sprinkle with the sugar. Refrigerate, covered, for 2 hours.

Serves 4

Stuffed Peaches

- **6 ripe peaches**
- **60 g (2 oz) amaretti biscuits (Italian almond cookies), crushed**
- **1 egg yolk**
- **2 tablespoons caster (berry) sugar**
- **20 g (⅔ oz) almond meal (ground almonds)**
- **1 tablespoon amaretto (almond-flavoured liqueur)**
- **¼ cup (60 ml/2 fl oz) white wine**
- **1 teaspoon caster (berry) sugar, extra**
- **20 g (⅔ oz) unsalted butter**

Preheat the oven to moderate 180°C (350°/Gas 4) and lightly grease a 30 × 25 cm (12 × 10 inch) ovenproof dish with butter.

Cut each peach in half and carefully remove the stones. Scoop a little of the pulp out from each and combine in a small bowl with the crushed biscuits (cookies), egg yolk, caster (berry) sugar, almond meal (ground almonds) and amaretto (almond-flavoured liqueur).

Spoon some of the mixture into each peach and place them cut-side-up in the dish. Sprinkle with the white wine and the extra sugar. Place a dot of butter on the top of each and bake for 20–25 minutes, until golden.

Note: When they are in season, you can also use ripe apricots or nectarines for this recipe.

Serves 6

Feuilleté with Cherries Jubilee

- 375 g (13¼ oz) puff pastry
- 1 egg, lightly beaten
- 20 g (⅔ oz) unsalted butter
- 20 g (⅔ oz) sugar
- 500 g (1 lb 2 oz) cherries, pitted
- 300 ml (10 fl oz) thick (double/heavy) cream
- ½ cup (125 ml/4¼ fl oz) brandy or Kirsch (cherry liqueur)
- icing (powdered) sugar, to dust

Roll the pastry out on a floured work surface and cut out four rectangles of 10 × 13 cm (4 × 5 inches) each. Put them on a baking tray (sheet) and brush with the egg glaze, being careful not to let any drip down the sides of the pastry. Refrigerate for 30 minutes. Preheat the oven to hot 220°C (425°F/Gas 7).

Melt the butter and sugar together in a saucepan and add the pitted cherries. Cook over high heat for about 1 minute, then reduce the heat and simmer for about 3 minutes, or until the cherries are tender. Reduce the heat to low and keep the cherries warm.

Bake the feuilleté on the top shelf of the oven for 15 minutes until golden and puffed, then cut them in half horizontally and gently pull any doughy bits out of the centre. Turn the oven off and put the feuilleté back in the oven and allow to dry out for a couple of minutes.

When you are ready to serve, whisk the cream until it reaches stiff peaks. Place a warm feuilleté base on each serving plate. Heat the brandy or Kirsch in a small saucepan and set it alight, then pour it over the cherries (keep a saucepan lid nearby in case the flames get too high). Spoon some cherries into each feuilleté and top with a little cream. Put the lids on and dust with icing (powdered) sugar before serving.

Serves 4

Pavlova Roll with Raspberry Coulis

- **4 egg whites**
- **1 cup (250 g/8¾ oz) caster (berry) sugar**
- **1 teaspoon cornflour (cornstarch)**
- **2 teaspoons lemon juice or vinegar**
- **⅔ cup (170 ml/5¾ fl oz) cream, whipped**
- **¼ cup (55 g/1⅞ oz) chopped fresh berries**

Raspberry Coulis
- **2 tablespoons brandy**
- **250 g (8¾ oz) fresh raspberries, washed and hulled**
- **1 tablespoon icing (powdered) sugar**

Brush a 25 × 30 cm (10 × 12 inch) Swiss roll tin with oil and line with non-stick baking paper extending up 2 sides. Preheat the oven to moderate 180°C (350°F/Gas 4). Beat the egg whites into soft peaks. Gradually add ¾ cup sugar and beat until thick and glossy. Combine 1 tablespoon sugar with the cornflour (cornstarch). Fold into the meringue with the lemon juice or vinegar. Spoon into the tin and smooth. Bake for 12–15 minutes until springy.

Put a large sheet of baking paper on top of a tea towel and generously sprinkle with the rest of the sugar. Turn the pavlova onto this, peel off the lining paper and leave for 3 minutes. Roll up pavlova from the long side using the tea towel to assist; cool. Fold berries into whipped cream.

Unroll the pavlova, fill with the cream mixture and re-roll without the tea towel and baking paper. Transfer to a plate and refrigerate.

To make Raspberry Coulis: Put the brandy, raspberries and icing (powdered) sugar in a food processor and process until well blended. Serve Pavlova Roll in slices with Raspberry Coulis.

Serves 8–10

215

Apple Galettes

- 2 cups (250 g/8¾ oz) plain (all-purpose) flour
- 250 g (8¾ oz) unsalted butter, chopped
- 8 apples

- ¾ cup (185 g/6½ oz) caster (berry) sugar
- 125 g (4⅓ oz) unsalted butter, chopped

Place the flour and butter in a bowl and cut the butter into the flour with two knives until it resembles large crumbs. Gradually add about ½ cup (125 ml/4¼ fl oz) chilled water, stirring with a knife and pressing together, until a rough dough forms. Turn onto a lightly floured board and roll into a rectangle. The dough will be crumbly and hard to manage at this point. Fold the pastry into thirds; turn it so the hinge is on your left and roll into a large rectangle. Always turn the pastry the same way so the hinge is on the left. Refrigerate in plastic wrap for 30 minutes.

Complete two more turns and folds before refrigerating the pastry for another 30 minutes. Repeat the process so that you have completed 6 folds and turns. Wrap the pastry in plastic wrap and refrigerate before use. The pastry can be stored in the refrigerator for 2 days or in the freezer for up to 3 months.

Preheat the oven to moderately hot 190°C (375°F/Gas 5). Roll the pastry out on a lightly floured surface until 3 mm (⅛ inch) thick. Cut into eight 10 cm (4 inch) rounds. Peel and core the apples and slice thinly. Arrange the apples in a spiral on the pastry. Sprinkle well with sugar and dot with unsalted butter. Bake on greased baking trays (sheets) for 20–30 minutes, until the pastry is crisp and golden. Serve warm.

Serves 8

Apple Strudel

- **4 green cooking apples**
- **30 g (1 oz) butter**
- **2 tablespoons orange juice**
- **1 tablespoon honey**
- **¼ cup (60 g/2 oz) sugar**
- **½ cup (60 g/2 oz) sultanas (golden raisins)**
- **2 sheets ready-rolled puff pastry**
- **¼ cup (45 g/1⅔ oz) ground almonds**
- **1 egg, lightly beaten**
- **2 tablespoons soft brown sugar**
- **1 teaspoon ground cinnamon**

Preheat the oven to hot 220°C (425°F/Gas 7). Brush two oven trays (sheets) lightly with melted butter or oil. Peel, core and thinly slice the apples. Heat the butter in a medium pan; add the apples and cook for 2 minutes until lightly golden. Add the orange juice, honey, sugar and sultanas (golden raisins). Stir over medium heat until the sugar dissolves and the apples are just tender. Transfer the mixture to a bowl and leave until completely cooled.

Place a sheet of the pastry on a flat work surface. Fold it in half; and make small cuts in the folded edge of the pastry at 2 cm (¾ inch) intervals. Open out the pastry and sprinkle with half of the ground almonds. Drain away the liquid from the apples and place half of the mixture in the centre of the pastry. Brush the edges with the lightly beaten egg, and fold together, pressing firmly to seal.

Place the strudel on a prepared tray (sheet), seam-side down. Brush the top with egg and sprinkle with half of the combined brown sugar and cinnamon. Repeat the process with the other sheet and the remaining filling. Bake for 20–25 minutes or until the pastry is golden and crisp. Serve hot with cream or ice cream, or at room temperature as a teatime treat.

Makes 2 strudels

Strawberry Meringue Stacks

- **4 egg whites**
- **1 cup (250 g/8¾ oz) caster (berry) sugar**

- **500 g (1 lb 2 oz) strawberries, hulled**
- **1¼ cups (315 ml/11 fl oz) cream, whipped**

Preheat oven to slow 150°C (300°F/Gas 2). Brush two 33 × 28 cm (13 × 11 inch) oven trays (sheets) with melted butter or oil. Cut non-stick baking paper to fit trays (sheets). Using an 8 cm (3 inch) round cutter as a guide, mark 12 circles onto paper, and place pencil-side down on trays (sheets).

Place egg whites in a medium, clean dry bowl. Using electric beaters, beat until soft peaks form. Add the sugar gradually, beating constantly until mixture is thick and glossy and all the sugar has dissolved. Spread meringue into rounds on the prepared trays (sheets). Bake for 40 minutes then turn off heat and allow meringues to cool in oven.

Place half the strawberries into a food processor or blender and blend until completely liquid. Slice the remaining strawberries and fold through whipped cream. To serve, sandwich two meringue rounds together with cream mixture and place on each plate. Pour some strawberry sauce around base of the meringue.

Note: The meringues can be made up to two days in advance and stored in an airtight container. Strawberry sauce can be made up to one day ahead. Make the strawberry cream mixture up to two hours in advance. Store the sauce and cream, covered, in the refrigerator. After assembling, serve immediately. If you prefer a sweeter sauce, a little caster (berry) sugar can be added. Garnish with strawberry leaves to serve, if you wish.

Serves 6

Cakes

Chocolate Mud Cake

- 250 g (8¾ oz) unsalted butter
- 250 g (8¾ oz) dark (semi-sweet) chocolate, chopped
- 2 tablespoons instant coffee powder
- 150 g (5¼ oz) self-raising flour
- 150 g (5¼ oz) plain (all-purpose) flour
- ½ teaspoon bicarbonate of soda (baking soda)
- ½ cup (60 g/2 oz) cocoa powder
- 2¼ cups (550 g/1 lb 3½ oz) caster (berry) sugar
- 4 eggs, lightly beaten
- 2 tablespoons oil
- ½ cup (125 ml/4¼ fl oz) buttermilk

Icing
- 150 g (5¼ oz) unsalted butter, chopped
- 150 g (5¼ oz) dark (semi-sweet) chocolate, chopped

Preheat the oven to 160°C (315°F/Gas 2–3). Lightly grease a deep 23 cm (9 inch) round cake tin and line with baking paper, making sure the paper around the side extends at least 5 cm (2 inches) above the top edge.

Put the butter, chocolate and coffee in a saucepan with ¾ cup (185 ml/6½ fl oz) hot water and stir over low heat until smooth. Remove from the heat.

Sift the flours, bicarbonate of soda (baking soda) and cocoa powder into a large mixing bowl. Stir in the sugar and make a well in the centre. Place the eggs, oil and buttermilk in a separate mixing bowl and mix until combined. Pour into the dry ingredients and mix together with a whisk. Gradually add the chocolate mixture, whisking well after each addition.

Pour the mixture (it will be quite wet) into the tin and bake for 1¾ hours. Test the centre with a skewer – the skewer may be slightly wetter than normal. Remove the cake from the oven. If the top looks raw, bake for another 5–10 minutes, then remove from oven. Leave in the tin until completely cold, then turn out and wrap in plastic wrap.

For the icing, combine the butter and chocolate in a saucepan and stir over low heat until the butter and chocolate are melted. Remove and cool slightly. Pour over the cake and allow it to run down the side.

Serves 8

Chocolate Nut Cake

- **250 g (8¾ oz) stellini (soup pasta)**
- **1 cup (140 g/5 oz) roasted hazelnuts, skinned**
- **1½ cups (150 g/5¼ oz) walnuts**
- **¾ cup (100 g/3½ oz) blanched almonds**
- **3 tablespoons cocoa powder**
- **1 teaspoon ground cinnamon**
- **⅔ cup (155 g/5½ oz) sugar**
- **1 tablespoon mixed peel**
- **grated rind of 1 lemon**
- **1 teaspoon vanilla essence**
- **2 tablespoons Cognac**
- **60 g (2 oz) butter**
- **100 g (3½ oz) dark (semi-sweet) chocolate, chopped**

Grease and line the base of a deep 20 cm (8 inch) round springform tin. Cook the pasta in boiling water until al dente. Rinse under cold water to cool. Drain thoroughly.

Place the nuts, cocoa powder, cinnamon, sugar, mixed peel, rind, vanilla essence and Cognac in a food processor. Process in short bursts until finely ground.

Melt the butter and chocolate in a small pan over low heat or in the microwave, until smooth.

Combine the pasta, nut mixture and melted chocolate and butter. Mix well. Spoon the mixture into the prepared tin. Press down firmly with a wet hand. Smooth the surface with the back of a wet spoon. Refrigerate overnight to firm. Remove from the tin and cut into wedges. Dust with a little cocoa powder and icing (powdered) sugar for serving. Delicious with whipped cream.

Serves 6–8

Layered Passionfruit Torte

- 6 eggs, separated
- ¾ cup (90 g/3¼ oz) icing (powdered) sugar
- ½ cup (125 g/4⅓ oz) sugar
- ½ teaspoon vanilla essence
- ½ cup (60 g/2 oz) cornflour (cornstarch)
- 1½ teaspoons baking powder
- ¼ cup (30 g/1 oz) plain (all-purpose) flour

Filling
- 1 tablespoon lemon juice

- 1 tablespoon gelatine
- pulp of 10 passionfruit
- 500 g (1 lb 2 oz) cream cheese
- 1½ cups (185 g/6½ oz) icing (powdered) sugar, sifted
- ¾ cup (185 ml/6½ fl oz) cream, lightly whipped
- ½ cup (125 ml/4¼ fl oz) cream, extra, whipped to stiff peaks
- pulp of 2 passionfruit, extra
- ¼ cup (40 g/1½ oz) roasted almonds or pistachios, chopped

Preheat the oven to 180°C (350°F/Gas 4). Lightly grease two shallow 23 cm (9 inch) round cake tins and line the bases with baking paper. Place the egg whites in a large dry mixing bowl. Beat with electric beaters until stiff peaks form. Add the sugar gradually, beating until all the sugar has dissolved and mixture is thick and glossy. Fold in the yolks and vanilla essence. Sift dry ingredients into the mixture and gently fold in until smooth. Spoon mixture evenly into the prepared tins. Bake for 20 minutes, or until the cakes shrink away from the sides of the tins. Leave the cakes in the tins for 5 minutes before turning out onto wire racks to cool completely.

To make the filling, combine the juice, gelatine and water in a small mixing bowl. Heat half the passionfruit pulp in a small saucepan until it boils. Add the gelatine mixture and stir over medium heat until dissolved. Strain the mixture through a sieve and add to remaining passionfruit pulp. Leave to cool slightly. Beat the cream cheese and sugar with electric beaters until the mixture is smooth and creamy. Add the passionfruit mixture. Fold in the lightly whipped cream.

To assemble the cake, cut each cake in half horizontally with a serrated knife. Place one layer on a serving plate and spread with one-fifth of filling. Continue layering, leaving enough filling to spread evenly over the top and side of the cake.

Place extra whipped cream in a piping bag and pipe rosettes on top of the cake. Spread extra passionfruit pulp over top. Sprinkle the nuts over the rosettes. Refrigerate for several hours.

Storage: Assemble up to 3 days in advance but add the rosettes and pulp just before serving.

Serves 8

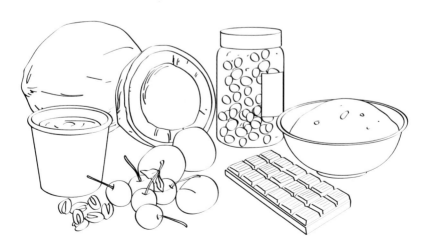

Baked Cheesecake

- 375 g (13¼ oz) plain sweet biscuits (cookies)
- 180 g (6⅓ oz) butter, melted

Filling
- 500 g (1 lb 2 oz) cream cheese
- 200 g (7 oz) caster (berry) sugar
- 4 eggs
- 300 ml (10 fl oz) cream
- 2 tablespoons plain (all-purpose) flour
- 1 teaspoon ground cinnamon
- ¼ teaspoon ground nutmeg
- 1 tablespoon lemon juice
- 2 teaspoons vanilla essence
- ground nutmeg and cinnamon, to serve

Preheat the oven to moderate 180°C (350°F/Gas 4). Grease a 23 cm (9 inch) shallow springform tin.

Put the biscuits (cookies) in a food processor and process until fine and crumbly. Add the melted butter and process for 10 seconds. Press into the base and side of the tin, then refrigerate.

Beat the cream cheese and sugar together until soft and creamy. Add the eggs and cream and beat for about 4 minutes. Fold in the flour, cinnamon, nutmeg, juice and vanilla essence. Pour the mixture into the chilled crust. Bake for 1 hour, or until firm. Let the cheesecake cool in the oven, turned off with the door open (to prevent sinking and cracking). Refrigerate overnight. Sprinkle with nutmeg and cinnamon. Delicious with cream and strawberries.

Serves 10

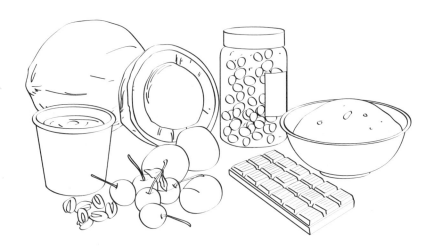

Custard Butter Cake

- 1 cup (125 g/4⅓ oz) self-raising flour
- ⅔ cup (85 g/3 oz) custard powder
- ½ teaspoon bicarbonate of soda (baking soda)
- 125 g (4⅓ oz) unsalted butter, chopped
- ¾ cup (185 g/6½ oz) caster (berry) sugar
- 3 eggs, lightly beaten
- ¼ cup (60 ml/2 fl oz) buttermilk

Icing
- 100 g (3½ oz) white chocolate
- ¼ cup (60 ml/2 fl oz) cream
- 200 g (7 oz) cream cheese, softened
- ⅓ cup (40 g/1½ oz) icing (powdered) sugar
- silver cachous (dragées) and crystallised (candied) violets, to decorate

Preheat the oven to 180°C (350°F/Gas 4). Lightly grease a deep 20 cm (8 inch) square cake tin and line the base with baking paper. Sift the flour, custard powder and soda into a bowl and make a well in the centre.

Melt the butter and sugar in a small saucepan over low heat, stirring until the sugar has dissolved. Remove from the heat. Add the butter mixture and combined egg and buttermilk to the dry ingredients and stir until just combined. Spoon into the prepared tin. Bake for 35 minutes, or until a skewer comes out clean when inserted into the centre. Leave in the tin to cool.

To make the icing, melt the chocolate and cream in a saucepan over low heat. Cool and add to the cream cheese and icing (powdered) sugar. Beat until smooth. Decorate with silver cachous (dragées) and crystallised (candied) violets.

Serves 8–10

225

Cashew Meringue Cake

Cashew Meringue
- 300 g (10½ oz) cashews
- 8 egg whites
- 1½ cups (375 g/13¼ oz) caster (berry) sugar
- 2 teaspoons vanilla essence
- 2 teaspoons white vinegar

Fillings
- 250 g (8¾ oz) unsalted butter, softened
- 1 cup (125 g/4⅓ oz) icing (powdered) sugar
- 4 tablespoons Crème de Cacao
- 2 cups (500 ml/17 fl oz) cream
- 1 tablespoon orange liqueur
- 2 teaspoons vanilla essence
- chocolate curls and cocoa powder, for decoration

To make Cashew Meringue: Preheat the oven to moderate 180°C (350°F/Gas 4). Spread the cashews on a baking tray (sheet) and toast them in the oven for 5 minutes or until golden, stirring occasionally to turn them over. Check frequently to make sure they don't burn. Remove the cashews from the oven and allow to cool. Place the cashews in a food processor and process them in short bursts until finely ground.

Reduce the oven temperature to slow 150°C (300°F/Gas 2). Line 4 oven trays (sheets) with non-stick baking paper and draw a 21 cm (8¼ inch) diameter circle on each piece of paper.

Beat the egg whites in a large, clean, dry bowl until soft peaks form. Gradually add the sugar to the bowl, beating well after each addition, until the whites are thick and glossy. Using a metal spoon, fold in the vanilla, vinegar and ground cashews.

Divide the mixture evenly among the 4 circles and carefully spread it to the edge of each circle. Bake the meringues for 45 minutes or until they are crisp. Turn the oven off and allow the meringues to cool in the oven, leaving the oven door ajar.

To make Fillings: Place the butter, icing (powdered) sugar and Crème de Cacao in a bowl and beat until the mixture becomes light and creamy. Set aside. Place the cream, orange liqueur and vanilla essence in a separate bowl and beat until soft peaks form.

Place 1 meringue circle on a serving plate and carefully spread it with half the butter mixture. Place a second meringue circle on top and spread it with half the orange cream mixture. Repeat with the remaining meringue circles, butter mixture and orange cream mixture.

The top of the meringue cake can be decorated with chocolate curls and dusted lightly with cocoa. Carefully cut into sections for serving.

Serves 8–10

Chocolate Collar Cheesecake

- 200 g (7 oz) plain chocolate biscuits (cookies), crushed
- 70 g (2½ oz) unsalted butter, melted

Filling
- 500 g (1 lb 2 oz) cream cheese, softened
- ⅓ cup (90 g/3¼ oz) sugar
- 2 eggs
- 1 tablespoon cocoa powder
- 300 g (10½ oz) sour cream
- 250 g (8¾ oz) good-quality dark (semi-sweet) chocolate, melted

- ⅓ cup (80 ml/2¾ fl oz) whiskey cream liqueur

Collar
- 50 g (1¾ oz) white chocolate, melted
- 150 g (5¼ oz) good-quality dark (semi-sweet) chocolate, melted
- 1¼ cups (315 ml/11 fl oz) cream, whipped
- cocoa powder and icing (powdered) sugar, to dust

Brush a 23 cm (9 inch) round springform tin with melted butter or oil and line the base and side with baking paper. Mix together the biscuit (cookie) crumbs and butter, press firmly into the base of the tin and refrigerate for 10 minutes. Preheat the oven to moderate 180°C (350°F/Gas 4).

Beat the cream cheese and sugar with electric beaters until smooth and creamy. Add the eggs, one at a time, beating well after each addition. Beat in the cocoa and sour cream until smooth. Beat in the cooled melted dark (semi-sweet) chocolate. Beat in the liqueur and pour over the base. Smooth the surface and bake for 45 minutes. The cheesecake may not be fully set, but will firm up. Refrigerate, overnight if possible, until cold.

Remove the cheesecake from the tin and put it on a board. Measure the height and add 5 mm (¼ inch). Cut a strip of baking paper this wide and 75 cm (29½ inches) long. Pipe or drizzle the melted white chocolate in a figure eight pattern along the paper. When just set, spread the dark (semi-sweet) chocolate over the entire strip of paper. Allow the chocolate to set a little, but you need to be able to bend the paper without it cracking.

Wrap the paper around the cheesecake with the chocolate inside. Seal the ends and hold the paper in place until the chocolate is completely set. Peel away the paper. Spread the top with cream. Dust with cocoa powder and icing (powdered) sugar.

Serves 8–10

Black Forest Gateau

- 125 g (4⅓ oz) unsalted butter
- 1 cup (250 g/8¾ oz) caster (berry) sugar
- 2 eggs, lightly beaten
- 1 teaspoon vanilla essence
- ⅓ cup (40 g/1½ oz) self-raising flour
- 1 cup (125 g/4⅓ oz) plain (all-purpose) flour
- 1 teaspoon bicarbonate of soda (baking soda)
- ½ cup (60 g/2 oz) cocoa powder
- ¾ cup (185 ml/6½ fl oz) buttermilk

Filling
- ¼ cup (60 ml/2 fl oz) Kirsch (cherry liqueur)
- 3 cups (750 ml/26 fl oz) cream, whipped
- 425 g (15 oz) can pitted morello or black cherries, drained

Topping
- 100 g (3½ oz) good-quality dark (semi-sweet) chocolate
- 100 g (3½ oz) milk chocolate
- cherries with stalks, to decorate

Preheat the oven to moderate 180°C (350°F/Gas 4). Brush a deep, 20 cm (8 inch) round cake tin with oil or melted butter. Line the base and side with baking paper.

Using electric beaters, beat the butter and sugar until light and creamy. Add the eggs gradually, beating well after each addition. Add the vanilla essence and beat until well combined. Transfer to a large bowl. Using a metal spoon, fold in the sifted flours, bicarbonate of soda (baking soda) and cocoa alternately with the buttermilk. Mix until combined and the mixture is smooth.

Pour the mixture into the tin and smooth the surface. Bake for 50–60 minutes, or until a skewer comes out clean when inserted into the centre. Leave the cake in the tin for 30 minutes before turning it onto a wire rack to cool. When cold, cut horizontally into 3 layers, using a long serrated knife. The easiest way to do this is to rest the palm of one hand lightly on top of the cake while cutting into it. Turn the cake every few strokes so the knife cuts in evenly all the way around the edge. When you have gone the whole way round, cut through the middle. Remove the first layer so it will be easier to see what you are doing while cutting the next one.

To make chocolate shavings, leave the chocolate in a warm place for 10–15 minutes, or until soft but still firm. With a vegetable peeler, and using long strokes, shave curls of chocolate from the side of the block. If the block is too soft, chill it to firm it up. Making curls takes a little practice to perfect.

To assemble, place one cake layer on a serving plate and brush liberally with Kirsch. Spread evenly with one-fifth of the whipped cream. Top with half the cherries. Continue layering with the remaining cake, cream and liqueur cherries, finishing with the cream on top. Spread the cream evenly on the outside of the cake. Coat the side with chocolate shavings by laying the shavings on a small piece of greaseproof and then gently pressing them into the cream. If you use your hands, they will melt, so the paper acts as a barrier. Pipe rosettes of cream around the top edge of the cake and decorate with fresh or maraschino cherries on stalks and more chocolate shavings.

Serves 8–10

Chocolate Hazelnut Torte

- **500 g (1 lb 2 oz) dark (semi-sweet) chocolate, chopped**
- **6 eggs**
- **2 tablespoons hazelnut-flavoured liqueur (see Note)**
- **1½ cups (165 g/5¾ oz) ground hazelnuts**
- **1 cup (250 ml/8½ fl oz) cream, whipped**
- **12 whole hazelnuts, lightly roasted**

Chocolate Topping
- **200 g (7 oz) dark (semi-sweet) chocolate, chopped**
- **¾ cup (185 ml/6½ fl oz) cream**
- **1 tablespoon hazelnut-flavoured liqueur**

Preheat the oven to slow 150°C (300°F/Gas 2). Grease a deep 20 cm (8 inch) round cake tin and line with baking paper.

Put the chocolate in a heatproof bowl. Half fill a saucepan with water and bring to the boil. Remove from the heat and place the bowl over the pan, making sure it is not touching the water. Stir occasionally until the chocolate is melted.

Put the eggs in a large heatproof bowl and add the liqueur. Place the bowl over a saucepan of barely simmering water over low heat, making sure it does not touch the water. Beat with an electric mixer on high speed for 7 minutes, or until the mixture is light and foamy. Remove from the heat.

Using a metal spoon, quickly and lightly fold the melted chocolate and ground nuts into the egg mixture until just combined. Fold in the cream and pour the mixture into the tin. Place the tin in a shallow baking dish. Pour in enough hot water to come halfway up the side of the tin.

Bake for 1 hour, or until just set. Remove the tin from the baking dish. Cool to room temperature, cover with plastic wrap and refrigerate overnight.

Cut an 18 cm (7 inch) circle from heavy cardboard. Invert the chilled cake onto the disc so that the base of the cake becomes the top. Place on a wire rack over a baking tray (sheet) and remove the baking paper. Allow the cake to return to room temperature before you start to decorate.

To make the topping, combine the chopped chocolate, cream and liqueur in a small pan. Heat gently over low heat, stirring, until the chocolate is melted and the mixture is smooth.

Pour the chocolate mixture over the cake in the centre, tilting slightly to cover the cake evenly. Tap the baking tray (sheet) gently on the bench so that the top is level and the icing runs completely down the side of the cake. Place the hazelnuts around the edge of the cake. Refrigerate just until the topping has set and the cake is firm. Carefully transfer the cake to a serving plate, and cut into thin wedges to serve.

Note: Brandy or whisky can also be used, if preferred. This is a very rich cake so you only need to serve small portions.

Serves 10

Banana Cake

- **125 g (4⅓ oz) butter**
- **½ cup (125 g/4⅓ oz) caster (berry) sugar**
- **2 eggs, lightly beaten**
- **1 teaspoon vanilla essence**
- **4 medium ripe bananas, mashed**
- **1 teaspoon bicarbonate of soda (baking soda)**
- **½ cup (125 ml/4¼ fl oz) milk**
- **2 cups (250 g/8¾ oz) self-raising flour**

Butter Frosting
- **125 g (4⅓ oz) butter**
- **¾ cup (90 g/3¼ oz) icing (powdered) sugar**
- **1 tablespoon lemon juice**
- **¼ cup (15 g/½ oz) flaked coconut, toasted**

Preheat the oven to moderate 180°C (350°F/Gas 4). Brush a 20 cm (8 inch) round cake tin with oil or melted butter and line the base with baking paper. Using electric beaters, beat butter and sugar in a small bowl until light and creamy. Add the eggs gradually, beating thoroughly after each addition. Add the vanilla and mashed banana and beat until combined.

Transfer the mixture to a large bowl. Dissolve the soda in the milk. Using a metal spoon, fold in the sifted flour alternately with the milk. Stir until all the ingredients are just combined and the mixture is smooth. Spoon into the prepared tin; smooth the surface. Bake for 1 hour or until a skewer comes out clean when inserted into the centre of cake. Leave in the tin for 10 minutes before turning onto a wire rack to cool.

To make Frosting: Using electric beaters, beat the butter, icing (powdered) sugar and lemon juice until smooth and creamy. Spread onto the cooled cake, sprinkle with toasted coconut flakes.

Serves 8

Orange Berry Sponge

- ½ cup (60 g/2 oz) plain (all-purpose) flour
- ¼ cup (30 g/1 oz) cornflour (cornstarch)
- 1 teaspoon baking powder
- ¼ cup (60 ml/2 fl oz) milk
- 50 g (1¾ oz) butter
- ¾ cup (185 g/6½ oz) caster (berry) sugar
- 3 eggs
- 3 egg yolks
- 1 teaspoon finely grated orange rind
- 1½ cups (375 ml/13 fl oz) cream
- 3–4 teaspoons icing (powdered) sugar
- 1–2 tablespoons triple sec liqueur
- 250 g (8¾ oz) strawberries, hulled and sliced
- 250 g (8¾ oz) blueberries
- 2 tablespoons flaked almonds, toasted
- icing (powdered) sugar, for dusting

Preheat the oven to moderate 180°C (350°F/Gas 4). Brush a 30 × 20 cm (12 × 8 inch) shallow cake tin with melted butter or oil. Line the base and sides with baking paper extending 3 cm (1¼ inches) over each edge. Sift the flours and baking powder twice onto a sheet of greaseproof paper. Place milk and butter in pan. Stir over medium heat until butter has melted. (Take care not to boil mixture, but keep it hot.)

Place the sugar, eggs and yolks in a large heatproof bowl. Stand the bowl over a pan of simmering water. Using electric beaters, beat the mixture over heat until pale yellow, thick and glossy and increased in volume. Remove bowl from heat. Stir in rind until well combined.

Using a metal spoon, fold in a third of the flour at a time. Fold in the hot butter mixture and stir until just smooth. (Do not over-mix. It is important to keep as much volume as possible in the mixture.) Spoon the mixture into the prepared tin. Bake for 25–30 minutes or until springy to touch. Leave in the tin to cool.

Turn the cake out onto a flat work surface. Using a sharp serrated knife, trim away any dark patches. Cut the cake into three even rectangles, around 10 × 20 cm (4 × 8 inches) each.

Beat the cream and icing (powdered) sugar with electric beaters until stiff peaks form. Stir in the liqueur.

Spread one quarter of the cream mixture over one layer of cake. Top with a third of the berries. Add a second layer of cake; press down lightly. Repeat the process with cream and berries, reserving some berries for the top and finishing with the third cake layer.

Spread the remaining cream evenly over the top and sides of the cake. Decorate the cake with the remaining berries and toasted flaked almonds. Dust the cake lightly with icing (powdered) sugar.

Note: To toast almonds, scatter on an oven tray (sheet) lined with baking paper. Place in a preheated moderate 180°C (350°F/Gas 4) oven for 5–10 minutes. Do not use frozen or canned berries in this recipe as they are too soggy. If blueberries are unavailable, substitute any berry in season, such as blackberries, or omit the second berry variety entirely, if you prefer.

Serves 8–10

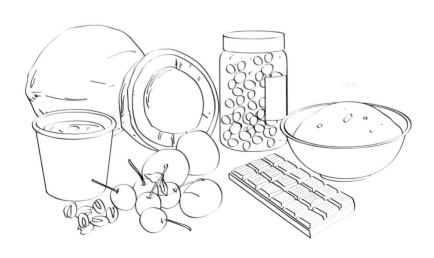

Light Fruit Cake

- 185 g (6½ oz) unsalted butter, softened
- ½ cup (125 g/4⅓ oz) caster (berry) sugar
- 3 eggs
- 1 cup (160 g/5⅔ oz) sultanas (golden raisins)
- ⅔ cup (100 g/3½ oz) dried currants
- ¼ cup (60 g/2 oz) chopped glacé (glazed) apricots
- ¼ cup (45 g/1⅔ oz) chopped glacé (glazed) figs
- 1 cup (240 g/8½ oz) coarsely chopped glacé (glazed) cherries
- ½ cup (80 g/2¾ oz) macadamia nuts, coarsely chopped
- 1½ cups (185 g/6½ oz) plain (all-purpose) flour
- ½ cup (60 g/2 oz) self-raising flour
- ½ cup (125 ml/4¼ fl oz) milk
- 1 tablespoon sweet sherry
- nuts or glacé (glazed) cherries, for decoration

Preheat the oven to 160°C (315°F/Gas 2–3). Grease and line a deep 20 cm (8 inch) round or 18 cm (7 inch) square cake tin.

Cream the butter and sugar in a small bowl until just combined. Add the eggs, one at a time, beating well after each addition.

Transfer the mixture to a large bowl and stir in the fruit and nuts. Sift in half the flours and half the milk, stir to combine, then stir in the remaining flours and milk, and the sherry. Spoon into the prepared tin and tap the tin on the bench to remove any air bubbles. Smooth the surface with wet fingers and decorate the top with nuts or cherries, or both. Wrap the outside of the tin with paper. Sit the tin on several layers of newspaper in the oven and bake for 1¾–2 hours, or until a skewer inserted into the centre of the cake comes out clean. The top may need to be covered with a sheet of baking paper if it colours too much.

Remove from the oven, remove the top baking paper and wrap the tin in a thick tea towel until cool. Remove any remaining paper and wrap the cake well in aluminium foil, or store in an airtight container. Keeps for up to 2 weeks.

Serves 8

Sour Cherry Cake

- **125 g (4⅓ oz) unsalted butter, softened**
- **¾ cup (185 g/6½ oz) caster (berry) sugar**
- **2 eggs, lightly beaten**
- **½ cup (95 g/3⅓ oz) ground almonds**
- **1 cup (125 g/4⅓ oz) self-raising flour**
- **½ cup (60 g/2 oz) plain (all-purpose) flour**
- **½ cup (125 ml/4¼ fl oz) milk**
- **680 g (1 lb 8 oz) jar pitted morello cherries, well drained**
- **icing (powdered) sugar, to dust**

Preheat the oven to 180°C (350°F/Gas 4). Grease and flour a 23 cm (9 inch) fluted baba tin (bundt pan), shaking out any excess flour. Beat the butter and sugar with electric beaters until pale. Add the beaten egg gradually, beating well after each addition.

Stir in the ground almonds, then fold in the sifted flours alternately with the milk. Gently fold in the cherries. Spoon the mixture into the prepared tin and smooth the surface. Bake for 50 minutes, or until a skewer comes out clean when inserted into the centre of the cake. Leave to cool in the tin for 10 minutes before turning out onto a wire rack to cool. Dust with icing (powdered) sugar before serving.

Note: This cake is best eaten on the day it is made.

Serves 8–10

Zesty Olive Oil Cake

- 2 eggs
- ⅔ cup (160 g/5⅔ oz) caster (berry) sugar
- 2 teaspoons finely grated orange rind
- 2 teaspoons finely grated lemon rind

- ½ cup (125 ml/4¼ fl oz) olive oil
- 1½ cups (185 g/6½ oz) self-raising flour
- ¼ cup (60 ml/2 fl oz) milk
- ¼ cup (60 ml/2 fl oz) orange juice

Preheat the oven to 180°C (350°F/Gas 4). Lightly grease a shallow 20 cm (8 inch) round cake tin and line the base with baking paper. Whisk the eggs and sugar in a large mixing bowl until well combined. Add the orange and lemon rind, then gradually stir in the olive oil.

Stir in the sifted flour alternately with the milk and orange juice. Stir the mixture gently for 30 seconds with a wooden spoon. Pour into the prepared tin. Bake for 45 minutes, or until a skewer comes out clean when inserted into the centre of the cake. Leave to cool in the tin for 5 minutes before turning out onto a wire rack.

Note: This cake can be dusted with icing (powdered) sugar before serving, if desired.

Serves 8

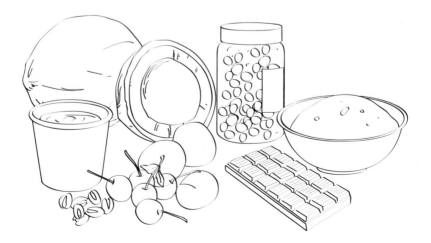

238

Yoghurt Cake with Syrup

- 185 g (6½ oz) unsalted butter, softened
- 1 cup (250 g/8¾ oz) caster (berry) sugar
- 5 eggs, separated
- 1 cup (250 g/8¾ oz) Greek-style yoghurt
- 2 teaspoons grated lemon rind
- ½ teaspoon vanilla essence
- 2¼ cups (280 g/9¾ oz) plain (all-purpose) flour
- ½ teaspoon bicarbonate of soda (baking soda)
- 2 teaspoons baking powder
- whipped cream, for serving

Syrup
- 1 cup (250 g/8¾ oz) caster (berry) sugar
- 1 cinnamon stick
- 4 cm (1½ inch) strip lemon rind
- 1 tablespoon lemon juice

Preheat the oven to moderate 180°C (350°F/Gas 4) and lightly grease a 20 × 10 cm (8 × 4 inch) loaf tin.

Cream the butter and sugar in a bowl with electric beaters until light and fluffy. Add the egg yolks gradually, beating well after each addition. Stir in the yoghurt, lemon rind and vanilla essence. Fold in the sifted flour, bicarbonate of soda (baking soda) and baking powder with a metal spoon.

Whisk the egg whites in a clean, dry bowl until stiff and gently fold into the mixture. Spoon into the tin and bake for 50 minutes, or until a skewer comes out clean when inserted into the centre of the cake. Cool, then turn out onto a wire rack.

Meanwhile, place the sugar and cinnamon stick in a small saucepan with ¾ cup (185 ml/6½ fl oz) cold water. Stir over medium heat until the sugar has dissolved. Bring to the boil, add the lemon rind and juice, then reduce the heat and simmer for 5–6 minutes. Strain, then pour the syrup over the hot cake and wait for most of it to be absorbed. Cut into slices and serve warm with whipped cream.

Serves 8–10

Coffee Liqueur Gateau

- 125 g (4⅓ oz) brazil nuts
- ⅔ cup (100 g/3½ oz) blanched almonds
- 80 g (2¾ oz) hazelnuts
- 2 tablespoons plain (all-purpose) flour
- ¾ cup (185 g/6½ oz) caster (berry) sugar
- 7 egg whites
- ¼ cup (60 ml/2 fl oz) coffee liqueur
- small chocolate buttons, to decorate (see Note)

- sifted icing (powdered) sugar, to dust

Coffee Cream
- 200 g (7 oz) butter
- 1 cup (150 g/5¼ oz) dark (semi-sweet) chocolate, melted
- 2–3 teaspoons icing (powdered) sugar
- 2 teaspoons warm water
- 3–4 teaspoons instant coffee powder

Preheat the oven to 180°C (350°F/Gas 4). Lightly grease a deep 20 cm (8 inch) round tin and line base and side with baking paper. Place the nuts on a baking tray (sheet) and roast for 5–10 minutes, or until golden. Rub the nuts vigorously in a clean tea towel to remove hazelnut skins. Place in a food processor and process until finely ground.

Transfer the ground nuts to a large bowl. Add the flour and 125 g (4⅓ oz) of the sugar and mix well. Using electric beaters, beat the egg whites in a large mixing bowl until soft peaks form. Gradually add the remaining sugar, beating until the mixture is thick and glossy and the sugar is dissolved. Using a metal spoon, fold the nut mixture into the egg mixture a third at a time. Spoon into the prepared tin and smooth the surface. Bake for 35–40 minutes, or until springy to the touch. Leave in the tin to cool.

To make the coffee cream, beat the butter in a small mixing bowl with electric beaters until light and creamy. Gradually pour in the melted chocolate, beating until well combined. Add the icing (powdered) sugar and combined water and coffee. Beat until smooth.

To assemble the gateau, turn the cake onto a flat working surface. Using a sharp serrated knife, carefully cut the cake horizontally into three layers. (Use the top layer of cake as the base of gateau.) Brush the first layer with half the liqueur. Spread with one fifth of the coffee cream.

Place the second cake layer on top. Brush with the remaining liqueur and spread with a quarter of the remaining coffee cream. Place the remaining layer on top. Spread top and sides with the remaining coffee cream.

Decorate with the chocolate buttons and dust with the icing (powdered) sugar. Refrigerate for 1 hour or until firm.

Storage: This cake can be prepared to 3 days in advance. Keep refrigerated in an airtight container.

Note: Make your own chocolate buttons with 150 g (5¼ oz) melted chocolate melts. Line two baking trays (sheets) with baking paper. Place half the chocolate in a small paper icing bag. Seal the end of the bag, then snip off tip. Pipe small chocolate buttons onto trays (sheets). Tap trays (sheets) lightly on bench to flatten buttons and leave to set. Peel off paper and use to decorate.

Serves 8–10

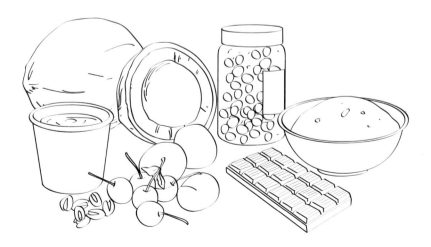

Chocolate Cherry Cake

- 200 g (7 oz) dark (semi-sweet) chocolate, chopped
- 250 g (8¾ oz) unsalted butter, chopped
- 1 cup (230 g/8¼ oz) firmly packed soft brown sugar
- 1 teaspoon vanilla essence
- 1¼ cups (155 g/5½ oz) self-raising flour
- ½ cup (45 g/1⅔ oz) desiccated (fine) coconut
- 2 eggs
- 1 cup (180 g/6⅓ oz) pitted sour cherries, drained
- icing (powdered) sugar, to dust
- fresh cherries, to garnish

Preheat the oven to 160°C (315°F/Gas 2–3). Lightly grease a 23 cm (9 inch) round cake tin and line the base with baking paper. Grease the paper. Place the chocolate, butter, sugar and vanilla essence in a heatproof bowl. Sit the bowl, making sure the base does not touch the water, over a saucepan of simmering water. Stir occasionally until the chocolate has melted and the mixture is smooth. Remove the saucepan from the heat and sit the bowl in a sink of cold water until cooled.

Combine the flour and coconut in a food processor. Add the chocolate mixture and eggs and process in short bursts until the mixture is just combined. Add the pitted sour cherries to the food processor and process until they are just chopped.

Pour the mixture into the prepared tin and bake for 1 hour 10 minutes, or until a skewer comes out clean when inserted into the centre of the cake. Leave the cake in the tin for 15 minutes before carefully turning out onto a wire rack to cool completely. If desired, dust with icing (powdered) sugar and decorate with fresh cherries.

Serves 8

Flourless Orange and Almond Cake

- 2 oranges
- 1½ cups (280 g/9¾ oz) ground almonds
- 1 cup (250 g/8¾ oz) caster (berry) sugar
- 1 teaspoon baking powder
- 1 teaspoon vanilla essence
- 1 teaspoon triple sec liqueur
- 6 eggs, lightly beaten
- icing (powdered) sugar, to dust

Wash the oranges well to remove any sprays or waxes. Place the whole oranges in a large saucepan, add enough water to cover them and place a small plate on top to keep the oranges submerged. Gradually bring the water to the boil, then reduce the heat and leave them to simmer for 40 minutes, or until the oranges are very soft. Preheat the oven to 180°C (350°F/Gas 4). Place the cake tin on a sheet of baking paper and trace around the outside, then cut out the shape with a pair of scissors. Lightly grease the tin, then place the baking paper, pencil-side down, onto the base of the tin and smooth out any bubbles.

Cut each of the oranges into quarters and leave the pieces to cool. Remove any pips, then place the oranges in the bowl of a food processor and blend until they form a very smooth pulp. Add the ground almonds, caster (berry) sugar, baking powder, vanilla essence and liqueur and, using the pulse button, process until all of the ingredients are combined. Add the egg and process again until just combined – take care not to over-process. Pour the orange mixture into the prepared tin and bake for 50 minutes, or until the cake is firm and leaves the side of the tin. Leave to cool completely in the tin. Dust with icing (powdered) sugar to serve.

Notes: This makes a great dessert cake served with fruit and cream. Try this cake with an orange syrup. Place 2 cups (500 ml/17 fl oz) of freshly squeezed and strained orange juice in a saucepan with ¾ cup (185 g/6½ oz) caster (berry) sugar and ¼ cup (60 ml/2 fl oz) Sauternes (white dessert wine). Place the saucepan over a medium heat and stir until the sugar is dissolved. Reduce the heat and simmer for about 20 minutes, or until the liquid is reduced by half and has become slightly syrupy. Skim off any scum that forms on the surface as you go. The syrup will thicken further as it cools. Poke some random holes in the top of the cake to let the syrup absorb, or just drizzle the syrup over the cake before dusting with icing (powdered) sugar and serving.

Serves 8

Flourless Chocolate Cake

- 500 g (1 lb 2 oz) good-quality dark (semi-sweet) chocolate, chopped
- 6 eggs
- 2 tablespoons hazelnut-flavoured liqueur or brandy
- 1½ cups (165 g/5¾ oz) ground hazelnuts
- 1 cup (250 ml/8½ fl oz) cream, whipped
- icing (powdered) sugar, to dust
- thick (double/heavy) cream, to serve (optional)

Preheat the oven to slow 150°C (300°F/Gas 2). Grease a deep 20 cm (8 inch) round cake tin and line the base with baking paper.

Half-fill a saucepan with water and bring to the boil. Remove from the heat and sit the chocolate in a heatproof bowl over the pan, making sure it is not touching the water. Stir occasionally until melted.

Put the eggs in a large heatproof bowl and add the liqueur or brandy. Place the bowl over a pan of just simmering water on low heat, making sure the bowl does not touch the water. Beat the mixture with electric beaters on high speed for 7 minutes, or until light and foamy. Remove from the heat.

Using a metal spoon, quickly and lightly fold the chocolate and nuts into the egg mixture until just combined. Fold in the cream and pour into the cake tin. Place the tin in a shallow roasting tin. Pour enough hot water into the roasting tin to come halfway up the side of the cake tin. Bake for 1 hour, or until just set. Remove from the roasting tin and cool to room temperature. Cover with plastic wrap and refrigerate overnight.

Invert the cake onto a plate and remove the baking paper. Cut into slices, dust lightly with icing (powdered) sugar and serve with thick (double/heavy) cream.

Serves 10

Carrot Cake

- 2½ cups (310 g/11 oz) self-raising flour
- 1 teaspoon bicarbonate of soda (baking soda)
- 2 teaspoons ground cinnamon
- 1 teaspoon mixed spice
- ½ cup (95 g/3⅓ oz) soft brown sugar
- ½ cup (60 g/2 oz) sultanas (golden raisins)
- 2 eggs, lightly beaten

- 2 tablespoons vegetable oil
- ⅓ cup (80 ml/2¾ fl oz) low-fat milk
- 140 g (5 oz) apple puree
- 300 g (10½ oz) carrot, coarsely grated

Ricotta Topping
- 125 g (4⅓ oz) ricotta
- ¼ cup (30 g/1 oz) icing (powdered) sugar
- ½ teaspoon grated lime rind

Grease a 10 × 18 cm (4 × 7 inch) loaf tin and line the base with baking paper. Preheat the oven to 180°C (350°F/Gas 4). Sift the flour, soda and spices into a large bowl. Stir in the sugar and sultanas (golden raisins).

Mix the eggs, oil, milk and apple puree and stir into the dry ingredients. Stir in the carrot. Spread into the tin and bake for 1¼ hours, or until a skewer comes out clean. Cool in the tin for 5 minutes, then on a wire rack.

To make the topping, beat the ingredients together until smooth. Spread over the cake.

Makes 14 slices

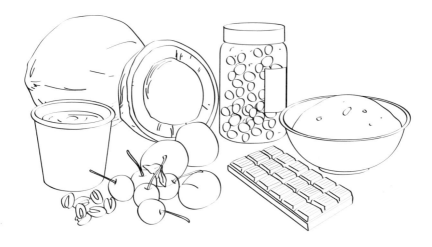

Lemon Berry Cheesecake

- 60 g (2 oz) plain biscuits (cookies), finely crushed
- 30 g (1 oz) butter, melted
- 300 g (10½ oz) ricotta
- 2 tablespoons caster (berry) sugar
- 2 × 130 g (4¼ oz) tubs low-fat fromage frais
- 2 × 130 g (4½ oz) tubs low-fat lemon fromage frais
- 2 teaspoons finely grated lemon rind
- 2 tablespoons fresh lemon juice
- 1 tablespoon gelatine
- 2 egg whites
- 250 g (8¾ oz) strawberries, halved

Lightly oil and line the base and sides of a 20 cm (8 inch) diameter springform tin with plastic wrap. Combine the biscuit (cookie) crumbs and butter in a small bowl and press evenly over the base of the tin. Refrigerate while making the filling.

Combine the ricotta and sugar in a food processor until smooth. Add all the fromage frais, the lemon rind and juice and mix well. Put ¼ cup (60 ml/2 fl oz) water in a small bowl, sprinkle the gelatine in an even layer onto the surface and leave to go spongy. Bring a small pan of water to the boil, remove from the heat and put the gelatine bowl in the pan. The water should come halfway up the side of the bowl. Stir the gelatine until clear and dissolved, then cool slightly. Stir the gelatine mixture into the ricotta mixture, then transfer to a large bowl. Beat the egg whites until soft peaks form, then fold into the ricotta mixture.

Pour the mixture into the prepared tin and refrigerate for several hours or overnight, until set. Carefully remove from the tin by removing the side and gently easing the plastic from underneath. Decorate with the halved strawberries.

Serves 12

Slices
and
Bars

Fudge Brownies

- cooking oil spray
- ½ cup (60 g/2 oz) plain (all-purpose) flour
- ½ cup (60 g/2 oz) self-raising flour
- 1 teaspoon bicarbonate of soda (baking soda)
- ¾ cup (90 g/3¼ oz) cocoa powder
- 2 eggs
- 1¼ cups (310 g/11 oz) caster (berry) sugar
- 2 teaspoons vanilla essence
- 2 tablespoons vegetable oil
- 200 g (7 oz) low-fat fromage frais
- 140 ml (4¾ fl oz) apple puree
- icing (powdered) sugar, for dusting

Preheat the oven to moderate 180°C (350°F/Gas 4). Spray a 30 × 20 cm (12 × 8 inch) shallow baking tin with oil and line the base of the tin with baking paper.

Sift the flours, bicarbonate of soda (baking soda) and cocoa powder into a large bowl. Mix the eggs, sugar, vanilla essence, oil, fromage frais and puree in a large bowl, stirring until well combined. Add to the flour and stir until combined. Spread into the prepared tin and bake for about 30 minutes, or until a skewer inserted in the centre comes out clean.

The brownie will sink slightly in the centre as it cools. Leave in the pan for 5 minutes before turning onto a wire rack to cool. Dust with icing (powdered) sugar before cutting into pieces to serve.

Makes 18 pieces

Chocolate Caramel Slice

- **125 g (4⅓ oz) plain sweet biscuits (cookies), crushed**
- **80 g (2¾ oz) unsalted butter, melted**
- **2 tablespoons desiccated (fine) coconut**
- **400 g (14 oz) can sweetened condensed milk**
- **125 g (4⅓ oz) butter**
- **⅓ cup (90 g/3¼ oz) caster (berry) sugar**
- **⅓ cup golden (corn) syrup**
- **250 g (8¾ oz) milk chocolate melts (see Variation)**
- **1 tablespoon vegetable oil**

Lightly grease a shallow 30 × 20 cm (12 × 8 inch) rectangular cake tin and line with aluminium foil. Grease the foil. Combine the biscuits (cookies), melted butter and coconut together in a medium mixing bowl. Press the mixture evenly into the prepared tin and smooth the surface.

Combine the condensed milk, butter, sugar and syrup in a small pan. Stir over low heat for 15 minutes or until the sugar has dissolved and the mixture is smooth, thick and lightly browned. Remove from heat and leave to cool slightly. Pour over the biscuit (cookie) base and smooth the surface.

Place the milk chocolate melts and oil in a small heatproof bowl. Stand over a pan of simmering water, stir until melted. Spread the chocolate mixture over caramel. Allow to partially set before marking into 24 triangles. Refrigerate until firm.

Storage: Slice may be stored in an airtight container for up to 2 days.

Variation: Use dark chocolate (semi-sweet) melts in place of milk chocolate.

Makes 24 triangles

Chocolate Peppermint Slice

- ⅔ cup (85 g/3 oz) self-raising flour
- ¼ cup (30 g/1 oz) cocoa powder
- ½ cup (45 g/1⅔ oz) desiccated (fine) coconut
- ¼ cup (60 g/2 oz) sugar
- 140 g (5 oz) unsalted butter, melted
- 1 egg, lightly beaten

Peppermint Filling
- 1½ cups (185 g/6½ oz) icing (powdered) sugar, sifted
- 30 g (1 oz) copha (white vegetable shortening), melted
- 2 tablespoons milk
- ½ teaspoon peppermint essence

Chocolate Topping
- 185 g (6 oz) dark (semi-sweet) chocolate, chopped
- 30 g (1 oz) copha

Preheat the oven to 180°C (350°F/Gas 4). Lightly grease a shallow tin measuring 18 × 28 cm (7 × 11 inches) and line with baking paper, leaving the paper hanging over on the two long sides. This makes it easy to lift the cooked slice out of the tin.

Sift the flour and cocoa into a bowl. Stir in the coconut and sugar, then add the butter and egg and mix well. Press the mixture firmly into the tin. Bake for 15 minutes, then press down with the back of a spoon and leave to cool.

For the peppermint filling, sift the icing (powdered) sugar into a bowl. Stir in the copha, milk and peppermint essence. Spread over the base and refrigerate for 5–10 minutes, or until firm.

For the chocolate topping, put the chocolate and copha in a heatproof bowl. Half fill a saucepan with water, bring to the boil, then remove from the heat. Sit the bowl over the saucepan, making sure the base of the bowl does not touch the water. Stir occasionally until the chocolate and copha have melted and combined. Spread evenly over the filling. Refrigerate the slice for 20 minutes, or until the chocolate topping is firm. Carefully lift the slice from the tin, using the paper as handles. Cut into pieces with a warm knife to give clean edges. Store in an airtight container in the refrigerator.

Makes 24 pieces

Berry Almond Slice

- 1 sheet puff pastry
- 150 g (5¼ oz) unsalted butter
- ¾ cup (185 g/6½ oz) caster (berry) sugar
- 3 eggs, lightly beaten
- 2 tablespoons grated lemon rind
- ⅔ cup (125 g/4⅓ oz) ground almonds
- 2 tablespoons plain (all-purpose) flour
- 150 g (5¼ oz) raspberries
- 150 g (5¼ oz) blackberries
- icing (powdered) sugar, to dust

Preheat the oven to 200°C (400°F/Gas 6). Lightly grease a 23 cm (9 inch) square shallow tin and line with baking paper, overhanging two opposite sides.

Place the pastry on a baking tray (sheet) lined with baking paper. Prick all over with a fork and bake for 15 minutes, or until golden. Ease pastry into the tin, trimming the edges if necessary. Reduce the oven to 180°C (350°F/Gas 4).

Using electric beaters, beat the butter and sugar in a mixing bowl until light and fluffy. Gradually add the egg, beating after every addition, then the lemon rind. Fold in the almonds and flour. Spread over the pastry base.

Scatter the fruit on top and bake for 1 hour, or until lightly golden. Cool in the tin before lifting out to cut. Dust with icing (powdered) sugar and serve.

Makes 15 pieces

Raspberry Linzer Slice

- 90 g (3¼ oz) butter
- ½ cup (125 g/4⅓ oz) caster (berry) sugar
- 1 teaspoon vanilla essence
- 1 egg, lightly beaten
- ⅔ cup (85 g/3 oz) plain (all-purpose) flour
- ⅓ cup (40 g/1½ oz) self-raising flour
- ¾ cup (240 g/8½ oz) raspberry jam (jelly), warmed

Hazelnut Topping
- 125 g (4⅓ oz) butter
- ⅓ cup (90 g/3¼ oz) caster (berry) sugar
- 1 egg, lightly beaten
- ½ cup (60 g/2 oz) plain (all-purpose) flour
- 1 tablespoon custard powder
- 1 teaspoon baking powder
- 1 cup (120 g/4¼ oz) firmly packed plain cake crumbs
- ½ cup (60 g/2 oz) ground hazelnuts
- ⅓ cup (80 ml/2¾ fl oz) milk

Preheat the oven to 180°C (350°F/Gas 4). Lightly grease a 20 × 30 cm (8 × 12 inch) shallow tin and line with baking paper, overhanging two opposite sides.

Using electric beaters, beat the butter, sugar and vanilla essence in a mixing bowl until light and creamy. Add the egg to the mixture gradually, beating well after each addition.

Sift the flours and fold into the mixture with a metal spoon. Spread into the tin and spread evenly with the raspberry jam (jelly).

To make the hazelnut topping, beat the butter and sugar with electric beaters until light and creamy. Add the egg gradually, beating well after each addition. Sift the flour, custard powder and baking powder and fold into the mixture with the cake crumbs and ground hazelnuts. Fold in the milk and spread over the base.

Bake for 45 minutes, or until firm and golden brown. Leave to cool in the tin before cutting to serve.

Makes 24 pieces

Chocolate Carrot Slice

- 1 cup (125 g/4⅓ oz) self-raising flour
- 1 teaspoon ground cinnamon
- ¾ cup (185 g/6½ oz) caster (berry) sugar
- ½ cup (80 g/2¾ oz) finely grated carrot
- 1 cup (185 g/6½ oz) mixed dried fruit
- ½ cup (90 g/3¼ oz) choc chips (bits/morsels)
- ⅓ cup (30 g/1 oz) desiccated (fine) coconut
- 2 eggs, lightly beaten
- 90 g (3¼ oz) unsalted butter, melted
- ⅓ cup (40 g/1½ oz) chopped walnuts

Cream Cheese Frosting
- 125 g (4⅓ oz) cream cheese
- 30 g (1 oz) unsalted butter
- 1½ cups (185 g/6½ oz) icing (powdered) sugar, sifted
- 1 teaspoon hot water

Preheat the oven to moderate 180°C (350°F/Gas 4). Brush a shallow 23 cm (9 inch) square cake tin with melted butter or oil and line the base and sides with baking paper.

Sift the flour and cinnamon into a large bowl. Add the caster (berry) sugar, grated carrot, mixed fruit, choc chips (bits/morsels) and coconut and stir until just combined. Add the beaten eggs and butter and then stir until combined.

Spread the mixture evenly into the prepared tin and smooth the surface. Bake for 30 minutes or until golden. Cool the cake in the tin and turn out onto a flat surface.

To make Cream Cheese Frosting: Using electric beaters, beat the cream cheese and butter in a small bowl until smooth. Add the icing (powdered) sugar and beat for 2 minutes or until the mixture is light and fluffy. Add the water and beat until well combined.

Spread the slice with frosting using a flat-bladed knife and sprinkle with walnuts. Cut into 16 squares, then cut each square into triangles.

Makes 32

Spiced Apple Slice

- 750 g (1 lb 10 oz) green apples
- ⅓ cup (90 g/3¼ oz) sugar
- ½ teaspoon ground cloves
- 2 tablespoons lemon juice
- 1 cup (125 g/4⅓ oz) plain (all-purpose) flour
- 1 cup (125 g/4⅓ oz) self-raising flour
- 1 teaspoon ground cloves, extra
- ½ teaspoon ground cinnamon
- 150 g (5¼ oz) butter
- ½ cup (125 g/4⅓ oz) caster (berry) sugar
- 1 teaspoon vanilla essence
- 1 egg, lightly beaten
- 1 tablespoon milk
- 1 tablespoon caster (berry) sugar, extra
- 1 teaspoon ground cinnamon, extra

Brush a 20 × 30 cm (8 × 12 inch) shallow tin with oil. Line the base with paper and grease the paper. Preheat the oven to 180°C (350°F/Gas 4). Peel, core and slice the apples and put in a pan with the sugar, cloves and juice. Stir over heat to warm. Cover and simmer, stirring often, for 20 minutes or until soft. Remove from the heat, drain and cool.

Sift the flours with the extra cloves and cinnamon. Beat the butter and sugar until light and creamy. Add the vanilla and egg and beat thoroughly. Fold in the flour in batches, mixing after each addition. If the mixture is too dry, add a little milk. Knead gently on a lightly floured surface until smooth. Divide in half, cover with plastic wrap and chill for 30 minutes.

Roll out one portion of pastry to fit the tin base. Spread with apple filling. Place the second pastry sheet on top of the filling and press down gently.

Brush the top with milk and sprinkle with the extra sugar and cinnamon. Bake for 30 minutes or until golden brown. Leave for 15 minutes, then turn onto a wire rack to cool.

Serves 8

Continental Slice

- 125 g (4⅓ oz) butter
- ½ cup (125 g/4⅓ oz) caster (berry) sugar
- ¼ cup (30 g/1 oz) cocoa
- 250 g (8¾ oz) shredded wheatmeal biscuits (graham crackers/digestive biscuits), crushed
- ¾ cup (65 g/2⅓ oz) desiccated (fine) coconut
- ¼ cup (30 g/1 oz) chopped hazelnuts
- ¼ cup (60 g/2 oz) chopped glacé (glazed) cherries
- 1 egg, lightly beaten
- 1 teaspoon vanilla essence

Topping
- 60 g (2 oz) butter
- 1¾ cups (215 g/7½ oz) icing (powdered) sugar
- 2 tablespoons custard powder
- 1 tablespoon hot water
- 1 tablespoon triple sec liqueur
- 125 g (4⅓ oz) dark (semi-sweet) chocolate
- 60 g (2 oz) copha (white vegetable shortening)

Line the base and sides of an 18 × 28 cm (7 × 11 inch) shallow tin with foil. Combine the butter, sugar and cocoa and stir over low heat until the butter melts and mixture is well combined. Cook, stirring, for 1 minute. Remove from the heat and cool slightly.

Combine the biscuit (cracker) crumbs, coconut, hazelnuts and cherries in a large bowl. Make a well in the centre; add the butter mixture, egg and vanilla all at once and stir well. Press the mixture firmly into the prepared tin. Refrigerate until firm.

Beat the butter until creamy. Gradually add the combined icing (powdered) sugar and custard powder, alternately with the combined water and liqueur. Beat the mixture until light and fluffy. Spread evenly over the base and then refrigerate until set.

Combine the chocolate and copha (shortening) in a heatproof bowl; stand bowl over a pan of simmering water and stir over low heat until chocolate melts and mixture is smooth. Spread over the slice. Refrigerate for 4 hours or until firm. Cut into squares to serve.

Makes 36

Thai Sticky Rice Slice

- 2½ cups (500 g/1 lb 2 oz) glutinous rice
- 2½ cups (600 ml/20 fl oz) coconut milk
- ½ cup (125 g/4⅓ oz) caster (berry) sugar

Topping
- 1 cup (90 g/3¼ oz) desiccated (fine) coconut
- ¼ cup (60 ml/2 fl oz) coconut milk, heated
- 90 g (3¼ oz) palm sugar, grated

Put the rice in a large glass bowl and cover with water. Soak for 8 hours or overnight; drain. Line a 30 × 20 cm (12 × 8 inch) shallow tin with baking paper, overlapping the two long sides. Line a large bamboo steamer with baking paper.

Spread the steamer base with rice, cover and place over a wok. Half-fill the wok with boiling water. Steam for 45–50 minutes, or until the grains are softened. Top up the wok with water when necessary.

Put the rice, coconut milk and sugar in a large heavy-based pan. Stir over low heat for 10 minutes, or until all the coconut milk is absorbed. Spoon into the tin and flatten the surface. Set aside to cool and firm.

For the topping, put the coconut in a small bowl and mix in the coconut milk. Put the palm sugar and 3 tablespoons water in a small pan and stir over low heat for 3 minutes, or until the sugar has dissolved and the syrup has thickened slightly. Stir in the coconut and continue to stir until the mixture holds together. Cover and set aside to cool. Spread the topping over the rice base. Cut into diamonds for serving. Serve at room temperature.

Note: These are best eaten on the same day. Chilling firms the mixture and it loses its flavour. Glutinous rice and palm sugar are available from Asian speciality stores. Palm sugar can be crushed with a rolling pin.

Makes 25–30

Hard Caramels

- 1 cup (250 g/8¾ oz) sugar
- 90 g (3¼ oz) butter
- 2 tablespoons golden (corn) syrup
- ⅓ cup (80 ml/2¾ fl oz) liquid glucose

- ½ cup (90 ml/3 fl oz) canned condensed milk
- 250 g (8¾ oz) dark (semi-sweet) chocolate, chopped

Grease the base and sides of a 20 cm (8 inch) square cake tin, then line with baking paper and grease the paper. Combine the sugar, butter, golden (corn) syrup, liquid glucose and condensed milk in a heavy-based saucepan. Stir over medium heat without boiling until the butter has melted and the sugar has dissolved completely. Brush the sugar crystals from the sides of the saucepan with a wet pastry brush.

Bring to the boil, reduce the heat slightly and boil, stirring, for about 10–15 minutes, or until a teaspoon of mixture dropped into cold water reaches hard ball stage (forming a firm ball that holds its shape). If using a sugar thermometer, the mixture must reach 120°C (250 °F). Remove from the heat immediately. Pour into the tin and leave to cool. While the caramel is still warm, mark into 49 squares with an oiled knife. When cold, cut through completely into squares.

Line two baking trays (sheets) with foil. Place the chocolate in a small heatproof bowl. Bring a saucepan of water to the boil, then remove the saucepan from the heat. Sit the bowl over the saucepan, making sure the bowl doesn't touch the water. Stir until the chocolate has melted. Remove from the heat and cool slightly. Using two forks, dip the caramels one at a time into the chocolate to coat. Lift out, drain the excess chocolate, then place on the trays (sheets) and leave to set.

Makes 49

Triple-Decker Fudge Slice

- ½ cup (60 g/2 oz) plain (all-purpose) flour
- 2 tablespoons cocoa powder
- 2 tablespoons caster (berry) sugar
- 60 g (2 oz) butter, melted
- 1 tablespoon milk
- ½ teaspoon vanilla essence

Vanilla Topping
- 250 g (8¾ oz) cream cheese, cubed
- ⅓ cup (90 g/3¼ oz) caster (berry) sugar
- 1 egg
- 1 teaspoon vanilla essence

Chocolate Topping
- 125 g (4⅓ oz) milk chocolate, chopped
- 125 g (4⅓ oz) butter, chopped
- 2 eggs, lightly beaten
- ½ cup (125 g/4⅓ oz) caster (berry) sugar
- ¼ cup (30 g/1 oz) plain (all-purpose) flour
- icing (powdered) sugar, to dust

Lightly grease an 18 × 28 cm (7 × 11 inch) shallow tin and line with baking paper, overhanging two opposite sides.

Sift the flour, cocoa and sugar into a bowl. Add the butter, milk and vanilla and mix well to form a dough. Gently knead for 1 minute, adding more flour if sticky. Press into the prepared tin and refrigerate for 20 minutes. Preheat the oven to 190°C (375°F/Gas 5).

Cover the pastry with baking paper, fill with baking beads or rice and bake for 10–15 minutes. Remove the paper and beads or rice and reduce the heat to 180°C (350°F/Gas 4). Bake for 5–10 minutes, then leave to cool.

To make the vanilla topping, beat the cream cheese in a mixing bowl until smooth. Gradually beat in the sugar, then the egg and vanilla essence. Beat well, pour over the base and refrigerate.

To make the chocolate topping, melt the chocolate and butter in a small saucepan, stirring over very low heat until smooth. Mix together the eggs and sugar. Stir in the chocolate mixture and flour until just combined.

Pour the chocolate topping over the cold vanilla topping and smooth with a spoon. Reduce the oven to 160°C (315°F/Gas 2–3) and bake for 35–40 minutes, or until just set. Leave to cool completely, then refrigerate for 2 hours, or until firm. Dust with icing (powdered) sugar before cutting and serving.

Makes 20 pieces

Passion Mallow Slice

- 150 g (5¼ oz) butter
- ¼ cup (60 g/2 oz) caster (berry) sugar
- ½ teaspoon vanilla essence
- 1 cup (125 g/4⅓ oz) plain (all-purpose) flour
- ½ cup (60 g/2 oz) self-raising flour

- 250 g (8¾ oz) white marshmallows
- ½ cup (125 ml/4¼ fl oz) milk
- 2 tablespoons caster (berry) sugar
- 2 teaspoons lemon juice
- 1¼ cups (315 ml/11 fl oz) cream, lightly whipped

Marshmallow Topping
- ½ cup (125 ml/4¼ fl oz) passionfruit pulp (or 5–6 passionfruit)

Preheat the oven to 180°C (350°F/Gas 4). Lightly grease an 18 × 28 cm (7 × 11 inch) shallow tin and line with baking paper, overhanging two opposite sides.

Using electric beaters, beat the butter and sugar in a mixing bowl until light and creamy, and the sugar has dissolved. Stir in the vanilla essence. Sift the flours into a bowl, then fold into the butter mixture and mix to a soft dough. Knead gently to bring together.

Press the dough into the prepared tin and smooth with the back of a spoon. Lightly prick the dough and bake for 25 minutes, or until golden. Remove from the oven and leave to cool completely.

To make the topping, put the passionfruit, marshmallows, milk and sugar in a pan and stir over low heat until the marshmallows have melted.

Stir in the lemon juice and transfer to a bowl to cool. Refrigerate, stirring occasionally, for 30 minutes, or until slightly thickened. Quickly fold in the cream so the marshmallow doesn't set, then pour over the slice and refrigerate overnight, or until set. Cut into squares to serve.

Makes 20 pieces

Brandy Alexander Slice

- **80 g (2¾ oz) unsalted butter, chopped**
- **60 g (2 oz) dark cooking (bittersweet) chocolate, chopped**
- **250 g (8¾ oz) packet plain chocolate biscuits (cookies), crushed**
- **300 g (10½ oz) ricotta cheese**
- **¼ cup (60 ml/2 fl oz) cream**
- **⅓ cup (40 g/1½ oz) icing (powdered) sugar, sifted**
- **½ cup grated milk chocolate**
- **1 tablespoon brandy**
- **1 tablespoon crème de cacao liqueur (see Variation)**
- **½ teaspoon ground nutmeg**
- **60 g (2 oz) dark (semi-sweet) chocolate melts**

Lightly grease a shallow 30 × 20 cm (12 × 8 inch) rectangular tin and line with baking paper. Place the butter and chocolate in a small heatproof bowl. Stand over a pan of simmering water. Stir until the chocolate is melted and mixture is smooth. Remove from heat. Using a flat-bladed knife, mix chocolate mixture with the biscuit (cookie) crumbs in a small mixing bowl.

Press the biscuit (cookie) mixture evenly over the base of the prepared tin and set aside.

Using electric beaters, beat the cheese, cream and sugar in a small mixing bowl on medium speed for 3 minutes, or until mixture is light and creamy. Add the chocolate, brandy and liqueur and beat until combined.

Spread the cheese mixture over the prepared base and sprinkle with the nutmeg. Refrigerate for several hours or overnight. Cut into 12 bars before serving. Place the chocolate melts in a small heatproof bowl and stand over simmering water until melted. Place in a small piping bag and pipe a design on top of each bar.

Storage: Store in the refrigerator for up to 2 days.

Variation: Use coffee liqueur in place of the crème de cacao.

Makes 12 bars

Lemon and Almond Slice

- ½ cup (60 g/2 oz) plain (all-purpose) flour
- ⅓ cup (40 g/1½ oz) self-raising flour
- 2 tablespoons icing (powdered) sugar
- 60 g (2 oz) butter, chopped
- 1 egg, lightly beaten
- whipped cream, to serve
- lemon zest, to garnish

Almond Cream
- 3 eggs, at room temperature
- ½ cup (125 g/4⅓ oz) caster (berry) sugar
- 2 teaspoons grated lemon rind
- ½ cup (125 ml/4¼ fl oz) lemon juice
- ⅔ cup (80 g/2¾ oz) ground almonds
- 1 cup (250 ml/8½ fl oz) cream

Preheat the oven to 190°C (375°F/Gas 5). Lightly grease a 23 cm (9 inch) square shallow tin.

Put the flours, sugar and butter in a food processor and process until the mixture resembles fine breadcrumbs. Add the egg and process briefly, until the dough just comes together, adding a small amount of water if necessary.

Press the dough into the base of the prepared tin and prick well with a fork. Bake for 10–12 minutes, or until pale. Allow to cool. Reduce the oven to 180°C (350°F/Gas 4).

To make the almond cream, beat the eggs and sugar with a wooden spoon. Stir in the lemon rind, juice, almonds and cream. Pour over the pastry and bake for 20–25 minutes, or until lightly set. Leave to cool in the tin. Serve with whipped cream and garnish with zested lemon rind.

Makes 15 pieces

Caramel Pecan Squares

- **250 g (8¾ oz) plain chocolate biscuits (cookies)**
- **1 tablespoon drinking chocolate**
- **1½ cups (150 g/5¼ oz) pecans**
- **185 g (6½ oz) butter, melted**

- **60 g (2 oz) butter**
- **400 g (14 oz) can sweetened condensed milk**
- **icing (powdered) sugar, to dust**
- **drinking chocolate, to dust**

Caramel Topping
- **½ cup (90 g/3¼ oz) lightly packed soft brown sugar**

Preheat the oven to 180°C (350°F/Gas 4). Lightly grease an 18 × 28 cm (7 × 11 inch) shallow tin and line with baking paper, overhanging two opposite sides.

Finely crush the biscuits (cookies), drinking chocolate and a third of the pecans in a food processor. Transfer to a mixing bowl and add the melted butter. Mix well and press firmly into the prepared tin. Press the rest of the pecans gently over the top.

To make the caramel topping, place the brown sugar and butter in a saucepan over low heat. Stir until the butter melts and the sugar dissolves. Remove from the heat, stir in the condensed milk, then pour over the biscuit (cookie) base.

Bake for 25–30 minutes, or until the caramel is firm and golden – the edges will bubble and darken. Cool, then refrigerate for at least 3 hours.

Trim off the crusty edges and cut the slice into squares. Before serving, hold a piece of paper over one half of each piece and sprinkle the other half with icing (powdered) sugar. Sprinkle the other side with drinking chocolate.

Makes 16 pieces

Apple Crumble Slice

- ¾ cup (90 g/3¼ oz) self-raising flour
- ¾ cup (90 g/3¼ oz) plain (all-purpose) flour
- 1 cup (90 g/3¼ oz) desiccated (fine) coconut
- 250 g (8¾ oz) unsalted butter
- ¾ cup (140 g/5 oz) lightly packed soft brown sugar
- 410 g (14½ oz) can pie apple (see Variation)
- ⅓ cup (35 g/1¼ oz) rolled oats
- ¼ cup (35 g/1¼ oz) currants (dried)
- ¼ teaspoon ground cinnamon

Preheat the oven to 180°C (350°F/Gas 4). Lightly grease an 18 × 28 cm (7 × 11 inch) shallow rectangular tin and line with baking paper, overhanging two opposite sides. Sift the flours into a large mixing bowl and add the coconut. Combine 200 g (7 oz) of the butter and sugar in a small saucepan. Stir over low heat until the butter has melted and sugar has dissolved. Remove from heat and pour the butter mixture into the dry ingredients. Using a wooden spoon, stir until well combined.

Reserve one cup of mixture. Press the remaining mixture into the prepared tin. Bake for 15 minutes and leave to cool completely.

Spread the pie apple over the cooled base. Combine reserved mixture, remaining butter, oats and currants. Using fingertips, crumble mixture over the apple. Dust with the cinnamon. Bake for 35 minutes. Cool, lift from tin and cut into squares.

Storage: The slice can be stored for up to 2 days in an airtight container.

Variation: Pie apricots can be used instead of the apple.

Makes 24 squares

White Chocolate and Mango Slice

- **100 g (3½ oz) butter**
- **½ cup (125 g/4⅓ oz) caster (berry) sugar**
- **2 eggs, lightly beaten**
- **1 teaspoon vanilla essence**
- **1½ cups (185 g/6½ oz) self-raising flour**
- **½ cup (125 ml/4¼ fl oz) buttermilk**
- **100 g (3½ oz) white chocolate, grated**
- **2 × 425 g (15 oz) cans mango slices, drained, or 2 large fresh mangos, sliced**
- **¼ cup (60 g/2 oz) caster (berry) sugar, extra**

Preheat the oven to 180°C (350°F/Gas 4). Lightly grease an 18 × 28 cm (7 × 11 inch) shallow tin and line with baking paper, overhanging two opposite sides.

Using electric beaters, beat the butter and sugar in a mixing bowl until light and creamy. Gradually add the egg and vanilla essence, beating until well combined.

Using a metal spoon, alternately fold the sifted flour and buttermilk into the mixture, stirring until just combined. Add grated chocolate. Pour into the prepared tin and smooth the surface. Arrange the mango over the top. Place the tin on an oven tray (sheet) to catch any drips. Bake for 35–40 minutes, or until golden brown.

Put the extra sugar in a small saucepan with 1 tablespoon of water and stir over low heat until dissolved. Bring to the boil, then simmer for 1–2 minutes. Brush the syrup over the slice as soon as it comes out of the oven. Cut into pieces and serve hot.

Makes 10 pieces

Jaffa Fudge Slice

- **200 g (7 oz) plain sweet chocolate biscuits (cookies)**
- **1 cup (125 g/4⅓ oz) chopped walnuts**
- **125 g (4⅓ oz) dark (semi-sweet) chocolate, chopped**
- **½ cup (60 g/2 oz) icing (powdered) sugar**
- **125 g (4⅓ oz) butter**
- **1 tablespoon grated orange rind**
- **125 g (4⅓ oz) dark (semi-sweet) chocolate, extra, melted**

Lightly grease an 18 × 28 cm (7 × 11 inch) shallow tin and line with baking paper or foil, overhanging two opposite sides.

Place the biscuits (cookies) and walnuts in a food processor and process until the mixture resembles coarse breadcrumbs. Transfer to a large mixing bowl and make a well in the centre.

Put the chopped chocolate, sifted icing (powdered) sugar and butter in a small saucepan and stir over low heat until melted and smooth. Remove from the heat, stir in the orange rind, then pour into the biscuit (cookie) mixture and stir until well combined.

Press the mixture firmly into the prepared tin. Chill for 10 minutes. Spread the melted chocolate over and chill for 30 minutes to set.

Storage: Slice can be kept in an airtight container for up to a week.

Makes 32 pieces

Puddings

Chocolate Pudding

- **90 g (3¼ oz) unsalted butter**
- **½ cup (95 g/3⅓ oz) soft brown sugar**
- **3 eggs, separated**
- **125 g (4⅓ oz) dark (semi-sweet) chocolate, melted and cooled**
- **1 teaspoon vanilla essence**
- **1 cup (125 g/4⅓ oz) self-raising flour**
- **1 tablespoon cocoa powder**
- **½ teaspoon bicarbonate of soda (baking soda)**

- **¼ cup (60 ml/2 fl oz) milk**
- **2 tablespoons brandy**

Chocolate Sauce
- **125 g (4⅓ oz) dark (semi-sweet) chocolate, broken**
- **¼ cup (60 ml/2 fl oz) cream**
- **1 tablespoon brandy**

Grease a 1.25 litre (1.3 US qt/1.1 UK qt) pudding basin and line the base with a circle of baking paper. Preheat the oven to moderate 180°C (350°F/Gas 4). Cream the butter and half the sugar until light and creamy. Beat in the egg yolks, chocolate and vanilla. Sift together the flour, cocoa and bicarbonate of soda (baking soda). Fold into the mixture, alternating with spoonfuls of the combined milk and brandy. Beat the egg whites until soft peaks form. Gradually beat in the remaining sugar, until stiff and glossy. Fold into the chocolate mix.

Pour into the pudding basin. Cover tightly with foil. Secure with string, put in a deep ovenproof dish and pour in enough hot water to come halfway up the side of the basin. Bake for 1¼ hours, or until a skewer comes out clean. Unmould onto a serving plate.

To make the chocolate sauce, combine the ingredients in a heatproof bowl set over a pan of steaming water and stir until smooth. Serve the pudding with the sauce and cream.

Serves 6

Lemon Delicious

- **60 g (2 oz) unsalted butter**
- **¾ cup (185 g/6½ oz) caster (berry) sugar**
- **3 eggs, separated**
- **1 teaspoon grated lemon rind**
- **⅓ cup (40 g/1½ oz) self-raising flour, sifted**
- **¼ cup (60 ml/2 fl oz) lemon juice**
- **¾ cup (185 ml/6½ fl oz) milk**
- **icing (powdered) sugar, to dust**

Preheat the oven to moderate 180°C (350°F/Gas 4). Brush a 1 litre (1.1 US qt/ 1.75 UK pt) ovenproof dish with oil. Using electric beaters, beat the butter, sugar, egg yolks and rind in a small bowl until the mixture is light and creamy. Transfer to a medium bowl.

Add the flour and stir with a wooden spoon until just combined. Add the juice and milk and stir to combine.

Place the egg whites in a small, dry bowl. Using electric beaters, beat until firm peaks form. Fold in the pudding mixture with a metal spoon until just combined.

Spoon into the ovenproof dish and place the dish inside a deep baking dish. Pour in boiling water to come one-third of the way up the side of the pudding dish. Bake for 40 minutes. Dust with icing (powdered) sugar.

Serves 4

Bread and Butter Pudding

- 60 g (2 oz) mixed raisins (dark raisins) and sultanas (golden raisins)
- 2 tablespoons brandy or rum
- 30 g (1 oz) unsalted butter
- 4 slices good-quality white bread or brioche loaf
- 3 eggs
- 3 tablespoons caster (berry) sugar
- 3 cups (750 ml/26 fl oz) milk
- ¼ cup (60 ml/2 fl oz) cream
- ¼ teaspoon vanilla essence
- ¼ teaspoon ground cinnamon
- 1 tablespoon demerara sugar

Soak the raisins (dark raisins) and sultanas (golden raisins) in the brandy or rum for about 30 minutes. Butter the slices of bread or brioche and cut each piece into 8 triangles. Arrange the bread in a 1 litre (1.1 US qt/1.75 UK pt) ovenproof dish.

Mix the eggs with the sugar, add the milk, cream, vanilla and cinnamon and mix well. Drain the fruit and add any liquid to the custard.

Scatter the soaked fruit over the bread and pour the custard over the top. Cover with plastic wrap and refrigerate for 1 hour.

Preheat the oven to moderate 180°C (350°F/Gas 4). Remove the pudding from the refrigerator and sprinkle with the demerara sugar. Bake for 35–40 minutes, or until the custard is set and the top crunchy and golden.

Note: It is very important that you use good-quality bread for this recipe. Ordinary sliced white bread will tend to go a bit claggy when it soaks up the milk.

Serves 4

Sticky Date Pudding

- 1 cup (185 g/6½ oz) pitted dates
- 1 teaspoon bicarbonate of soda (baking soda)
- 90 g (3¼ oz) butter, softened
- ½ cup (115 g/4 oz) firmly packed soft brown sugar
- 2 eggs, lightly beaten
- 1 teaspoon vanilla essence
- 1½ cups (185 g/6½ oz) self-raising flour

Sauce
- 1 cup (230 g/8¼ oz) firmly packed soft brown sugar
- 1 cup (250 ml/8½ fl oz) cream
- 90 g (3¼ oz) butter
- ½ teaspoon vanilla essence

Preheat the oven to moderate 180°C (350°F/Gas 4). Brush a deep 18 cm (7 inch) square cake tin with melted butter and line the base with baking paper. Put the chopped dates and soda in a heatproof bowl and add 1 cup (250 ml/8½ fl oz) boiling water. Stir and leave for 15 minutes.

Using electric beaters, beat the butter and brown sugar until light and creamy. Beat in the eggs gradually. Add the vanilla essence. Fold in half of the sifted flour then half of the date mixture. Stir in the remaining flour and dates, mixing well. Pour into the prepared tin and cook for 50 minutes, or until cooked when tested with a skewer. Leave the pudding in the tin to cool for 10 minutes before turning out. Serve warm with the hot sauce.

To make the sauce, put the sugar, cream, butter and vanilla in a pan and bring to the boil while stirring. Reduce the heat and simmer for 5 minutes.

Serves 8

271

Sticky Black Rice Pudding

- **2 cups (400 g/14 oz) black rice**
- **3 fresh pandan leaves (see Notes)**
- **2 cups (500 ml/17 fl oz) coconut milk**
- **80 g (2¾ oz) palm sugar, grated**
- **¼ cup (55 g/2 oz) caster (berry) sugar**
- **coconut cream, to serve**
- **mango or papaya cubes, to serve**

Put the rice in a large glass or ceramic bowl and cover with water. Leave to soak for at least 8 hours, or preferably overnight. Drain, then put in a saucepan with 1 litre (1.1 US qt/1.75 UK pt) water and slowly bring to the boil. Cook at a low boil, stirring frequently, for 20 minutes, or until tender. Drain.

Pull your fingers through the pandan leaves to shred them and then tie them in a knot. Pour the coconut milk into a large saucepan and heat until almost boiling. Add the palm sugar, caster (berry) sugar and pandan leaves and stir until the sugars have dissolved.

Add the cooked rice to the pan of coconut milk and cook, stirring, for 8 minutes without boiling. Turn off the heat, cover and leave for 15 minutes to absorb the flavours. Remove the pandan leaves.

Spoon into bowls and serve warm with coconut cream and fresh mango.

Notes: The long flat leaves of the pandanus are crushed and used as a flavouring in many Thai sweets. They are sold fresh, frozen, dried or as a flavouring essence or paste.

Don't refrigerate the black rice pudding or it will dry out and harden.

Variation: Any fresh tropical fruit, such as banana, pineapple or lychee is also delicious served with this dish.

Serves 6–8

Nursery Rice Pudding

- ⅔ cup (140 g/5 oz) arborio or short-grain rice
- 1 litre (1.1 US qt/1.75 UK pt) milk
- ⅓ cup (80 g/2¾ oz) caster (berry) sugar
- 1 teaspoon natural vanilla extract
- ½ cup (125 ml/4¼ fl oz) cream

Rinse the rice in a colander until the water runs clear. Drain well and place in a heavy-based pan with the milk, sugar and vanilla.

Bring to the boil while stirring, then reduce the heat to the lowest setting and cook for about 45 minutes, stirring frequently, until the rice is thick and creamy.

Remove the pan from the heat and leave to stand for 10 minutes. Stir in the cream. Serve warm with stewed fruit, if desired.

Variations: Add a cinnamon stick and a strip of lemon zest to the rice in place of vanilla extract. Or add a small sprig of washed lavender to the rice while cooking.

Serves 4–6

Steamed Pudding

- 1¼ cups (155 g/5½ oz) self-raising flour
- salt
- 120 g (4¼ oz) softened butter
- ⅔ cup (160 g/5⅔ oz) sugar
- 3 eggs

Grease the base and side of a 1 litre (1.1 US qt/1.75 UK pt) pudding basin with melted butter. Place a round of baking paper in the bottom. Put the empty basin in a pan on an upturned saucer and pour in enough cold water to come halfway up the side of the basin. Remove the basin and put the water on to boil.

Sift the self-raising flour into a bowl. Add a pinch of salt, the softened butter, sugar and eggs and beat together well. Pour into the basin.

Cover a sheet of foil with a sheet of baking paper, and make a large pleat in the middle. Grease the paper with melted butter. Place paper-side-down on top of the basin and tie with string securely around the rim of the basin and over the top to make a handle.

Lower the basin into the simmering water and cover with a tight-fitting lid. Cook for 1 hour 45 minutes. Check the water level after an hour and top up to the original level with boiling water as needed. Try putting a coin in the base of the pan – it will stop rattling when the water is getting low.

Note: To reheat a steamed pudding after cooking, bring it back to room temperature and reboil for half the original cooking time. Alternatively, cut it into slices and reheat gently in the microwave individually.

Serves 4

Mini Fruit Truffle Puddings

- **500 g (1 lb 2 oz) fruit cake**
- **2 tablespoons desiccated (fine) coconut**
- **⅓ cup (80 ml/2¾ fl oz) dark rum**
- **⅓ cup (30 g/1 oz) flaked almonds, toasted and crushed**
- **400 g (14 oz) dark (semi-sweet) chocolate buttons, melted**
- **2 teaspoons oil**
- **150 g (5¼ oz) white chocolate, melted**
- **1 stick of angelica (see Note), chopped**
- **8 red glacé (glazed) cherries, chopped**

Finely chop the fruit cake in a food processor. Combine in a bowl with the coconut, rum, almonds and 150 g (5¼ oz) of the melted dark (semi-sweet) chocolate buttons and mix thoroughly. Roll two teaspoons of the mixture at a time into balls and place on a baking tray (sheet) covered with baking paper.

Place the remaining melted dark (semi-sweet) chocolate buttons and oil in a small bowl and stir well. Sit each truffle on a fork and dip in the chocolate to coat. Carefully remove, allowing any excess to drain away. Place back on the paper and leave to set. Do not refrigerate.

When the chocolate is set, spoon the white chocolate into a small piping bag or a small plastic bag, snip off the end of the bag and drizzle chocolate on top of each pudding and down the sides (to look like custard). Before the chocolate sets, decorate with small pieces of angelica and cherry.

Note: Angelica, sold in health-food stores, is crystallised (candied) stems or leaf ribs of a parsley-like plant.

Makes about 44

275

Rich Chocolate Self-Saucing Pudding

- 1½ cups (185 g/6½ oz) self-raising flour
- ¼ cup (30 g/1 oz) cocoa powder
- ¾ cup (185 g/6½ oz) caster (berry) sugar
- 90 g (3¼ oz) butter, melted
- ¾ cup (185 ml/6½ fl oz) milk
- 2 eggs, lightly beaten

Sauce
- 1½ cups (375 ml/13 fl oz) milk
- 1 cup (250 ml/8½ fl oz) water
- 185 g (6½ oz) dark (semi-sweet) chocolate, chopped

Preheat oven to moderate 180°C (350°F/Gas 4). Brush a 9-cup-capacity deep ovenproof dish with oil or melted butter.

Sift flour and cocoa into a large bowl; add sugar, make a well in the centre. Add butter and combined milk and eggs. Using a wooden spoon, stir until just combined and smooth; do not over-beat. Pour into prepared dish.

To make Sauce: Place the milk, water and chocolate in a small pan; stir over low heat until melted and smooth. Pour slowly over the pudding mixture. Bake for 45–50 minutes, until firm to the touch. Serve with cream or ice cream and fresh fruit, if desired.

Serves 6

276

Almond Cream Pudding

- **2 cups (500 ml/17 fl oz) milk**
- **75 g (2⅔ oz) caster (berry) sugar**
- **2 tablespoons cornflour (cornstarch)**
- **2 tablespoons ground rice**
- **75 g (2⅔ oz) ground blanched almonds**

- **1 teaspoon rosewater**
- **2 tablespoons flower blossom honey**
- **2 tablespoons shelled pistachio nuts, chopped**

Place the milk and sugar in a saucepan and heat over medium heat, stirring until the sugar has dissolved.

Combine the cornflour (cornstarch) and ground rice with ¼ cup (60 ml/2 fl oz) water and mix to a paste. Add to the milk and cook, stirring occasionally, over low heat for 20 minutes. Add the almonds and cook for 15 minutes, then add the rosewater. Spoon into shallow serving dishes and refrigerate for 1 hour. Serve drizzled with a little honey and sprinkled with pistachios.

Serves 4

Caramel Bread Pudding

- ⅔ cup (160 g/5⅔ oz) caster (berry) sugar
- 500 g (1 lb 2 oz) panettone or brioche
- ½ cup (125 g/4⅓ oz) caster (berry) sugar, extra

- 2 cups (500 ml/17 fl oz) milk
- 2 wide strips lemon rind, white pith removed
- 3 eggs, lightly beaten
- fresh fruit and cream, optional, for serving

Preheat the oven to moderate 180°C (350°F/Gas 4). Lightly brush a 23 × 13 × 7 cm (9 × 5 × 2¾ inch), 1.25 litre (1.3 US qt/1.1 UK qt) loaf tin with oil or melted butter.

Place the caster (berry) sugar with 2 tablespoons water in a small pan over medium heat and stir, without boiling, until the sugar has completely dissolved. Bring to the boil, reduce the heat slightly and simmer, without stirring, for about 10 minutes, until the syrup becomes a rich golden colour. Watch carefully towards the end of cooking to prevent burning. As soon as it reaches the colour you desire, pour into the loaf tin and leave to cool.

Using a large serrated knife, cut the panettone or brioche into 2 cm (¾ inch) thick slices and remove the crusts. Trim into large pieces to fit the tin in three layers, filling any gaps with panettone cut to size.

Stir the extra caster (berry) sugar, milk and lemon rind in a pan over low heat until the sugar has dissolved. Bring just to the boil, remove from the heat and transfer to a jug to allow the lemon flavour to be absorbed and the mixture to cool. Remove the lemon rind and whisk in the beaten eggs. Pour the mixture gradually into the tin, allowing it to soak into the panettone after each addition. Set aside for 20 minutes to let the panettone soak up the liquid.

Place the loaf tin into a large baking dish and pour in enough hot water to come halfway up the sides of the tin. Bake the pudding for 50 minutes, until just set. Carefully remove the tin from the baking dish and set aside to cool. Refrigerate the pudding overnight.

When ready to serve, turn out onto a plate and cut into slices. Serve with fresh fruit and cream, if desired.

Serves 6–8

Custard Pudding with Stewed Apple

- 180 g (6⅓ oz) unsalted butter
- ½ cup (125 g/4⅓ oz) caster (berry) sugar
- 2 eggs
- 1¼ cups (155 g/5½ oz) self-raising flour
- ¼ cup (30 g/1 oz) custard powder
- ¼ cup (45 g/1⅔ oz) ground almonds
- 1 cup (250 ml/8½ fl oz) cream

- 4 cooking apples
- 2 tablespoons sugar
- icing (powdered) sugar, to dust

Custard
- 1½ tablespoons custard powder
- ½ cup (125 ml/4¼ fl oz) milk
- 1 tablespoon sugar
- ⅓ cup (90 g/3¼ oz) sour cream

To make the custard, combine the custard powder and a little of the milk in a bowl and mix until smooth. Add the remaining milk and mix together. Pour into a pan, add the sugar and sour cream and stir over medium heat until the custard thickens and boils. Remove from the heat and cover the surface with plastic wrap to prevent a skin forming.

Preheat the oven to moderate 180°C (350°F/Gas 4). Beat the butter and sugar together until light and creamy. Add the eggs one at a time, beating well after each addition. Fold in the sifted flour, custard powder and ground almonds alternately with the cream.

Place half the pudding mixture in a 2 litre (2.1 US qt/1.75 UK qt) ovenproof dish and spoon the custard over it. Top with the remaining pudding mixture. The mixture will be a little stiff, pile it on top of the custard and smooth it out gently with the back of a spoon. Bake for 45–50 minutes, or until the pudding is firm to the touch. Dust with icing (powdered) sugar.

Meanwhile, peel, core and thinly slice the apples and place in a pan with the sugar and 2 tablespoons water. Bring to the boil, reduce the heat and simmer, covered, for 10 minutes, until the apples are tender. Serve the pudding from the dish, accompanied by the warm apples.

Serves 6

Chinese Almond Pudding

- **1 cup (100 g/3½ oz) ground almonds**
- **½ cup (90 g/3¼ oz) glutinous rice flour**
- **2½ cups (625 ml/21 fl oz) milk**
- **½ cup (115 g/4 oz) caster (berry) sugar**

Combine the ground almonds and rice flour in a heavy-based saucepan and mix in about ⅓ cup (80 ml/2¾ fl oz) cold water to form a thick, smooth paste. Add a little more water if necessary. Then stir in the milk until smooth.

Place the pan over low heat and cook, stirring almost constantly so that it does not catch, for about 1¼ hours, or until thick and smooth. Gradually add the sugar, stirring until dissolved.

Pour the mixture into six small Chinese rice bowls. You can either serve the pudding warm, or allow to cool slightly, then refrigerate for 3 hours, or until firm. When chilled, it is nice served with fresh mango.

Variation: Stir in 50 g (1¾ oz) pitted and chopped jujubes (Chinese dates).

Serves 6

Sticky Orange and Passionfruit Pudding

- 3 cups (375 g/13¼ oz) plain (all-purpose) flour
- 1½ teaspoons baking powder
- 200 g (7 oz) chilled unsalted butter, chopped
- ½ cup (45 g/1⅔ oz) desiccated (fine) coconut
- 300 ml (10 fl oz) cream

- ½ cup (160 g/5⅔ oz) orange marmalade
- 2 tablespoons passionfruit pulp

Passionfruit Syrup
- ½ cup (125 ml/4¼ fl oz) orange juice
- ¾ cup (185 g/6½ oz) caster (berry) sugar
- ¼ cup (60 g/2 oz) passionfruit pulp

Sift the flour, baking powder and a pinch of salt into a bowl. Rub in the butter with just your fingertips until fine and crumbly. Stir in the coconut. With a flat-bladed knife, mix in most of the cream. Add the rest, if needed, to bring the mixture together. Press together into a soft dough and roll between 2 sheets of baking paper to make a 25 × 40 cm (10 × 16 inch) rectangle.

Spread marmalade over the dough and drizzle with passionfruit pulp. Roll up lengthways like a Swiss roll. Chill for 20 minutes, or until firm.

Preheat the oven to 180°C (350°F/Gas 4). Brush a deep 20 cm (8 inch) round cake tin with melted butter or oil; line the base with baking paper. Cut the rolled dough into 2 cm (¾ inch) slices; arrange half over the base of the tin. Place a second layer over the gaps where the bottom slices join. Place the tin on a baking tray (sheet).

To make the passionfruit syrup, put all the ingredients with ¼ cup (60 ml/2 fl oz) water in a pan. Stir over low heat, without boiling, until the sugar has dissolved. Bring to the boil, then pour over the pudding. Bake for 50 minutes, or until a skewer comes out clean. Leave for 15 minutes before turning out.

Serves 6

Summer Pudding

- 150 g (5¼ oz) blackcurrants
- 150 g (5¼ oz) redcurrants
- 150 g (5¼ oz) raspberries
- 150 g (5¼ oz) blackberries
- 200 g (7 oz) strawberries, hulled and quartered or halved
- caster (berry) sugar, to taste
- 6–8 slices good-quality white bread, crusts removed
- cream, for serving, optional

Put all the berries except the strawberries in a large pan with ½ cup (125 ml/ 4¼ fl oz) water and heat gently until the berries begin to collapse. Add the strawberries and turn off the heat. Add sugar, to taste (how much you need will depend on how ripe the fruit is). Set aside to cool.

Line six 150 ml (5 fl oz) moulds or a 1 litre (1.1 US qt/1.75 UK pt) pudding basin with the bread. For the small moulds, use 1 slice of bread for each, cutting a circle to fit the bottom and strips to fit the sides. For the large mould, cut a large circle out of 1 slice for the bottom and cut the rest of the bread into fingers. Drain a little juice off the fruit mixture. Dip one side of each piece of bread in the juice before fitting it, juice-side-down, into the mould, leaving no gaps. Do not squeeze it or flatten it or it will not absorb the juices as well.

Fill the centre of the mould with the fruit and add a little juice. Cover the top with a layer of dipped bread, juice-side-up, and cover with plastic wrap. Place a plate which fits inside the dish onto the plastic wrap, then weigh it down. Stack the small ones on top of each other to weigh them down. Refrigerate overnight. Carefully turn out the pudding and serve with any extra mixture and cream.

Serves 4–6

Notes

Notes

Page 244 — Gluten free
   243 —

Index